BOOKED

The Last 150 Years
Told through Mug Shots

BOOKED

The Last 150 Years
Told through Mug Shots

GIACOMO PAPI

translated by Jamie Richards

Seven Stories Press
NEW YORK ◊ TORONTO

First Seven Stories Press edition, April 2006

Originally published in Italian as *Accusare: Storia del Novecento in 366 foto segnaletiche* by ISBN Edizioni, Italy, 2004.

Seven Stories Press
140 Watts Street
New York, NY 10013
http://www.sevenstories.com/

In Canada:
Publishers Group Canada, 250A Carlton Street, Toronto, ON M5A 2L1

College professors may order examination copies of Seven Stories Press titles for a free six-month trial period. To order, visit www.sevenstories.com/textbook/ or send a fax on school letterhead to 212-226-1411.

Book design by Phoebe Hwang

LIBRARY OF CONGRESS CATALOGING-IN-PUBLICATION DATA
Papi, Giacomo.
[Accusare : storia del Novecento in 366 foto segnaletiche. English]
Booked : the last 150 years told through mug shots / Giacomo Papi ; translated by Jamie Richards.— A Seven Stories Press 1st ed.
p. cm.
ISBN-13: 978-1-58322-717-6 (pbk. : alk. paper)
ISBN-10: 1-58322-717-2 (pbk. : alk. paper)
1. Celebrities—Portraits. 2. Criminals—Portraits. 3. Identification photographs.
4. Portrait photography. 5. Biography—Portraits. 6. Photography. I. Title.
TR681.F3P3613 2005
779'.2—dc22
2005034974

Printed in the USA

9 8 7 6 5 4 3 2 1

CONTENTS

INDEX OF NAMES

THE MUG SHOTS

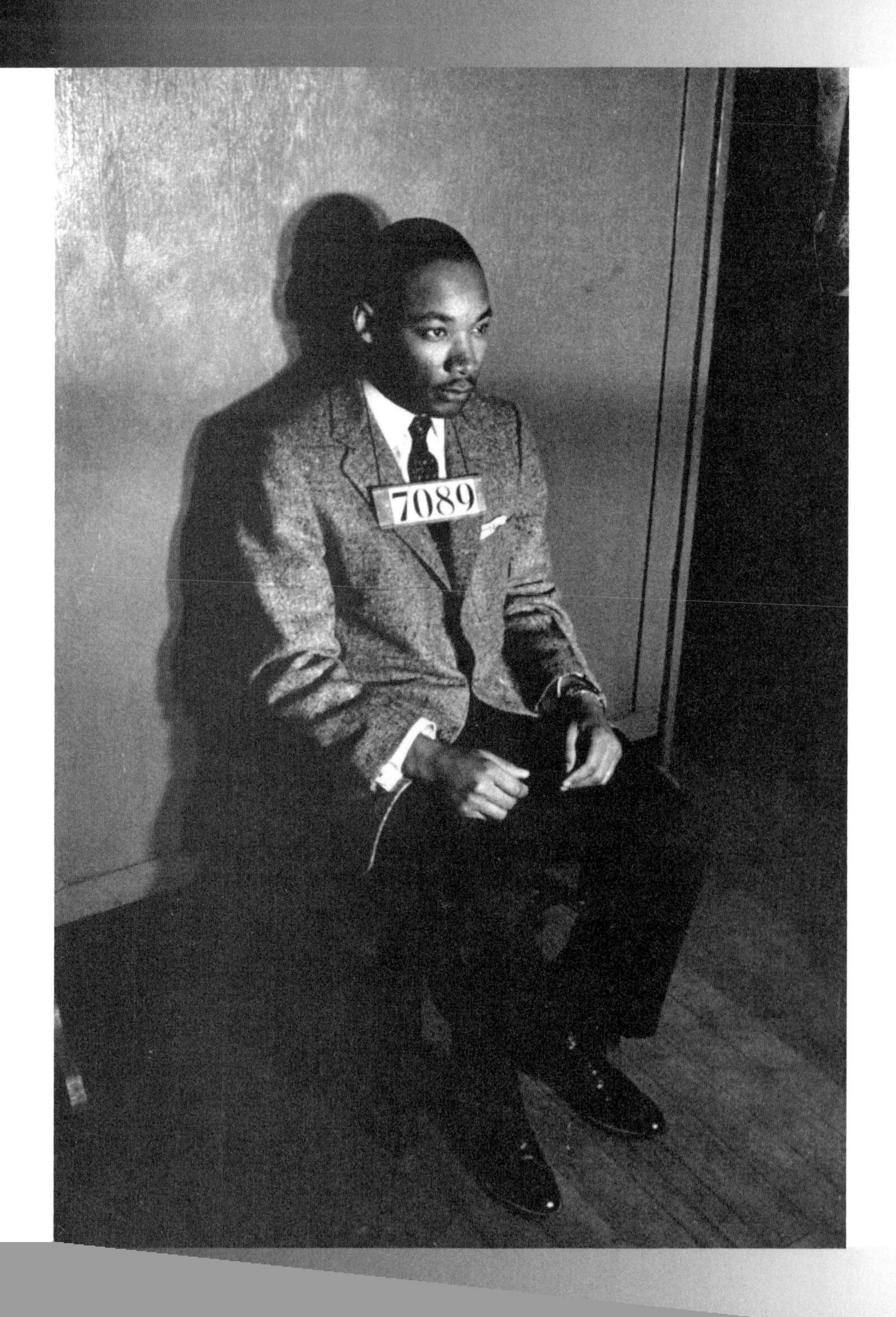
7089

MARTIN LUTHER KING JR.

MONTGOMERY, ALABAMA, 09/03/1958

These are more than just two mug shots. On the previous page, *Time*'s Don Cravens photographs Martin Luther King Jr. from above, while at the same time the police photographer snaps him from the front. To gauge the difference between the two shots in distance and in tone, compare the placement of his hands and legs, the posture of his head and shoulders, his elegant clothing, his stately air, his focused gaze, his manly pride with the mug shot in the foreground. The time and the booking number are the same, but the perspective has changed.

Reverend King was arrested on September 3, 1958, in Montgomery, Alabama, for failing to obey an officer and was released on one-hundred-dollar bail. The mug shot disappeared for forty-six years. It resurfaced in the summer of 2004, when it was discovered at the home of a recently deceased sheriff. A note was added to the mug shot that changes its meaning. With a blue ball-point pen, someone etched the word "dead" and the date—April 4, 1968—on the picture.

Leader of the Civil Rights movement in America and winner of the Nobel Peace Prize in 1964, King was killed at the age of thirty-nine in Memphis, Tennessee. The first witnesses described the assassin as "trim, white, about thirty-five years old, wearing a dark suit and a white shirt." A block away from the assassination, the police found a .30-06 caliber Remington rifle.

King was hit in the neck as he was talking with friends outside his room at the Lorraine Motel in Memphis. Among them was a musician, Ben Branch, another was Reverend Jesse Jackson, who, in subsequent decades, would try to unite King's human, religious, and political legacy with varying success.

King was in Memphis to support a sanitation workers' strike that had led to violence. After he won the Nobel Prize, his wife had declared, "we have lived with the threat of death always present."

Two months later, James Earl Ray, a common criminal known for his hatred toward blacks, was arrested in London. He confessed, recanted three days later, but was sentenced to ninety-nine years in prison. For twenty-nine years, until his death from cirrhosis of the liver, Ray continued to profess his innocence.

A few months before the homicide, the head of the FBI, J. Edgar Hoover, wanted to "prevent the rise of a messiah who could unify, and electrify, the militant black nationalist movement." Over the years, King's family has become convinced that Ray is innocent.

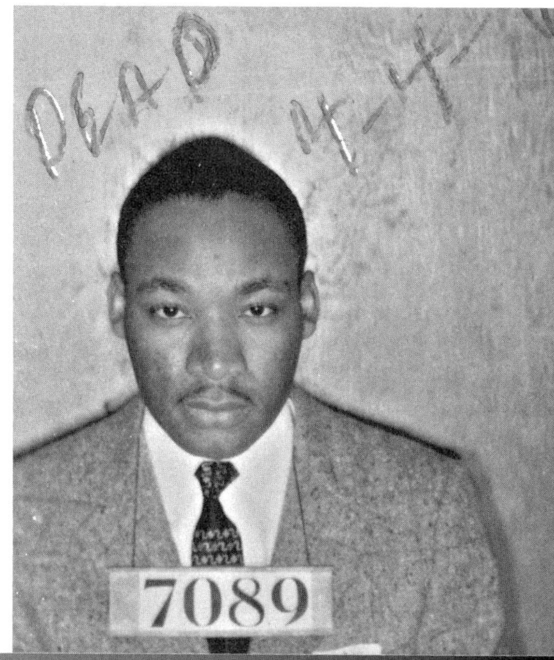

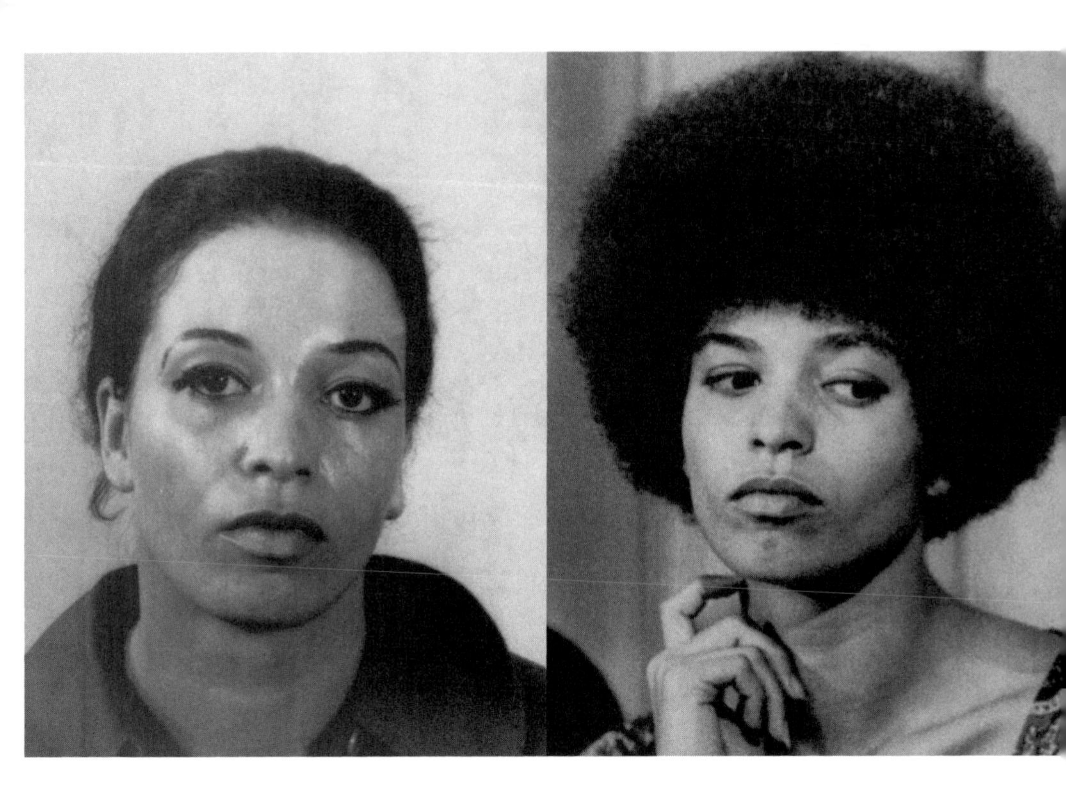

ANGELA DAVIS

NEW YORK CITY, 10/13/1970

A pop icon. A political icon. Beauty of ideas. Beauty of the body. In this dance of the personal and the political, of the sex symbol and the role model, nobody comes close to Angela Davis except maybe Ernesto "Che" Guevara.

Along with her mug shot, the police were wise enough to include a photograph from Davis's daily life, where she's showing off her classic afro. In both hemispheres of the world, unlikely perms cropped up on left-leaning women.

She was born in Alabama on January 26, 1944. The world started to hear about her in 1968 when she was fired for being a Communist from the University of California, Los Angeles, where she taught philosophy. Accused of assisting in a Black Panthers kidnapping of a San Rafael judge during which four people were murdered, she was arrested in a Manhattan motel on October 13, 1970. After an international campaign, she was acquitted in 1972.

During the trial, she admitted to being involved with George Jackson, the black communist leader who was killed in a California prison on August 21, 1971.

Today, Angela Yvonne Davis is a professor at the University of California, Santa Cruz.

JANIS JOPLIN

TAMPA, FLORIDA, 11/17/1969

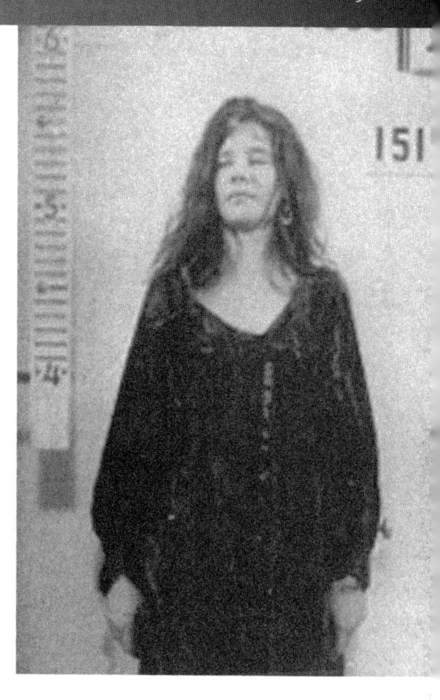

In 1962, at the University of Texas at Austin, where she was studying art, she was voted "Ugliest Man on Campus." Janis Joplin was nineteen and, for her, this was nothing new. In Port Arthur, Texas, where she was born and raised, things had been the same. She moved to San Francisco in 1966 and achieved success in 1968 with her album *Cheap Thrills*. No white woman had ever had a voice like that, like sandpaper soaked in heroin, sex, and Southern Comfort, the bittersweet liquor that nourished her spirit and her voice. In November 1969, she was arrested (and released) for verbally assaulting a police officer. She belonged to a generation of young people who "insult their parents, march against the government, consume vast quantities of drugs, screw everything that moves," writes Charles Shaar Murray, Jimi Hendrix biographer. On October 3, 1970, she recorded "Buried Alive in the Blues," her last song.

Jopliln started using heroin again in mid-September 1970. She was staying at the Landmark in Los Angeles, which was known as a hotel for pushers. On the evening of October 4, she was waiting for two lovers, one male and one female, but remained alone. She shot up, went to talk to the hotel clerk, and was found dead eighteen hours later. "The ugliest man on campus," "the greatest female singer in the history of rock n' roll," died from a heroin overdose—the first in a long line of rock stars—on October 5, 1970.

JIM MORRISON

TALLAHASSEE, FLORIDA, 09/28/1963

Under "James Douglas Morrison"—who was born in Melbourne, Florida, on December 8, 1943, and died in Paris on July 3, 1971—the FBI lists ten arrests. Most of the ninety-six-page file remains undisclosed.

One report from March 4, 1969, states: "Morrison's program lasted one hour during which time he sang one song and for the remainder he grunted, groaned, gyrated and gestured" in order to "provoke chaos."

This mug shot captures the future Doors frontman's first arrest. The only one whose reason is still unknown.

BERKELEY STUDENTS

BERKELEY, CALIFORNIA, 12/03/1964

The '68 revolution started yesterday. Yesterday is December 2, 1964, the same day that Beatle Ringo Starr had his tonsils removed. Students at UC Berkeley had been in a state of unrest since October 1 when a student was arrested for distributing pamphlets.

Berkeley president Clark Kerr's vision of a university didn't include politics; for him, the university was a factory that filled empty heads, shaped them, and made them work for the system.

The day before the group mug shot pictured below, 1,000 students gathered in Berkeley's Sproul Hall. Similar sit-ins occurred in hundreds of other meeting halls. And suddenly, '68 was born.

Mario Savio, a twenty-two-year-old student, born to Sicilian immigrants and raised in Queens, NY, took off his shoes so he wouldn't be charged with damages and climbed onto the roof of a police car. He took a megaphone and said: "If President Kerr in fact is the manager, then I'll tell you something: the faculty are a bunch of employees, and we're the raw material! But we're a bunch of raw materials that don't mean to have any process upon us, don't mean to be made into any product, don't mean to end up being bought by some clients of the University, be they the government, be they industry, be they organized labor, be they anyone! We're human beings! There is a time when the operation of the machine becomes so odious, makes you so sick at heart, that you can't take part; you can't even passively take part, and you've got to put your bodies upon the gears and upon the wheels, upon the levers, upon all the apparatus, and you've got to make it stop. And you've got to indicate to the people who run it, to the people who own it, that unless you're free, the machine will be prevented from working at all!" Then Joan Baez started singing "We Shall Overcome."

In the following months, protests at Berkeley spread to many universities in America and throughout the world, and later led to the movement against the Vietnam War.

The day after Savio's speech, the police, called by the university president, burst onto campus and arrested 792 students. But the machine got jammed. To proceed with the booking, someone proposed a group mug shot, which is pretty rare.

Mario Savio chose, at that moment, to move out of the spotlight. He had only taken off his shoes and said a few words, but he changed history. He died of heart failure in 1996 at just fifty-three years of age.

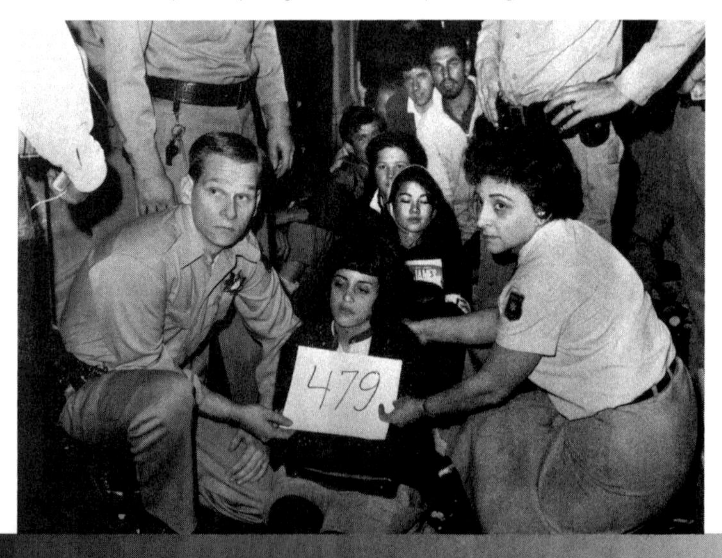

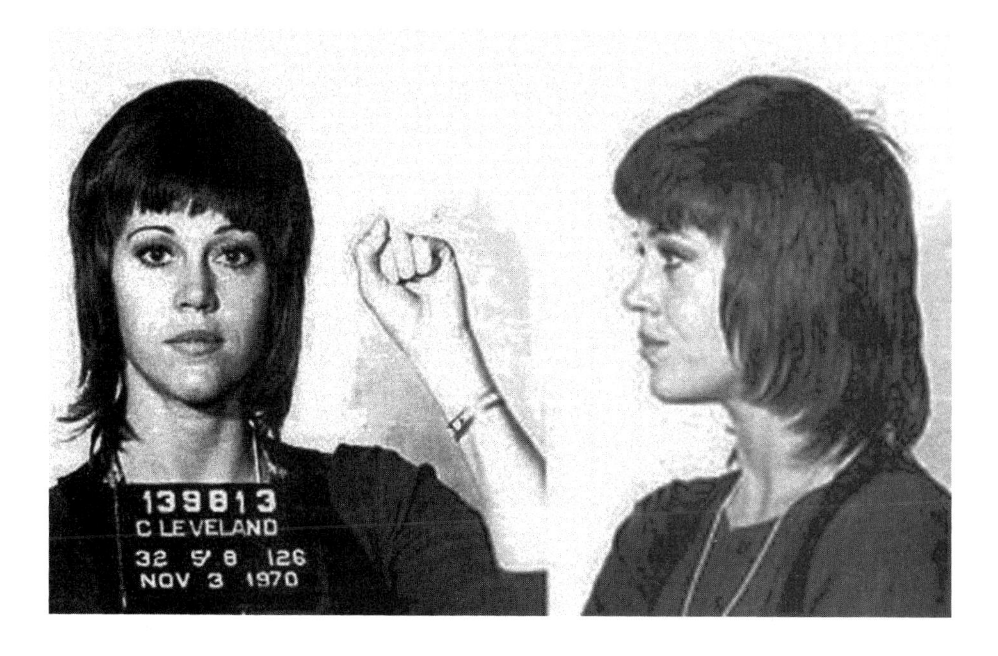

JANE FONDA

CLEVELAND, OHIO, 11/03/1970

If it weren't for Dorothy Pennebaker, Marlon Brando's mother, Henry Fonda would never have made his debut in an Omaha theater. He would never have become a famous actor. He would never have married a New Yorker from good stock. And his actor children, Jane and Peter, would never have been born.

Before releasing aerobics videos, before marrying CNN founder Ted Turner, before getting divorced in 2001 and becoming a born-again Christian (like George W. Bush), Jane Fonda represented the entire left, shaking things up beneath the American sky. "Hanoi Jane" was a symbol of the Vietnam antiwar protest, along with veteran John Kerry. In 1964, she appeared nude in *La Ronde*, a film by her first husband, Roger Vadim. She said: "Revolution is an act of love. We are the children of revolution . . . It runs in our blood."

She's beautiful, anticonformist, liberal, and liberated. In 1970, she was arrested twice. The first, in March, after a protest at Fort Lawton in Seattle. The second, shown in the photo, in November at the Cleveland airport. She was arrested after kicking a police officer who found her carrying some suspicious pills. The charge was dropped when they turned out to be vitamins.

LENNY BRUCE

LOS ANGELES, CALIFORNIA, 04/27/1963

He was a sort of comic American Socrates, except that Socrates only had to go through one trial. Between 1961 and 1963, Lenny Bruce appeared before judges a dozen times on obscenity charges for two of his sketches—one in which he declared, "Eleanor Roosevelt has the nicest tits of any lady in office," and another in which he said Jacqueline Kennedy "hauled ass to save her ass" after the president's assassination—and for talking about sex with chickens, as well as excessive use of the verb "to come" to indicate having an orgasm.

Onstage after one New York arrest, he reflected: "What does it mean to be found obscene in New York? This is the most sophisticated city in the country . . . If anyone is the first person to be found obscene in New York, he must feel utterly depraved . . ."

Born Leonard Schneider in 1925 in a Jewish area of Long Island, he died on August 3, 1966, in Hollywood Hills from a morphine overdose. In those forty-one years, he wrote *How to Talk Dirty and Influence People*, inspired the film *Lenny* (Bob Fosse, 1974, with Dustin Hoffman), and scandalized thousands of people. But he made even more laugh.

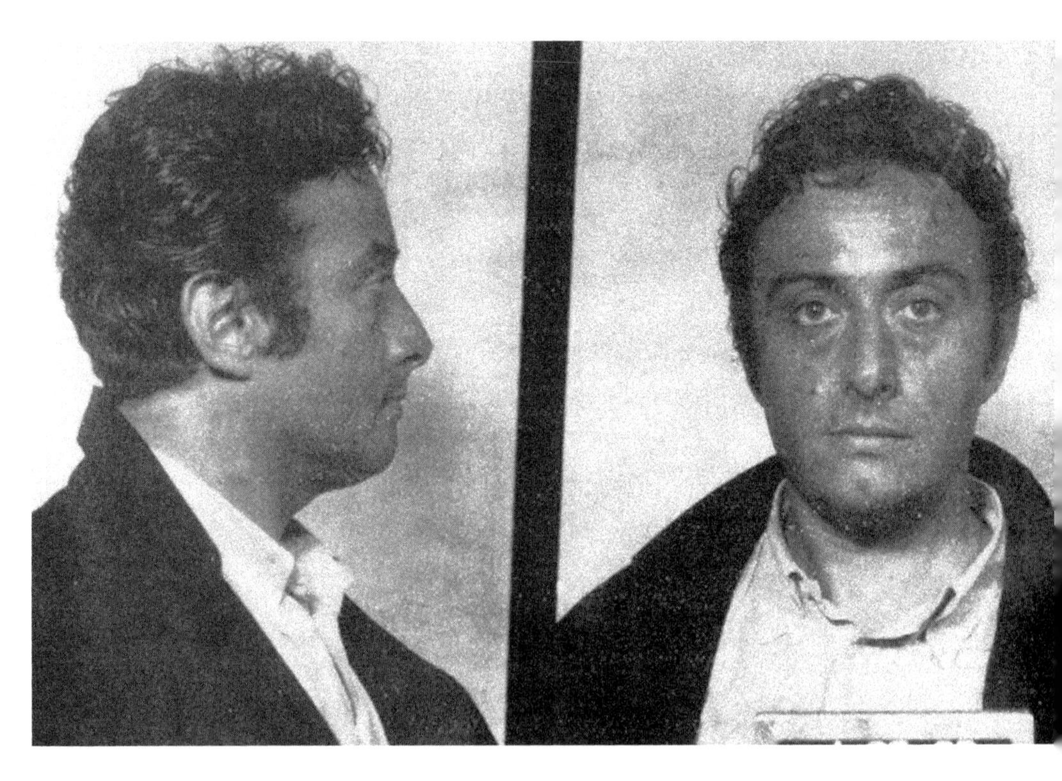

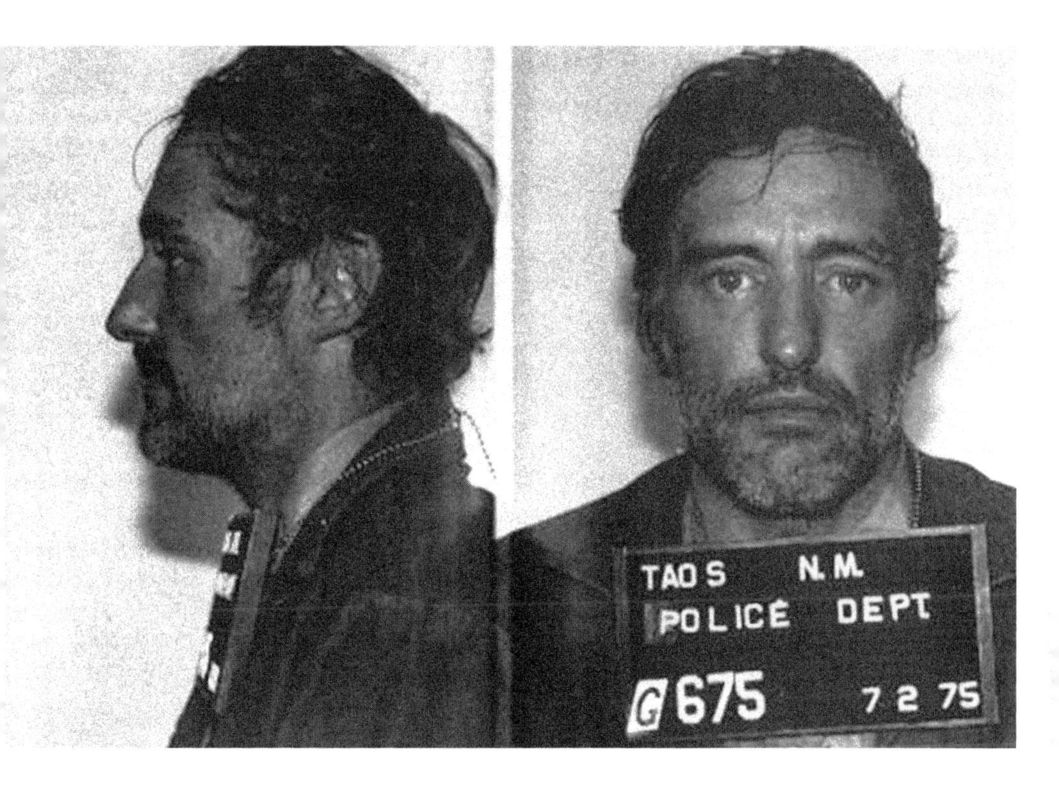

DENNIS HOPPER

TAOS, NEW MEXICO, 07/02/1975

"You want to hear about insanity? I was found running naked through the jungles in Mexico. At the Mexico City airport, I decided I was in the middle of a movie and walked out on the wing on takeoff. My body . . . my liver . . . okay, my brain . . . went."

He started acting at the age of ten but entered film history in 1955, at nineteen, working alongside James Dean in Nicholas Ray's *Rebel Without a Cause*. The two became friends and a year later came together again for George Stevens's *Giant*. After James Dean's fatal accident, Hopper did everything he could to take his place, imitating both his genius and his excesses. He was blacklisted from Hollywood for several years.

In 1969, he came back to life in another era of cinema and of young rebellion. The movie was *Easy Rider*, which he directed and wrote, along with Henry Fonda and Terry Southern. On July 2, 1975, the motorcyclist caused a crash and rode off before alerting the police. He was arrested for leaving the scene of an accident and reckless driving. In 1999 he was caught with a bit of marijuana. He may run naked through the Mexican jungle, but he is still an heir to James Dean's legacy.

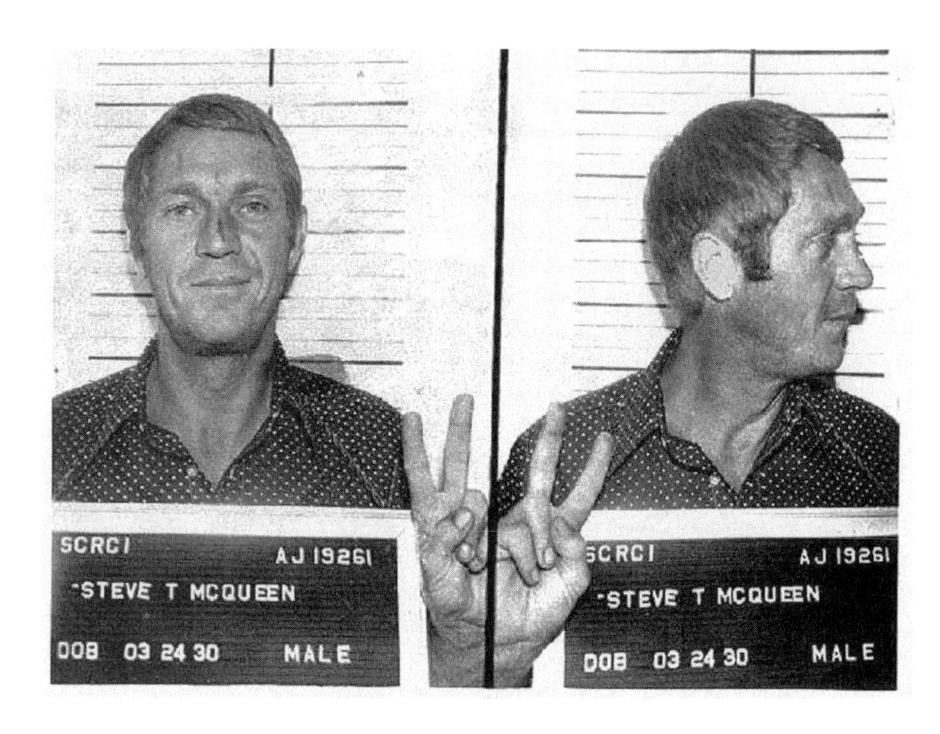

STEVE McQUEEN

ANCHORAGE, ALASKA, 1972

The Great Escape, the film that brought him fame, came to theaters in 1963. In real life, nine years later, his situation was somewhat similar. Maybe that's why he's laughing. The reason for the arrest was one of the most common: driving under the influence.

Terence Steven McQueen's daredevil life began on March 24, 1930, in Beech Grove, Indiana. In 1947 he enlisted in the Marines. He was honorably discharged in 1950. McQueen was married three times and divorced twice. He died on November 7 from a rare form of lung cancer caused by asbestos exposure from his racing gear.

In life and on screen, he did nothing but flee, from the Nazis, from the police, and in a moving car when he started to race for a living. He was handsome and kind, with a penchant for death and for fun, the shining symbol of his ill-fated life. In 1973, the Rolling Stones released "Star Star." The song contains the line "Givin' head to Steve McQueen." In Italy he was consecrated with Vasco Rossi's "Vita Spericolata" (daredevil life) sung at the 1983 Sanremo Festival: "Voglio una vita come Steve McQueen" (I want a life like Steve McQueen's).

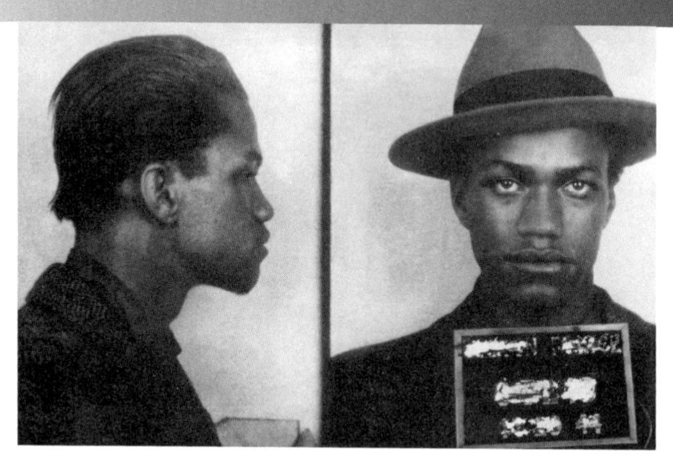

MALCOLM X

BOSTON, MASSACHUSETTS, 01/12/1946

"Louise Little, my mother, who was born in Grenada, in the British West Indies, looked like a white woman. Her father was white. She had straight black hair, and her accent did not sound like a Negro's. Of this white father of hers, I know nothing except her shame about it. I remember hearing her say she was glad that she had never seen him. It was, of course, because of him that I got my reddish-brown 'mariny' color of skin, and my hair of the same color. I was the lightest child in our family. (Out in the world later on, in Boston and New York, I was among the millions of Negroes who were insane enough to feel that it was some kind of status symbol to be light-complexioned—that one was actually fortunate to be born thus. But, still later, I learned to hate every drop of that white rapist's blood that is in me.)"

Unlike Michael Jackson, Malcolm X, the other leader of the American Civil Rights movement besides Martin Luther King Jr., sought the purity of his origins, hating the traces of the rape that history had tattooed upon him. His autobiography continues:

> They took Shorty and me, handcuffed together, to the Charlestown State Prison.
>
> I can't remember any of my prison numbers. That seems surprising, even after the dozen years since I have been out of prison. Because your number in prison became part of you. You never heard your name, only your number. On all of your clothing, every item, was your number, stenciled. It grew stenciled on your brain.

In prison, he got stoned by smoking nutmeg, found Islam, painstakingly copied a dictionary cover to cover, and relearned to read and write. He joined Elijah Mohammed's Nation of Islam, the Black Muslims, a group that advocated the return to Africa for American blacks, and professed the superiority of black people and the inherent evil of whites. He got a law degree and became a lawyer. In just a few years, because of his extraordinary oratory abilities, he became a leader who outshined the group's founder, Elijah Mohammed.

When his pilgrimage to Mecca made him realize that the division was not between blacks and whites but between the poor and the rich, Malcolm broke away from Elijah. This caused him to be shunned by many Black Muslims, even Muhammad Ali, who had been a close friend. In his last interview he declared, "I'm a marked man" and "I live like a man who's already dead." He was murdered at the age of thirty-nine, on February 21, 1965, as he was giving a speech in New York. He was shot fifteen times in public, after the American tradition that began with President Abraham Lincoln.

LEWIS POWELL

WASHINGTON, D.C., 04/17/1865

Public assassination became an American institution. America was where assassination transformed history into epic and epic into history. A formula first tested with Abraham Lincoln in 1865, followed by the assassination of John F. Kennedy in Dallas a century later. The idea was reformulated in fiction in "Theme of the Traitor and Hero" from Jorge Luis Borges's *Ficciones*, which inspired Bernardo Bertolucci's film, *The Spider's Stratagem*. Public assassination was an American exclusive. At least until September 11, 2001.

Lincoln was assassinated on April 14, 1865 at Ford's Theatre in Washington, D.C., during a performance of *Our American Cousin*, a play by Tom Taylor. Five days earlier, on April 9 in the town of Appomattox, Virginia, Confederate General Robert E. Lee surrendered to General Ulysses S. Grant's Union army. The North had won. The Civil War was over.

At the trial, the defendant most striking to ladies and journalists was Lewis Powell, a handsome yet aloof Southern boy. His photo demonstrates how, even 140 years later, scarcely a moment has passed between Oscar Wilde's aesthetic ideal and Calvin Klein's.

It was a grandiose plan. John Wilkes Booth, head of the conspirators financed by the Confederate States of America, was to get rid of all the leaders of the victorious Union. While Booth killed the president, shooting him point blank in the head and then fleeing the theater on horseback, his men were in charge of eliminating the possible successors. Jacob Thompson, head of the Confederate secret service, wanted to "leave the government entirely without a head" because there was "no provision in the Constitution of the United States by which, if these men were removed, they could elect another President."

Lewis Powell was assigned the task of assassinating Secretary of State William Seward, who was sick in bed at his home in Washington. On April 14, at 10:00 p.m., Powell came to his door, saying that the doctor had sent him to deliver a prescription. But Seward's son, Frederick, stopped him, so he bludgeoned him with the gun (leaving the young man in a coma for sixty days). Then he barged into Seward's room, shouting, "I'm mad! I'm mad!" and stabbed him several times. He escaped on his bay mare. He was captured on the seventeenth at the home of Mary Surratt, who would become the first woman to be executed in the U.S. There were bloodstains on Powell's clothes. The initials JWB were printed on the inside of his boots.

Powell was the youngest of eight brothers in an Alabama family, though they soon moved to Georgia. At seventeen in Live Oak, Florida, he enlisted in the Confederate army. Powell was an introverted young man who loved fishing and animals. Wounded on July 2, 1863, in the Battle of Gettysburg, he was taken prisoner by Union troops and transferred to a hospital in Baltimore. He soon escaped and crossed the lines to Virginia. He returned to Baltimore in 1965, posing as a Union sympathizer, and was introduced to Booth by a Confederate operative.

During the arraignment, his lawyer portrayed Powell as a country boy who had gotten swept up by circumstances. He declared, "We know now that slavery made him immoral, that war made him a murderer, and that necessity, revenge, and delusion made him an assassin." Sitting on the bench, a steel bar restraining his hands, he would "sit like a statue" and "smile as one who fears no earthly terrors." In prison, he tried to commit suicide by banging his head against the wall of his cell. He confessed to a warden that he was "tired of life." Powell was hanged along with the others (except for Booth, who was shot and killed before he could be arrested) on July 7, 1865.

In 1992, his skull was discovered among a collection of Native American skulls at the Anthropology Department of the Smithsonian Institute. It was returned to one of his descendants to be buried with the rest of his body in Geneva, Florida.

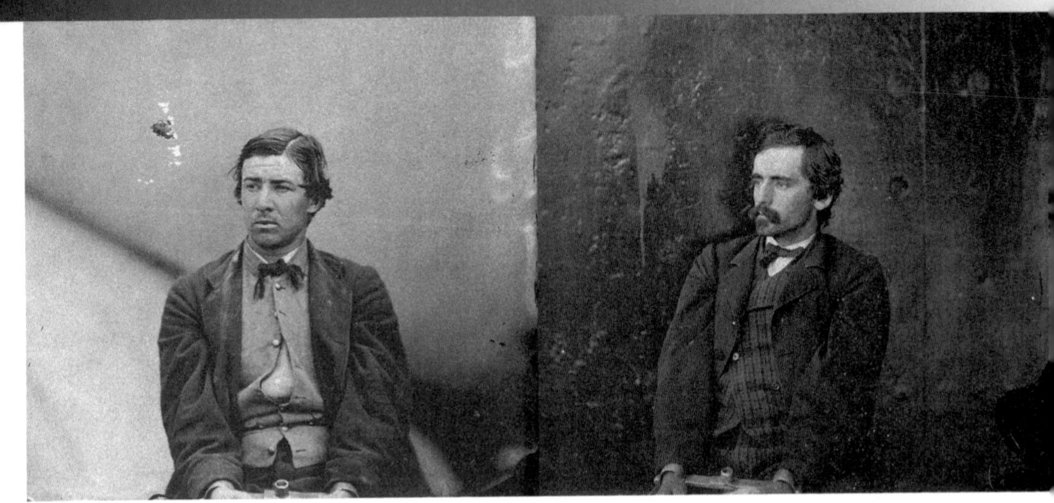

DAVID HEROLD **MICHAEL O'LAUGHLEN**

THE LINCOLN ASSASSINATION

WASHINGTON, D.C., 04/14/1865

John Wilkes Booth, mastermind of the conspiracy against and assassination of Abraham Lincoln, is not part of this lineup. His mug shot doesn't exist, because he wisely decided to get himself killed before he could be caught and hanged. Trapped in a barn, he refused to surrender. He shouted to David Herold, who was coming out with his hands up, "[You're] a damned coward." Booth stepped forward armed and was shot. Dying, he had time to whisper, "Tell mother I die for my country."

Things were even worse for David Herold, who had stood guard for Lewis Powell during the assassination attempt on the secretary of state. During the trial, his lawyer said Herold "was only wax in the hands of a man like Booth." A witness for the defense stated, "In mind, I consider him about eleven years of age."

In a corner, nearly forgotten, sat Michael O'Laughlen. He had grown up in Baltimore on the same street as Booth, but his actual role in the plot has never been clear. Perhaps he was to kill General Grant, or perhaps he was supposed to extinguish the theater lights to help Booth. Perhaps.

What sealed his fate was a telegram from his old friend summoning him to Washington. The defense claimed that he was in the capital to celebrate the Union's victory and that he had walked through the streets with everyone else during "the night of illumination," when all public buildings in Washington were lit with candles.

George Atzerodt, a German native, emigrated with his family to Maryland when he was eight years old. Booth convinced him to participate in Lincoln's kidnapping, but when the plan escalated to assassinating the president, he was given the task of killing the vicepresident, Andrew Johnson. On April 14, he checked into room 126 of the Kirkwood Hotel, where Johnson was staying. However, instead of going through with the murder, he ended up just wandering around town. The police found a loaded gun and a hunting knife under his pillow. His defense was based entirely on his cowardice. Before going up to the scaffold to be hanged, he politely bid the journalists farewell: "May we meet in another world."

During the Civil War, Edman Spangler, a.k.a. Ned, worked at Ford's Theatre. His job was changing the sets and handling the carpentry.

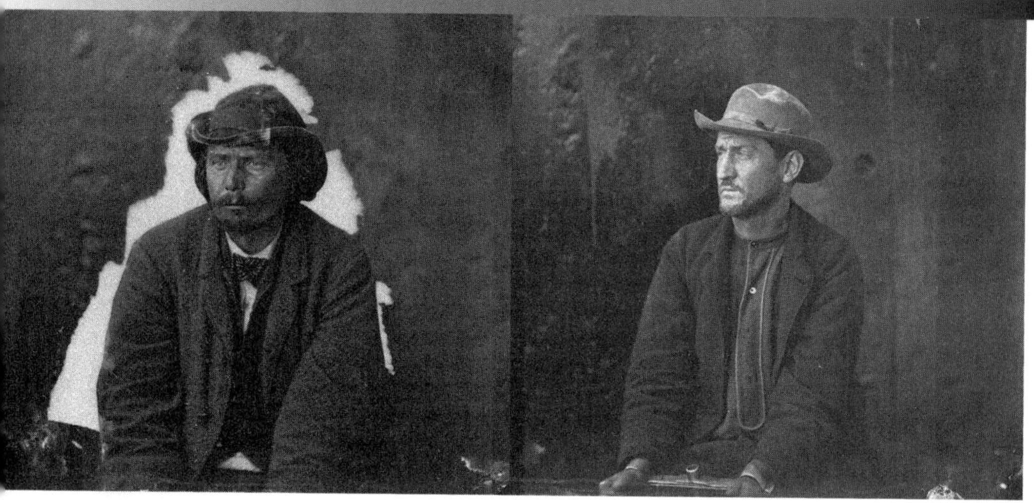

GEORGE ATZERODT

EDMAN SPANGLER

When Booth killed Lincoln, shouting, "Revenge for the South," Spangler held the emergency exit door open and made sure that the getaway horse was ready. The defense focused on his ignorance of the targets: even if there was no doubt that Spangler had helped Booth, there was no evidence that he was aware of his entire plan. Witnesses claimed that on April 14, as Spangler was preparing the presidential box, he had said, "Damn the president!" That didn't help, but he only got six years in jail. Pardoned by President Johnson in 1869, he resumed life on a farm and died in 1875.

Samuel Arnold, Booth's classmate at the military academy in Baltimore, was unemployed. When he found work, he backed out of the plot. A letter he had written to Booth saved his life. He was pardoned in 1869 and died in 1906 at the age of seventy-two.

Missing from the group, aside from the head conspirator with his droopy moustache, is Mary Surratt, whose house was a meeting spot for the plotters, and her son John, who was captured in Egypt in 1866. At 1:30 p.m. on July 7, 1865, Powell, Atzerodt, Herold, and Mary Surratt, the first woman ever executed in United States history, were hanged at the Old Arsenal Building in Washington, D.C. Proof against her was a *carte de visite* titled *Morning, Noon, and Night* with a photo of Booth on the back. The advent of the photographic visiting card, invented by André Adolphe-Eugène Disdéri in 1854, signals the birth of the photo I.D.

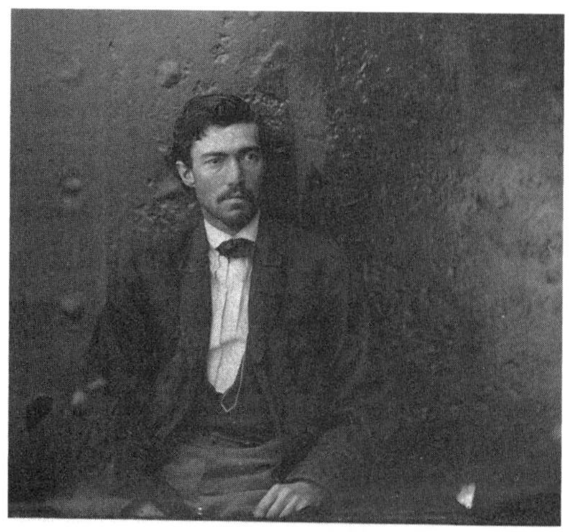

SAMUEL ARNOLD

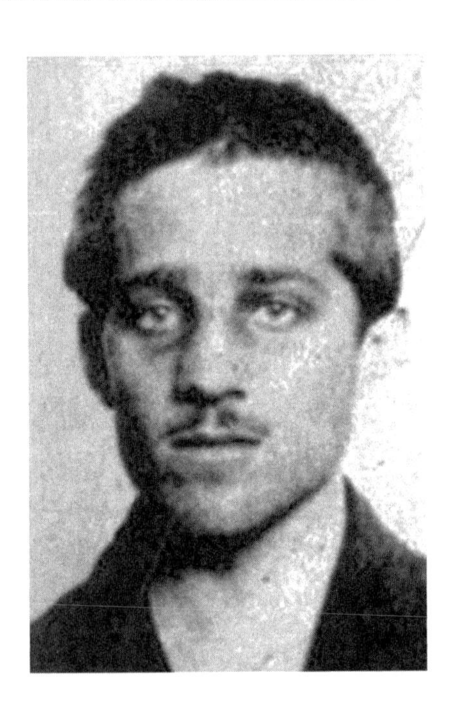

GAVRILO PRINCIP

SARAJEVO, AUSTRO-HUNGARIAN EMPIRE, 1914

Archduke Franz Ferdinand, heir to the Austro-Hungarian throne, desperately wanted to appear elegant. On June 28, 1914, in Sarajevo, the Serbian irredentist student Gavrilo Princip shot him, and his tight uniform delayed and rendered vain any attempt at rescue. The archduke and his wife died. World War I broke out, even though nobody really cared about the heir's death. Austria, almost out of obligation, attacked Serbia. Russia, which could have stayed out of it, intervened. Everyone else followed. The conflict spread over the whole continent like an irrational fever. The twentieth century had begun. But the armies were still nineteenth century. It was a bloodbath.

Winston Churchill wrote his wife: "I wondered whether those stupid Kings & Emperors cd not assemble together . . . but we all drift on in a kind of dull cataleptic trance. As if it was somebody else's operation!" Over the course of the Great War, the first mass photographic documentation occurred. Soldiers lined up for photographs, cigarettes in hand, wearing pressed uniforms. In Italy, there was even an edict requiring it. That way, their corpses could be identified.

Gavrilo Princip perished in prison in 1918, after the end of the war, without ever thinking he was to blame.

GAETANO BRESCI

MONZA, ITALY, 07/29/1900

He returned to Italy from New Jersey to kill the king. On July 29, 1900, in Monza, Italy, Umberto I was shot by a young anarchist wielding a Hamilton & Booth revolver. The king died. A month later the attacker was given a life sentence. Bresci died on May 22, 1901, by hanging himself with a towel in his jail cell.

In 1902, the Italian criminologist Cesare Lombroso wrote: "Bresci, 35, born in Goiano, part of Prato; his father, recently deceased, was a farmer; a brother, nearly retarded, is a cobbler . . . He suffered greatly from his family's misery . . .; but later trained in weaving, he did well enough, even earning up to twenty lire a week at the age of twenty-five." Lombroso describes him: "One does not notice in him any trait that would designate him a madman, degenerate, or criminal. He was of average stature, with pale skin, strong musculature, a black moustache, black eyes, small and deep-set, a cold gaze; there is a very slight exaggeration of development in the cheekbone and a bit of a flaw on the brow." And he concludes: "Crime of insanity, crime of passion, and inherent criminality are to be ruled out in him. He remains a criminal of opportunity . . . It is probable that the anarchy lectures, heard during the formative period . . . had an excessive influence on the content of his mind."

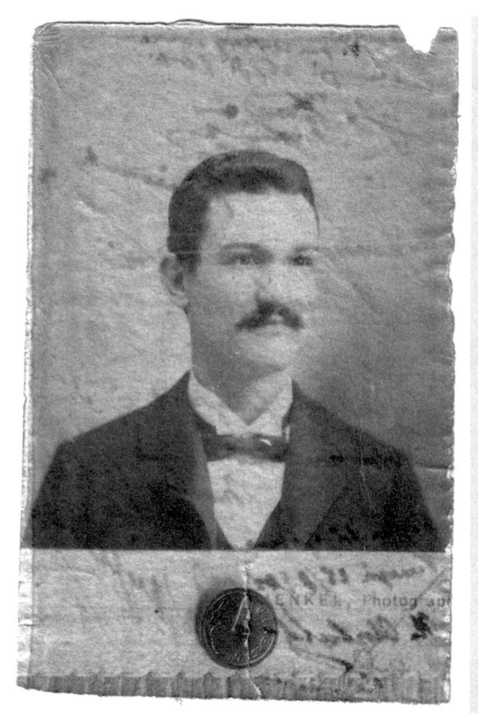

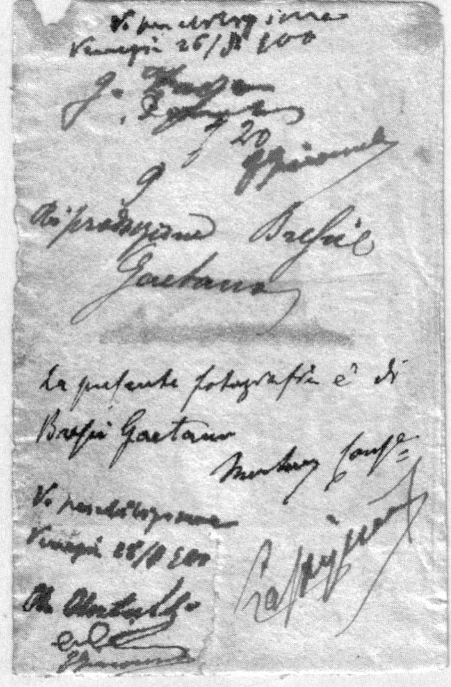
La presente fotografia e' di
Bresci Gaetano

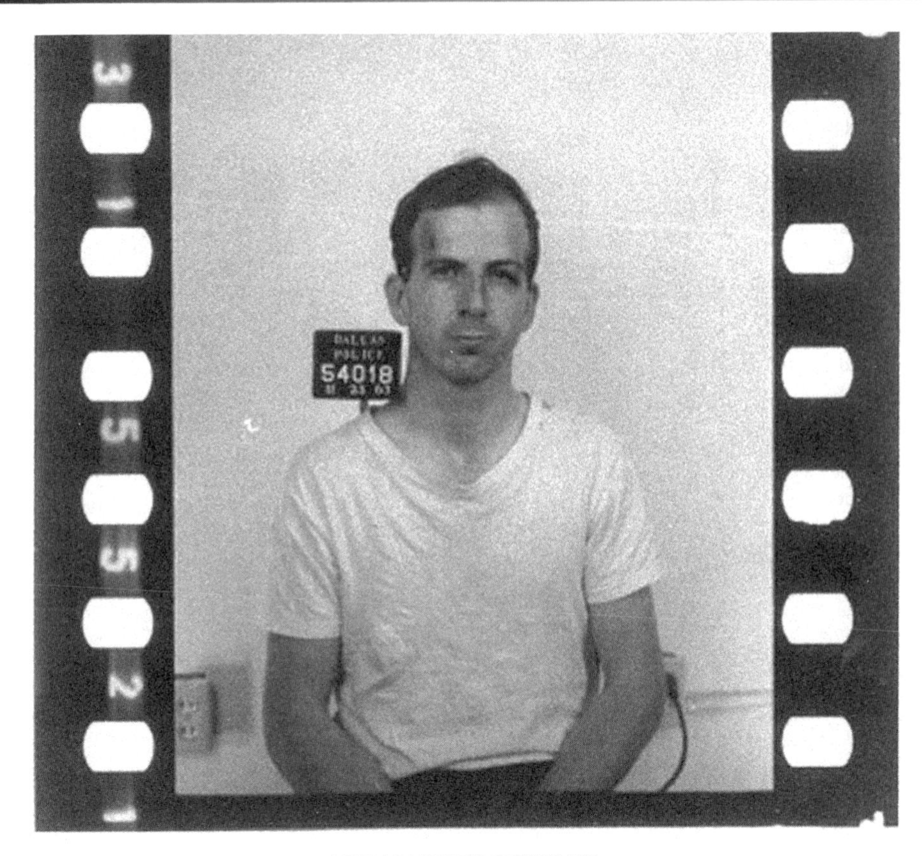

LEE HARVEY OSWALD

DALLAS, TEXAS, 11/22/1963

Disturbed, aggressive, dyslexic, Marine, pro-Soviet, pro-Castro, assassin. The life of Lee Harvey Oswald ended on November 22, 1963, the date of the assassination of President John Fitzgerald Kennedy in Dallas. After the shots were fired, witnesses saw him fleeing the building where he worked, the very building thought to be the source of the bullets that killed JFK. An identikit picture was released, and a police officer tried to stop him, but Oswald shot him. They arrested him inside the Texas Theatre, where he had entered without paying. He yelled to reporters, "I didn't shoot anyone," and later declared, "I am only a patsy." He didn't make it to trial alive.

Two days later, Jack Ruby a.k.a. Sparky, a petty criminal of Polish origins, shot Oswald as he was transferring prisons. Photography and television fixed that moment in history forever.

One of the bullets that killed JFK matched a case found at Edwin Walker's house. A former general, Walker was an outspoken segregationist and anticommunist politician whom Oswald had tried to kill in February 1963. At Oswald's house, documents were found that proved his involvement in the attack. Even now, there are still doubts as to the real co-conspirators and the actual perpetrators of the Kennedy assassination.

JACK RUBY

DALLAS, TEXAS, 11/24/1963

On November 22 and 24, 1963, history traveled through the airwaves to television screens. Two days after the filming of John F. Kennedy's assassination was filmed by an amateur, a murder—of his presumed assassin—was broadcast on live television for the first time. It was 11:21 a.m. when Lee Harvey Oswald was brought to journalists during his transfer to another prison. Dozens of flashes went off in the assassin's face, as did a .38 caliber Colt Cobra, serial number 2744LW, registered to one Jack Ruby.

Jacob Leon Rubenstein, born in Chicago in 1911 to a family of Jewish Poles, had a modest criminal career under his belt at the service of the only power that counted in Chicago at that time—Al Capone's organization. During World War II he served in the American army without once shooting a gun. After moving to Dallas, he scraped by, managing nightclubs and prostitutes. In 1959 he went to Cuba, a gambling and prostitution mecca, to visit Lewis McWillie, a gangster also linked to Meyer Lansky and Santo Trafficante, who would be incarcerated by Fidel Castro in 1963.

As to the killer's motives, there seems to be confusion. He might have wanted to show that "even Jews have guts" and to spare the widowed Jackie the strain of a trial. Theories on the case are a waste. For some, Ruby had acted on mafia orders; some held that he wanted to democratically avenge Kennedy's assassin; others thought he had been involved in the plot to begin with and was eliminating a possible informer. Still others insisted that he was just a crazy fanatic.

At the trial, Ruby's lawyer, Melvin Belli, unsuccessfully pursued the insanity angle. On March 14, 1964, the court sentenced him to death. The condemned man wrote to the Warren Commission, which was busy shedding light on the president's assassination, asking to be heard. The request was approved after the press published a letter from Ruby's sister. In the summer of 1964, Earl Warren and President Gerald Ford reached Dallas. Ruby begged to be transferred to Washington, D.C., because he feared for his life.

The Texas Supreme Court ordained to have the trial moved to another location, because the city of Dallas could not guarantee the accused the proper impartiality of judgment. On January 3, 1967, awaiting his new trial, Ruby died of pulmonary embolism at fifty-six at Parkland Hospital in Dallas. He was buried at Westlawn Cemetery in Chicago, his hometown.

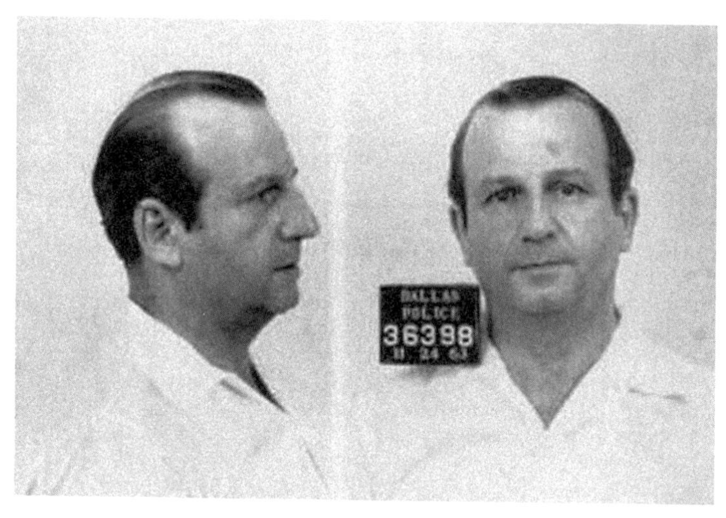

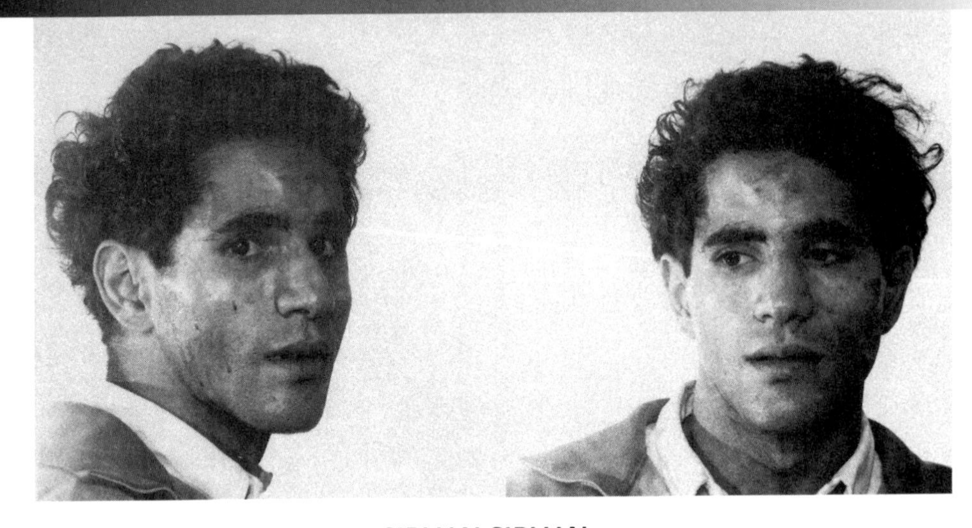

SIRHAN SIRHAN

FRESNO, CALIFORNIA, 01/08/1998

He was the first Palestinian to play a role on the stage of international politics. After more than thirty years, the role has continued to displease him. Only two months had passed since the assassination of Martin Luther King Jr. Just after midnight on June 5, 1968, Robert F. Kennedy, JFK's younger brother, recent winner of the Democratic primaries, was leaving Los Angeles's Ambassador Hotel, passing through the kitchen. He was ambushed near the stoves. Three bullets fired from an eight-cylinder Iver-Johnson pistol struck Bobby, who died the next day at the hospital.

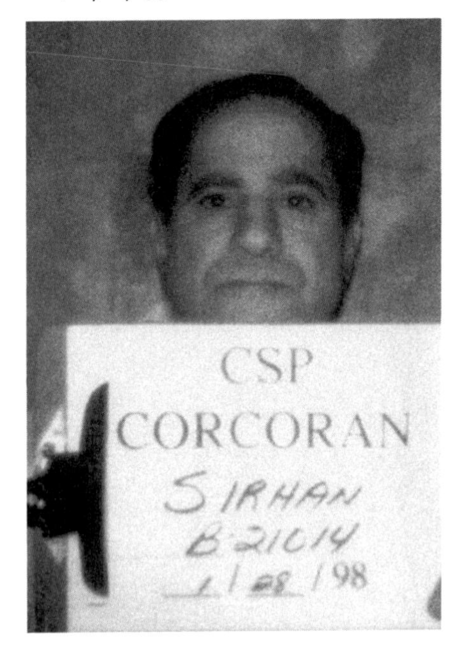

The gun was in the hands of Sirhan Bishara Sirhan, a twenty-four-year-old Palestinian immigrant. He claimed he was innocent, though there were many who would testify the opposite. He asserted that he had been brainwashed by someone who used him like a puppet. His defense was lame, but there were so many dubious elements of the conviction that, four months later, although he was sentenced to capital punishment, it was later commuted to life imprisonment. One such element was that nine bullets had been fired from an eight-cylinder gun. Sirhan Sirhan, as can be seen from his photos, has aged, but continues to declare his innocence. He has submitted twelve applications for parole, all denied.

LEON CZOLGOSZ

BUFFALO, NEW YORK, 09/06/1901

His idol was anarchist Gaetano Bresci, who in July 1900 in Monza killed the king of Italy to avenge the protestors whose massacre he had ordered General Bava-Beccaris to carry out. At the Buffalo Pan-American Exposition on September 6, 1901, anarchist Leon Czolgosz (born in Detroit, 1873) shot U.S. president William McKinley twice at point-blank range. McKinley died from his wounds eight days later. Czolgosz's trial only lasted nine hours, verdict included. He died at 7:12 a.m. on October 29, in prison in Auburn, New York, from three 1700-volt shocks. He declared: "I killed the president because he was an enemy of the good people—the good working people. I am not sorry for my crime." Sulfuric acid was poured in his coffin so that his body would disintegrate.

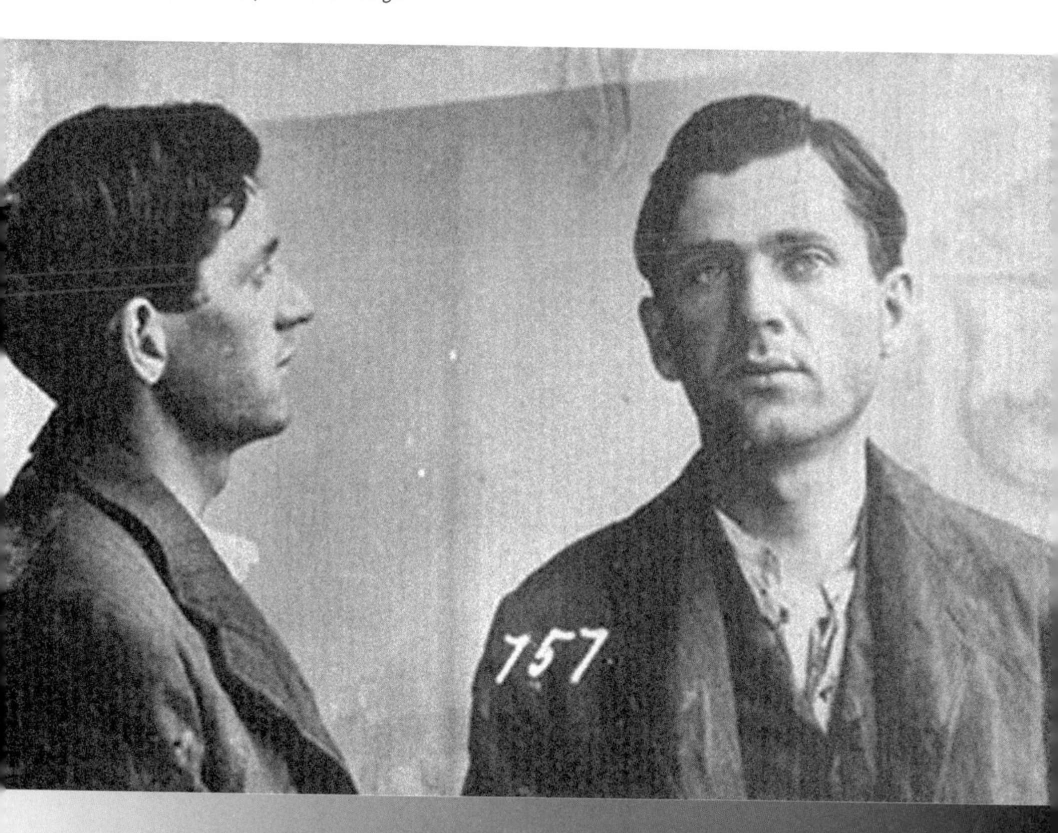

RAMÓN MERCADER DEL RÍO

MEXICO CITY, 08/20/1940

"Cuadro que demuestra la identidad de Ramón Mercader del Río," also known by the name Jacques Mornard. What's remarkable about the file on the assassin of Leon Trotsky—who was killed with an ice pick in Mexico City on August 20, 1940—isn't the photos, but the fingerprints. In *Wanted!* (Bruno Mondadori, 2003), Ando Gilardi writes: "Positive identification occurred not through the almost incomparable portraits shown at the bottom, but from these prints of the right index finger, the first taken in Spain in 1935, the second in Mexico City in 1940, after the crime was committed. The brevity of this primer doesn't allow for discussion of the complex dialectic relationship between the photographic portrait and the dactylogram, as the fingerprint was first called. But after William Herschel, duty obliges us to remember Francis Gallon who, discovering a classification method for these very diverse and irregular signs, made a 'plate' of them that was a thousand times more accurate than Herschel's physiognomy." The defeat of Bertillon's theory ushered us into the twentieth century. It is ironic that, in the history of crime and punishment, the pointer finger has become something of such fundamental importance.

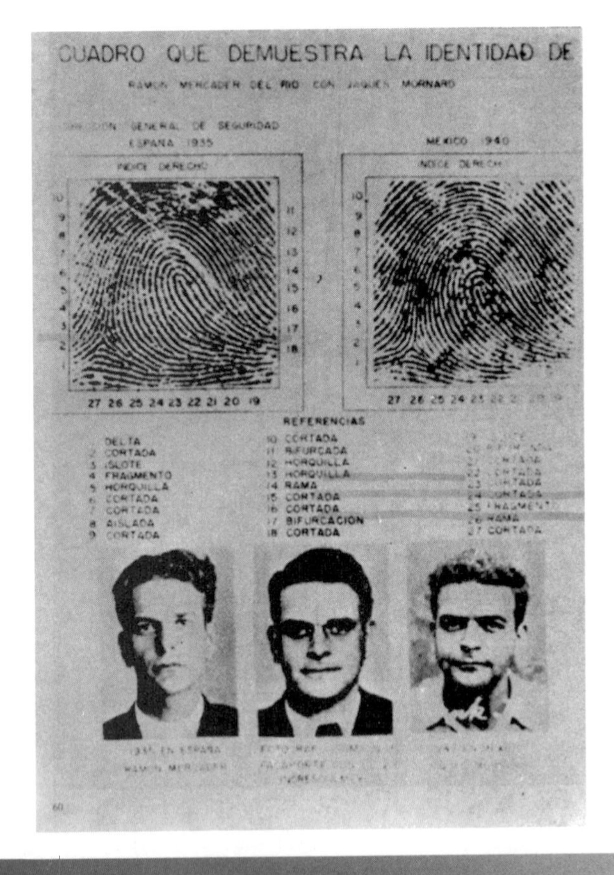

MARK DAVID CHAPMAN

NEW YORK CITY, 03/06/1998

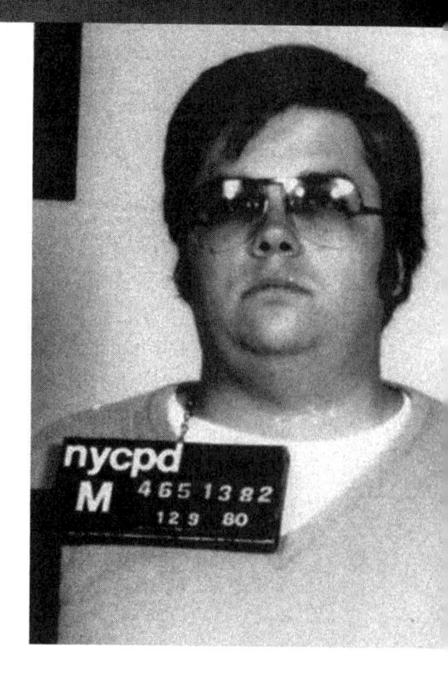

John Lennon's murderer is one of the few who have described the feeling of having a mug shot taken. This happened eleven years after the homicide, on June 28, 1991, in an long interview with Jack Jones for the Rochester *Democrat and Chronicle*. Here is an extract:

"There was nothing that felt like I was in a womb. There was nothing that felt like I was Holden Caulfield . . . even though, in a police car, I did say, 'I am *The Catcher in the Rye*.' I felt more of a . . . a panic . . . more of a . . . of being sucked in a giant wave . . . And I remember one officer . . . or rather one detective . . . either next to me, or . . . or sitting beside the man next to me . . . said, 'Mark, why . . . why did you do it?' And I remember I said to him, without hesitation . . . 'I can't understand what's going on in the world and . . . and what's it become . . .'"

"I remember he told me to remove my sweater. And I was removing it, he just came up and just pulled it off of me, just like, you know, 'Come on!' And . . . and took mug shots of me. One of these mug shots, from what I heard later, had disappeared and turned up in the press. And it was printed in *The New York Post* . . . a very ugly picture. They told me to turn sideways and face forward, and . . . mug shots . . ."

On December 8, 1980, leaving his New York home, John Lennon died from four gunshot wounds, fired by a fan.

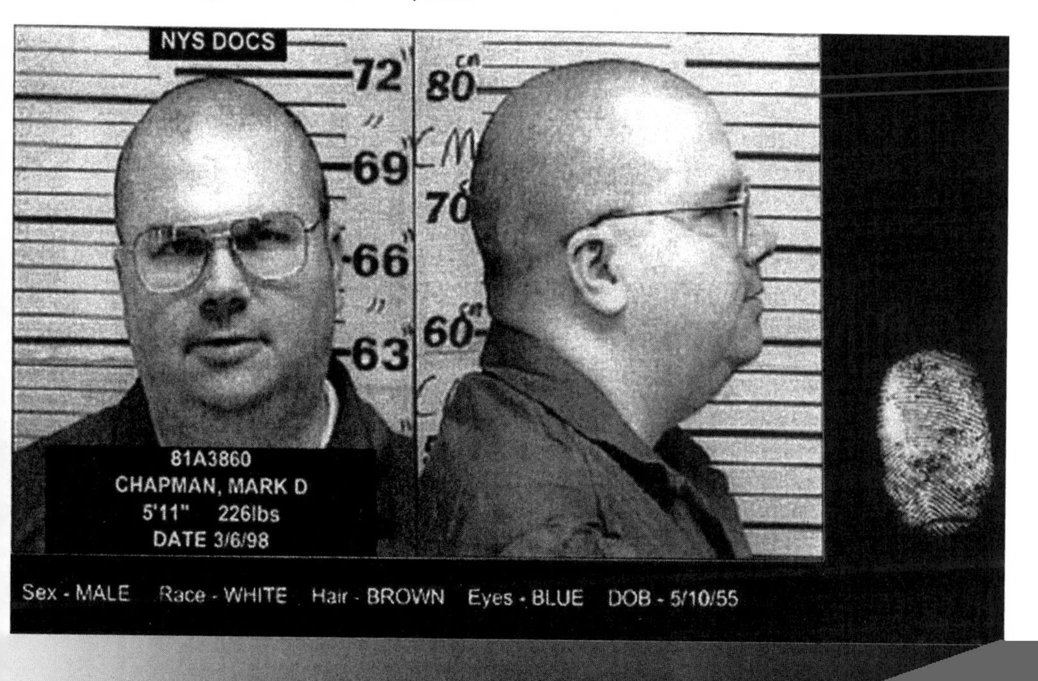

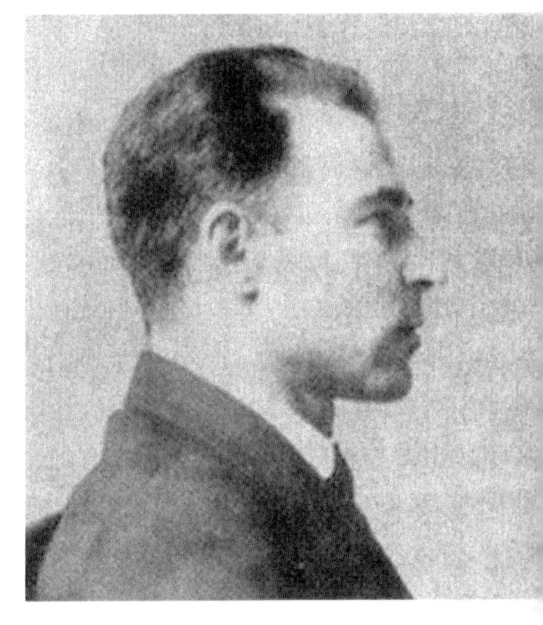

NICOLA SACCO, BARTOLOMEO VANZETTI

WEST BRIDGEWATER, MASSACHUSETTS, 05/05/1920

On August 23, 1927, the *New York Times* ran the headline "Sacco Cries 'Long Live Anarchy'; Vanzetti Insists on His Innocence." The article reads:

> Charlestown State Prison, Mass., Tuesday, Aug. 23—Nicola Sacco and Bartolomeo Vanzetti died in the electric chair early this morning, carrying out the sentence imposed on them for the South Braintree murders of April 15, 1920. Sacco marched to the death chair at 12:11 and was pronounced lifeless at 12:19. Vanzetti entered the execution room at 12:20 and was declared dead at 12:26. To the last they protested their innocence, and the efforts of many who believed them guiltless proved futile, although they fought a legal and extra legal battle unprecedented in the history of American jurisprudence. With them died Celestino F. Madeiros, the young Portuguese, who won seven respites when he 'confessed' that he was present at the time of the South Braintree murder and that Sacco and Vanzetti were not with him.

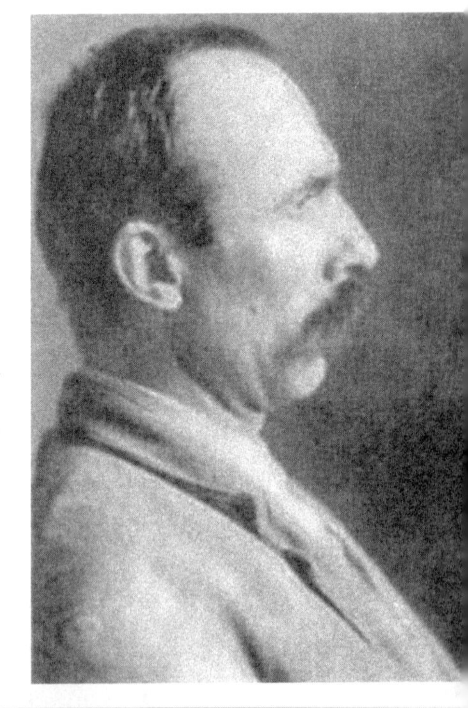

The story began on April 15, 1920, when in South Braintree, Massachusetts, during a holdup that yielded $15,776.51, banker Frederick A. Parmenter and security guard Alessandro Berardelli were killed. Nicola Sacco (born in Torremaggiore, Italy, 1891) and Bartolomeo

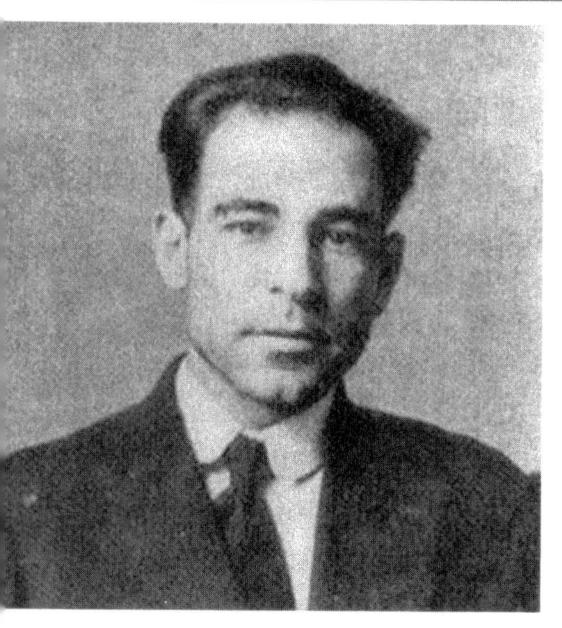

Vanzetti (born in Villafalletto, Italy, 1888), both anarchists, were arrested May 5. On July 14, 1921, a jury found them guilty. On February 14, 1923, Sacco started a hunger strike. On April 24, he returned to prison from the Bridgewater Hospital. He was deemed to be of sound mind.

On November 25, 1925, the young Portuguese Celestino Madeiros, convicted of a separate murder, cleared them by incriminating the gang of a certain Morelli, but the U.S. Supreme Court refused to reopen the case. On April 9, 1927, Judge Webster Thayer sentenced them to death. More investigations. More requests denied. Writer John Dos Passos wrote, "we are two nations."

From 1946–47, Woody Guthrie composed *Ballads of Sacco & Vanzetti*, which came out years later. Guthrie wrote to his producer, Moses Asch, founder of Folkways Records: "I feel like the trip to Boston was just a little bit hurried and hasty. I did not get to go to all the spots plainly mentioned in the pamphlets and books . . . So I say, let's forget about the Sacco and Vanzetti album for the time being. It will be lots better when I can get a car and my own way of traveling from one scene to the other one. I'm drunk as hell today, been that way for several days . . . I refuse to write these songs while I'm drunk and it looks like I'll be drunk for a long time."

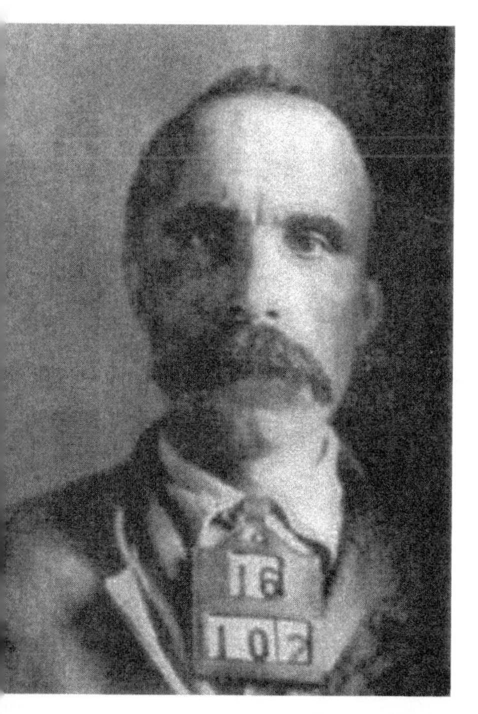

JULIUS ROSENBERG

NEW YORK CITY, 07/17/1950

ETHEL ROSENBERG

NEW YORK CITY, 8/11/1950

Accused of being Soviet spies, the Rosenbergs died on the electric chair on June 19, 1953. Since dawn, a crowd had gathered in New York to protest the verdict. The next day, William R. Conklin's feature appeared in the *New York Times*:

> OSSINING, N. Y., June 19—Stoic and tight-lipped to the end, Julius and Ethel Rosenberg paid the death penalty tonight in the electric chair at Sing Sing Prison for their war-time atomic espionage for Soviet Russia.
>
> The pair, first husband and wife to pay the supreme penalty here, and the first in the United States to die for espionage, went to their deaths with a composure that astonished the witnesses.
>
> Julius, 35 years old, was first to enter the glaringly lighted, white-walled death chamber. He walked slowly behind Rabbi Irving Koslowe, a chaplain at Sing Sing, who was intoning the Twenty-third Psalm, "The Lord is my shepherd, I shall not want." As Rosenberg neared the brown-stained oak chair he seemed to sway from side to side.
>
> Guards quickly placed him in the chair. He was clean-shaven, no longer wearing his mustache, and wore a white T-shirt. At 8:04 p.m. the first shock of 2,000 volts, with its ten amperes, coursed through his body. After two subsequent shocks his life ended at 8:06 p.m.
>
> Dr. H.W. Kipp and Dr. George McCracken applied stethoscopes to his chest, and Dr. Kipp said: "I pronounce this man dead."
>
> Ethel Rosenberg, the 37-year-old wife, entered the death chamber a few minutes

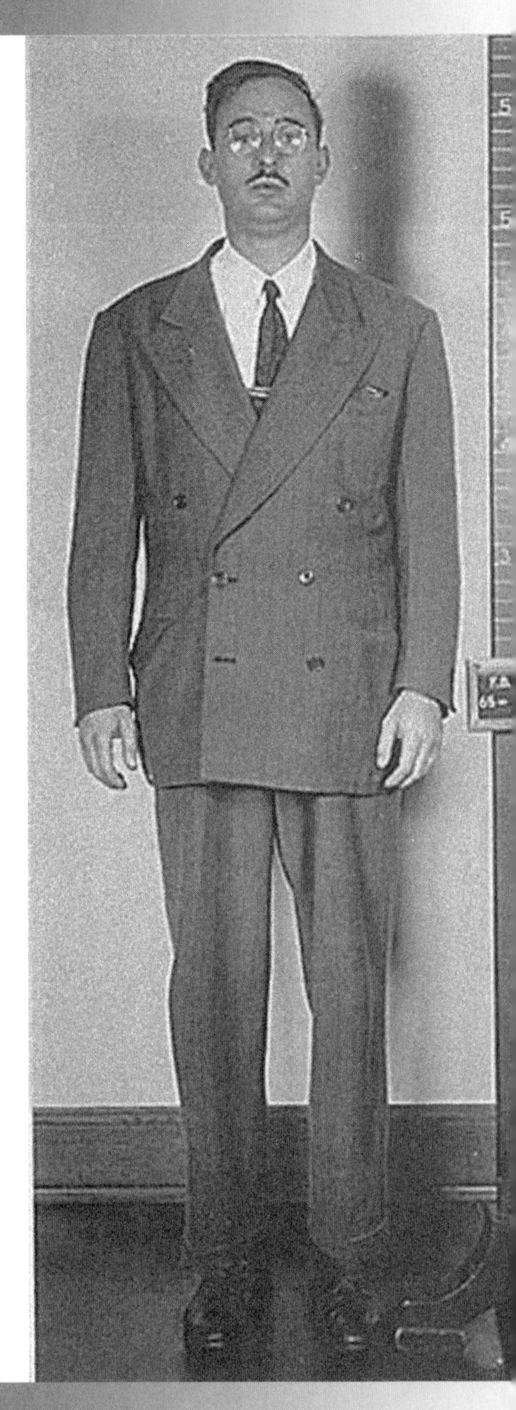

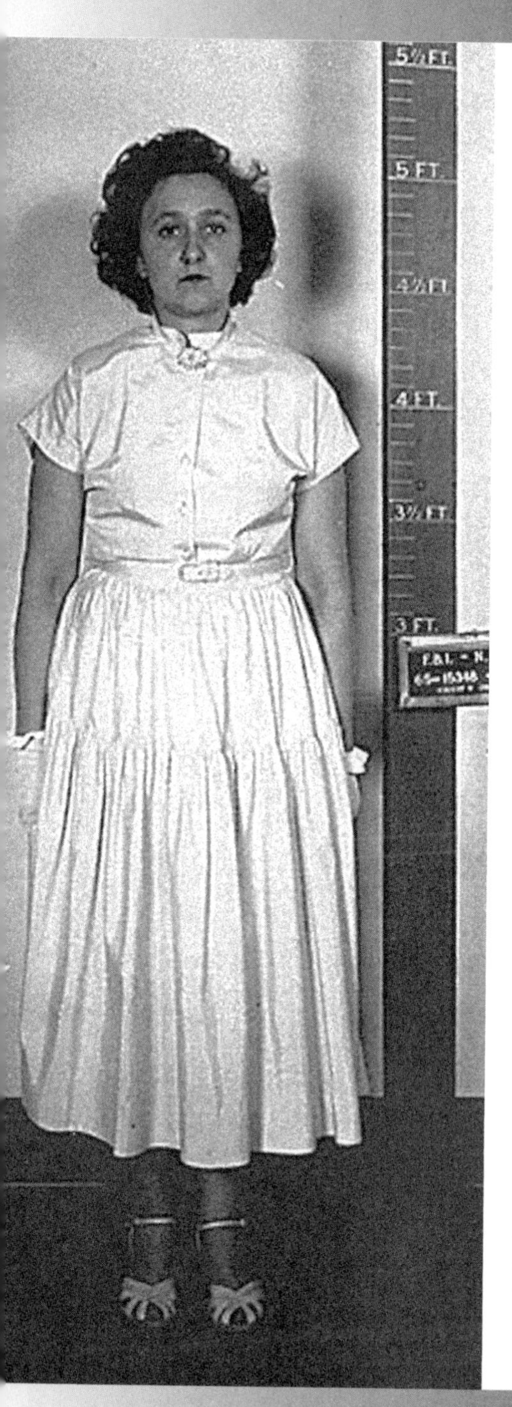

after the body of her husband had been removed. She wore a dark green print dress with white polka dots, and, like her husband, was shod in loafer-type cloth slippers. Her hair was close-cropped on top to permit contact of an electrode.

Just before she reached the chair the five-foot, 100-pound woman held out her hand to Mrs. Helen Evans, a matron. As Mrs. Evans grasped her hand, Mrs. Rosenberg drew her close and kissed her lightly on the cheek . . .

Mrs. Rosenberg sat in the electric chair 'with the most composed look you ever saw,' one witness said.

She winced a bit as the electrode came in contact with her head, but her arms relaxed under their binding straps. Silent, she waited while the guards dropped a leather mask over her face. To her right stood Joseph P. Francel, the state executioner, in an alcove.

The first of three successive shocks was applied at 8:11 p.m. After the third shock the two doctors applied their stethoscopes and found she was still alive. After two more applications of the current Mrs. Rosenberg was pronounced dead at 8:16 p.m.

Both executions of the death sentence had been advanced from the usual Sing Sing hour of 11 p.m. so that they would not conflict with the Jewish Sabbath. The last rays of a red sun over the Hudson River were casting a faint light when the double execution was completed.

The couple heard early this afternoon that both the Supreme Court and President Eisenhower had rejected their final appeals.

The couple left behind two young sons, Michael and Robert, who eventually changed their last name to Meeropol and became university professors. In 1990, Robert created the Rosenberg Fund for Children, an organization working to help the children of targeted progressive activists around the world.

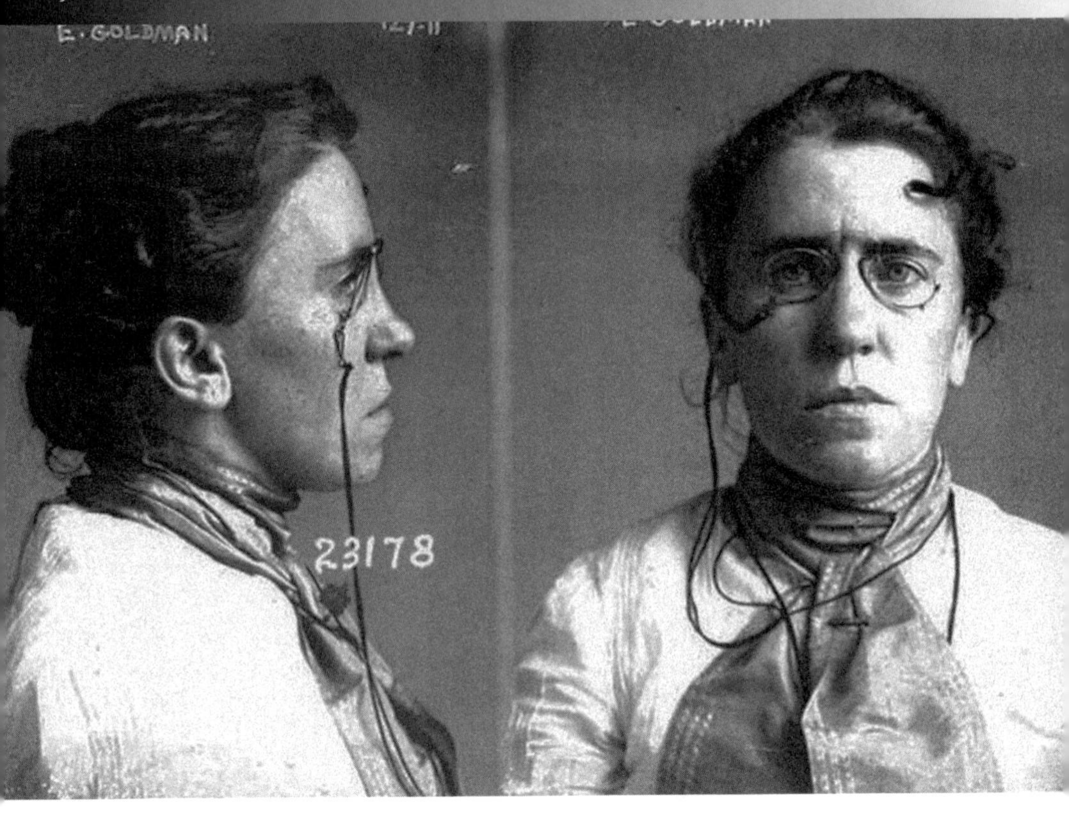

EMMA GOLDMAN

NEW YORK CITY, 02/11/1916

Anarchist, revolutionary, feminist. Born in a Russian ghetto in 1869. As a teenager, she emigrated to Rochester, New York. After four anarchists were hanged for the May 4, 1886, Haymarket Riot, she became increasingly political and eventually moved to New York City, where she helped Alexander Berkman plan the murder of industrialist Henry Clay Frick. To get money for a gun, she even tried prostitution (though unsuccessfully). The plan failed. She went to jail for urging a crowd of unemployed workers to take food, for distributing brochures on contraception, and finally, in 1917, for conspiracy.

She was deported to Russia just in time for the Revolution. She later wrote, "Never before in all history has authority, government, the State, proved so inherently static, reactionary, and even counter-revolutionary." After many travels, she repaired to England where she married a Welsh anarchist friend in order to gain citizenship. At sixty-seven, after Berkman's suicide, she went to support the Spanish Civil War. When she died in 1940, she was buried in Chicago, not far from the Haymarket martyrs.

She responded to the reproach of a friend who had seen her dancing in public, "our cause could not expect me to behave as a nun . . . I want freedom, the right to self expression, everybody's right to beautiful, radiant things."

PATRICIA HEARST

SAN MATEO, CALIFORNIA, 09/19/1975

In a 1994 interview, she said that sometimes she couldn't walk down the street without fifty heads turning to look at her. When the Symbionese Liberation Army kidnapped her in February 1974, the granddaughter of mass media magnate William Randolph Hearst (the man who inspired Orson Welles's *Citizen Kane*) was about to turn twenty and was studying at UC Berkeley. She was dating her former high school math tutor, who she'd just moved in with, and she was majoring in art history. Her family met the kidnappers' demands, paying them two million dollars in food to feed the needy in San Francisco. After that, the Hearst Corporation shelled out another four million.

On April 15, 1974, the security cameras at the Hibernia Bank in San Francisco taped Patricia Campbell Hearst wielding a submachine gun during a robbery. The newspapers jumped on the story. On her first shooting outside a Los Angeles sporting goods store on May 16: "(Hearst) pointed an M-1 carbine and fired the whole clip," an FBI agent recalled. "And then she took another rifle and shot some more." She was arrested the following year, in September 1975.

Her battle name was Tania, a tribute to Che Guevara's fearless agent in Bolivia. Her attorney, F. Lee Bailey, would manage to get O. J. Simpson acquitted a few decades later. The defense argued that Patty had been brainwashed and forced, through deprivation and threats, to follow her kidnappers' orders. The jury did not believe the defense, and in 1976 Patricia Hearst got seven years in prison. In 1979, after only two years, the sentence was commuted by Democratic president Jimmy Carter, and Patty was able to leave.

Two months later, she married her bodyguard and moved to Connecticut. In the last twenty-five years she has given birth to two daughters, written an autobiography, and appeared in seven films. In 2000, she played the mother of one of the young kidnappers of the famous actress Honey Whitlock (played by Melanie Griffith) in John Waters's *Cecil B. Demented*.

She was pardoned in 2001, President Clinton's final act before the end of his second term. She just wanted to be forgotten. This wish was somewhat hindered by the trial of Kathleen Ann Soliah, another member of the Simbionese Liberation Army, who was arrested in 1999. For twenty-five years she had lived as a fugitive as Sara Jane Olson, a housewife in Minnesota.

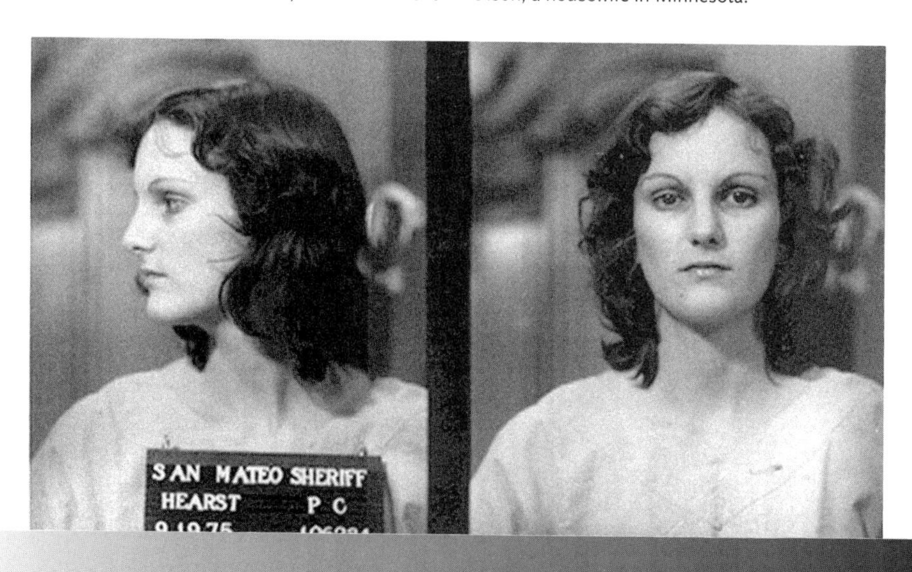

GUS HALL

LEAVENWORTH, KANSAS, 11/18/1954

Arvo Kusta Halberg, the son of Finnish immigrants, was born in 1910 in Minnesota. The area was teeming with steel mills and labor conflicts. At seventeen he joined the Communist Party, and in 1942 voluntarily enlisted in the Navy. His first conviction was for conspiracy in 1948, and he remained in prison for eight-and-a-half years. He got out when the Supreme Court declared the law that had convicted him unconstitutional. In 1959 he was elected chairman of the American Communist Party. He died in 2000, at the age of ninety. In 1992, he said: "I did what I believe in. I believe socialism is inevitable."

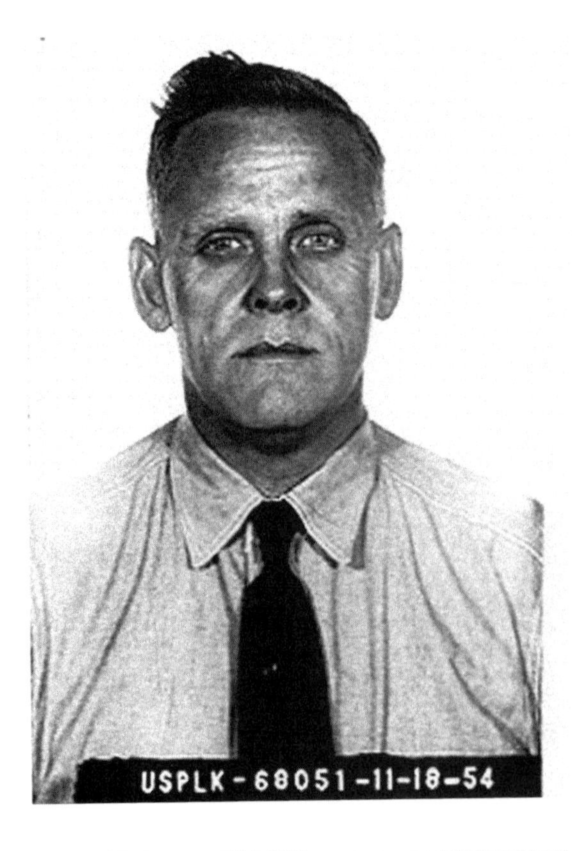

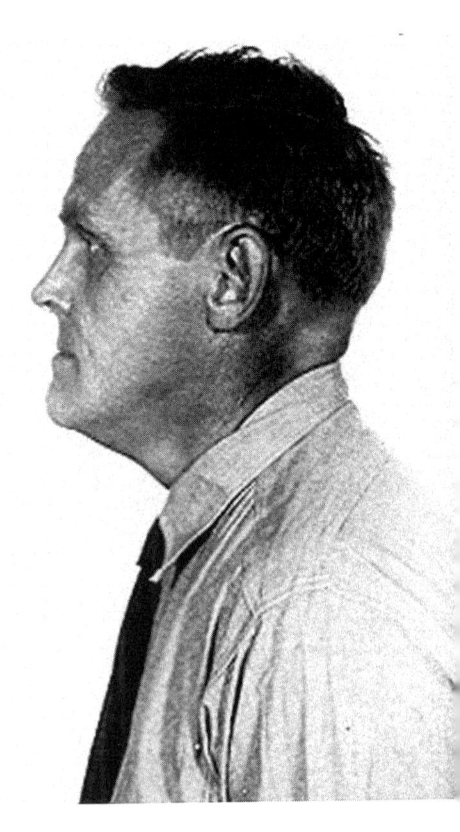

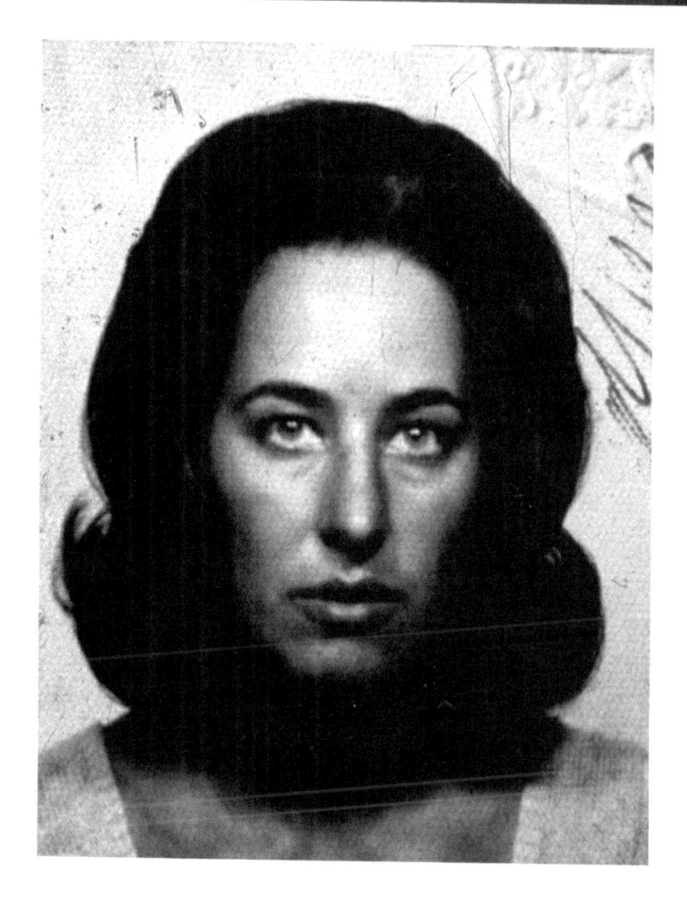

MARA CAGOL

"Margherita Cagol has fallen in battle—Mara, Communist leader and member of the Executive Committee of the Red Brigades. Her life and death are an example that no freedom fighter will ever forget . . . May a thousand arms reach out to take her gun. We, as a final farewell, say to her: Mara, a flower has blossomed, and the Red Brigades will continue to cultivate this flower of freedom until we are victorious." This is her memorial from the Red Brigades, most likely written by her husband, Renato Curcio.

Born in Trent in 1945 to a Catholic family, she received her diploma in guitar at the conservatory and a degree in sociology in 1969, with Francesco Alberoni as her adviser. Six days later, on August 2, she married Renato Curcio in a little church in San Romedio. She and her husband moved to Milan, where the couple, along with Alberto Franceschini, founded the Red Brigades.

Mara Cagol died on June 4, 1975, during the kidnapping of winemaker Vallarino Gancia, in a shootout with the Dalla Chiesa police at the Spiotta di Arzello farm in Monferrato. Her body was taken to the hospital in Acqua Terme, where her two sisters made the identification, later confirmed by her fingerprints, taken in 1972.

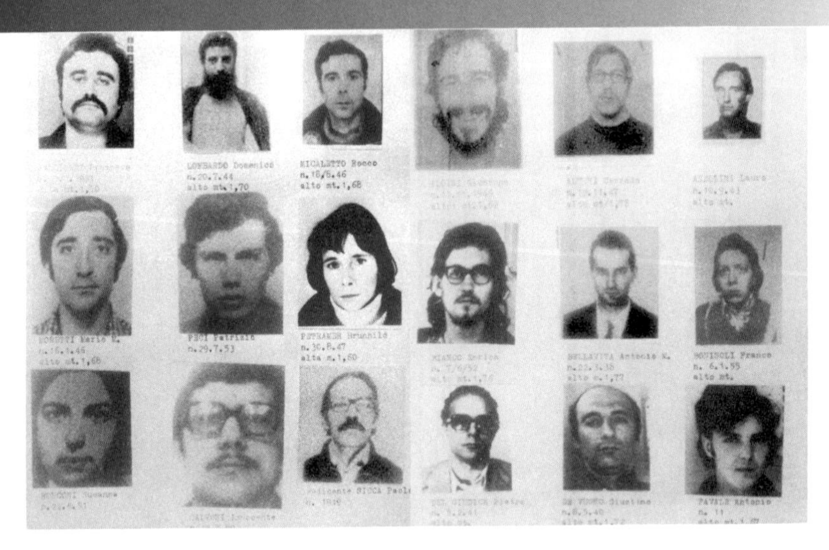

RED BRIGADES / RED ARMY FACTION

ITALY—GERMANY, 1978

At the end of the seventies, police photography started to write history as it was happening. In response to a previously inconceivable challenge, the State began mass-producing the image of the enemy so that he could be recognized, isolated, and rendered harmless.

It was precisely in the mug shot that the challenge from the Red Brigades (BR) in Italy and from the Red Army Faction (RAF) in Germany found its most visible form of representation. To confer some political sense to the kidnapping of Aldo Moro, president of the Christian Democrats and former prime minister of Italy, and of Hanns-Martin Schleyer, president of the German industry association, the terrorists themselves could find no better way than to replicate the judicial practices of the State they wanted to destroy. Thus the people's judgment was placed alongside the people's police photo.

The authorities' response to this iconographic challenge—in which powerful men were reduced, through photography, to the rank of common criminal—was connected to another use of police photography: the "wanted" poster, especially the collective wanted poster. In this case, the photo of the wicked doesn't enable, for symbolic or documentary ends, eventual arrest, but exactly the opposite. It publicly announces that the face's owner must be punished or stopped and asks a society of conformists to join the hunt. The Italian and German terrorists wanted, in the same year, for the kidnappings of Moro and Schleyer are part of that same gallery of mug shots.

Collective wanted posters represent an investigatory practice that, like the identikit picture, rarely yields positive results. Very few criminals have been recognized by such posters. Instead there are numerous cases of innocent people mis-identified, and convicted, thanks to them. It has been calculated that the RAF poster was seen by fifty million people without any of the terrorists being identified. Given the system's inefficiency and expense, it is plausible that the motives behind the use of wanted posters are political and aesthetic.

The public loves to see the faces of the wicked and therefore the media loves to broadcast them. Institutions, meanwhile, warn the good about the existence of evil. They reassure them that everyone's faces are catalogued. And they warn the evil that their faces have already been arrested.

In other words, the mug shot demonstrates an acquired possession of evil. The wanted poster affirms, while the battle is still in progress, that the good are strong and the bad are hunted.

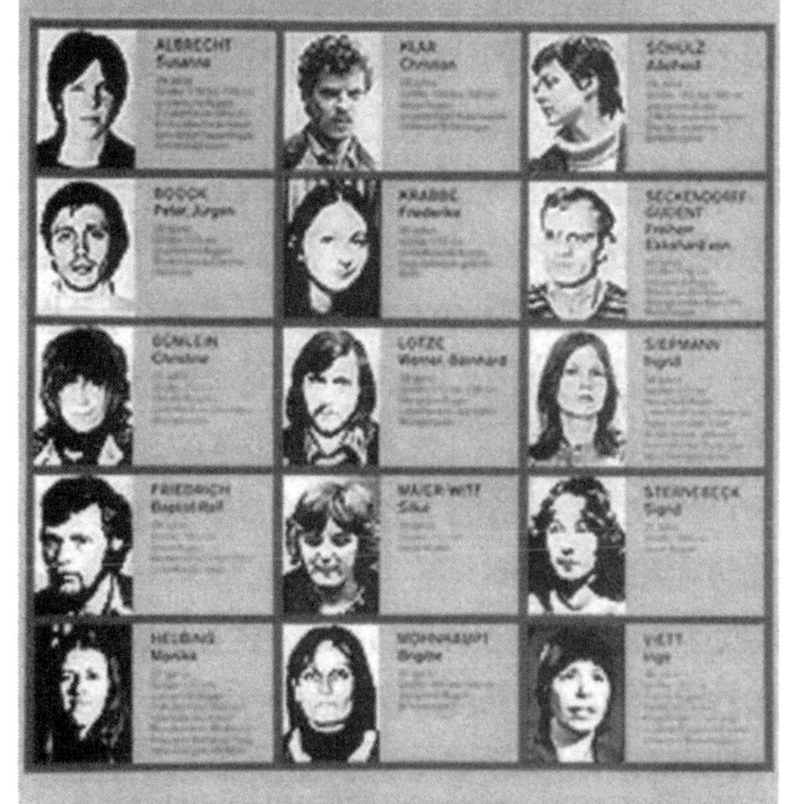
Terroristen
Vorsicht Schußwaffen!

HANNS-MARTIN SCHLEYER

VOLKSGEFÄNGNIS, GERMANY, 10/13/1977

Wednesday, October 19, 1977, 4:21 p.m. In a phone call to the Stuttgart headquarters of Deutsche Presse Agentur, a woman's voice claimed responsibility for the assassination of the president of the German industry association on behalf of the RAF:

"After forty-three days, we have ended Hanns-Martin Schleyer's miserable and corrupt existence. Herr Schmidt, who from the start has been reckoning with Schleyer's death in his power calculations, can find him in a green Audi 100 with Bad Homburg plates in the rue Charles Peguy in Mulhouse. His death is of no significance in our pain and rage at the slaughter of Mogadishu and Stammheim. The fascist drama staged by the imperialists to destroy the liberation movement does not surprise Andreas, Gudrun, Jan, Irmgard, and ourselves. We will never forgive Schmidt and the imperialists who support him for the blood that has been shed. The fight has only just begun. Freedom through the armed anti-imperialist struggle." The same evening, at 9:10 p.m., Schleyer's body was found, with three gunshots to the head. The mug shot, until then a practice exercised by power, bursts into history as a practice to oppose power. Institutions and revolution look each other in the eyes through the mirror of photography.

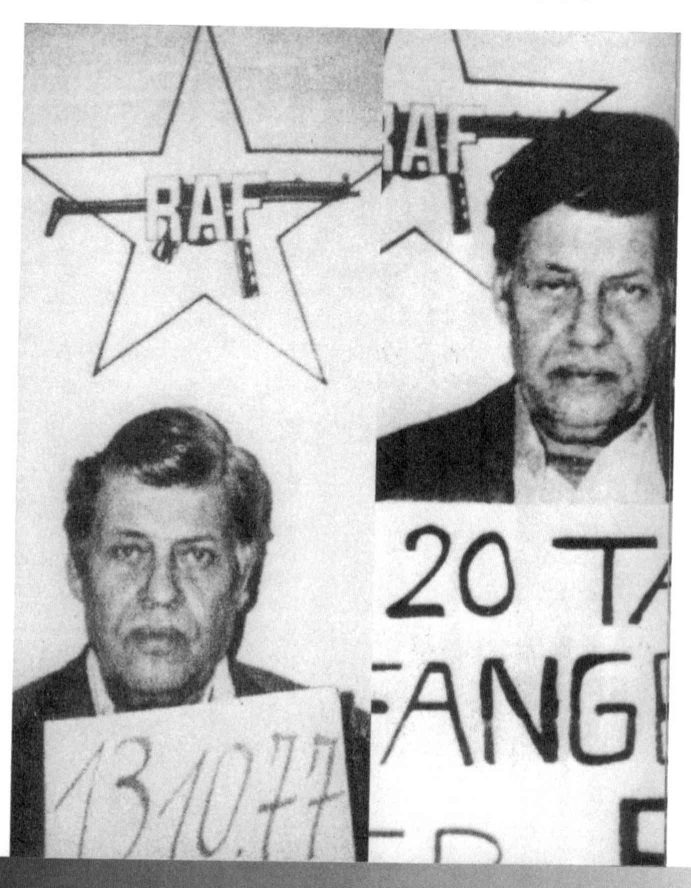

ALDO MORO

PRIGIONE DEL POPOLO, ITALY

On March 29, 1978, Francesco Cossiga, then Minister for the Christian Democrats, read a letter from Aldo Moro, president of the party who had been kidnapped by the Red Brigades on March 16 on Via Fani in Rome during an operation that led to the killing of five guards. The letter said: "Dear Francesco, . . . Although I know nothing either of what occurred after my abduction or of how it came about, it is certain—I have been explicitly informed of this—that I am seen as a political prisoner subject, as President of the Christian Democratic Party, to a trial aimed at exposing my responsibilities over the past thirty years (a trial at present restricted to political terms, which grows more threatening every day) . . . As I see it, the serious charge which is being brought against me concerns me in my capacity as official representative of the Christian Democratic Party as a whole in the administration of its political programme."

The body was found the morning of May 9, 1978, in the trunk of a red Renault 4 on Via Caetani in Rome, right in the middle of the street between the headquarters of two major Italian parties. When the first picture reached the press, the satirical newspaper *Il Male*—referencing a popular ad—published it with the caption "Scusate, abitualmente vesto Marzotto" ("Sorry, I usually wear Marzotto").

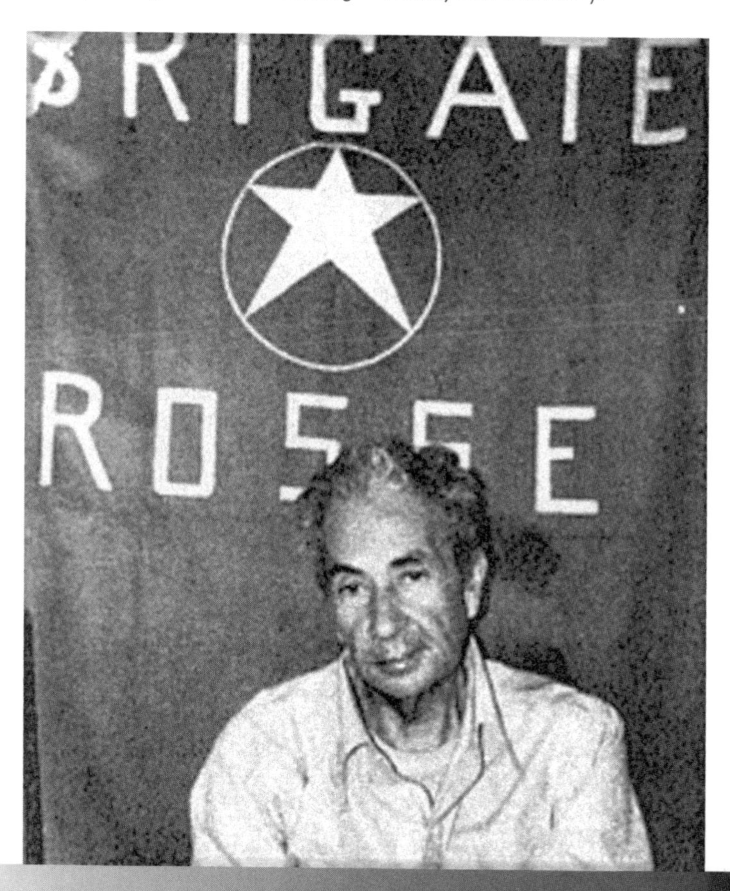

PALMIRO TOGLIATTI

From the song "Ricordo di Togliatti" by Borzacchini and Tical: "He had such a desire to learn / he studied hard, and with passion / since Palmiro was a model student / he received a scholarship / for the University of Turin / where he met Antonio Gramsci / and they wrote for the paper *Avanti!* / but then the Great War called to him." The secretary of the biggest communist party in Europe was born in Genoa in 1893. At the war's end, as the minister of justice, he granted amnesty to ex-fascists. For Italian journalist Giorgio Bocca, there was one primary reason for the cultural hegemony of the Italian Communist Party (PCI), conceptualized by Gramsci and achieved by Togliatti: "Communists read."

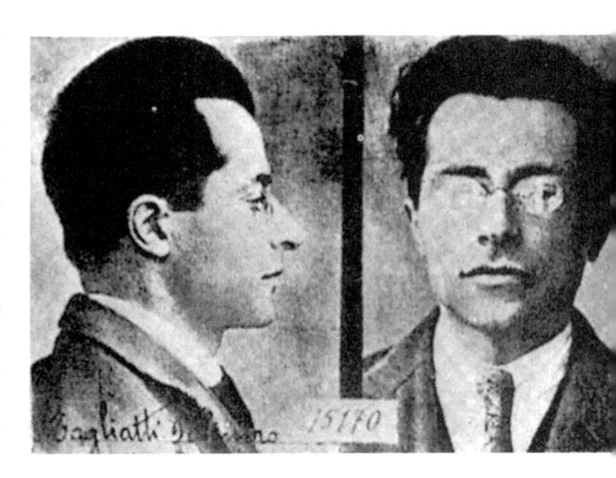

ANTONIO GRAMSCI

FORMIA, ITALY, 1937

"The first little sparrow was much nicer than the current one. It was very proud, very lively. This one is modest in the extreme, with a servile spirit and no initiative. The first immediately became master of the cell. It conquered all the existing peaks and therefore settled for quite a while to savor the sublime peace. Reaching the top of the bottle of tamarind juice was its perpetual quest: and consequently it fell once into a receptacle full of refuse from the cafeteria and was nearly buried. What I liked about this sparrow was that it didn't want to be touched."

The greatest Italian intellectual of the twentieth century, born in Ales, Sardinia, 1891. In 1911 he won a scholarship for low-income students (he came in ninth, Togliatti second) and moved to Turin. At the Livorno Congress in 1921, he was among the founding members of the Italian Communist Party.

Mussolini had him arrested in 1926 as he was leaving the Chamber of Deputies. He left behind two mug shots. In the first, he is young. In the second, eleven years later in 1937, he's an old man. The Formia prison required front and profile shots of inmates who needed to be hospitalized. He died in the Quisisana clinic in Rome, on April 27 of the same year.

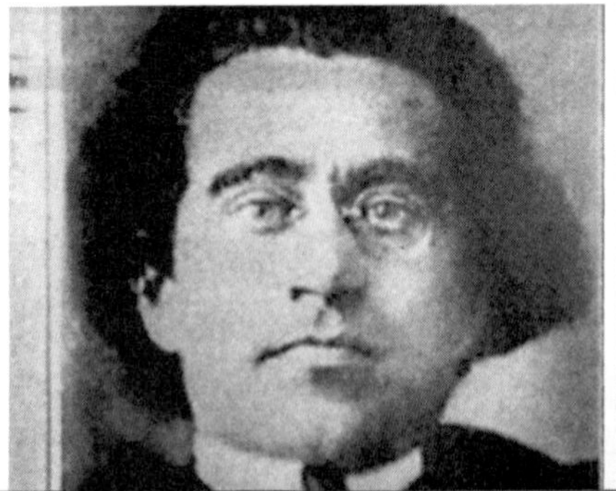

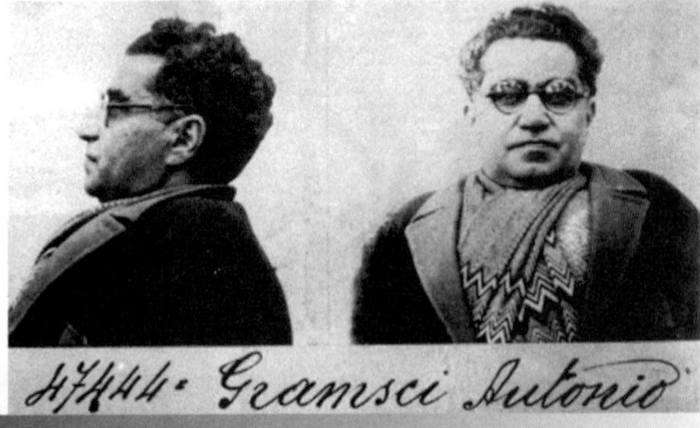

SANDRO PERTINI

STELLA, ITALY, 05/22/1925

In China they have a saying for newborns: "May you live in interesting times." Alessandro Pertini, born in Stella, in the province of Savona (now Liguria), on September 25, 1896, found interesting times on his path. And he lived them.

From a family of landowners, with four brothers (the youngest killed by the Nazis in Flossenburg), he returned from World War I with a silver medal. The following year, he joined the Unitarian Socialist Party and moved to Florence where he frequented the circle of the Rosselli brothers and Gaetano Salvemini.

He was arrested on May 22, 1925, for distributing the clandestine newspaper *Sotto il barbaro dominio fascista*. Accused of "instigating hatred among the social classes" (see article 120 of the Zanardelli Code), he was sentenced to eight months in prison. On December 4, 1926, another conviction and five months in confinement. He went into hiding. In Milan, housed by Carlo Rosselli, he was among the organizers of Filippo Turati's escape to France. In Nice, he became Jean Gauvrin and earned a living as a laborer, washing taxis, being an extra in films. He set up a clandestine radio broadcast, and the Nice tribunal sentenced him to a month in jail. He returned to Italy, to Pisa, on March 29, 1929.

Fifteen days later he was arrested again, referred to the special tribunal and sentenced to ten years and nine months in prison plus three under special surveillance. In Regina Coeli, he became ill and was moved to the Turi prison, where he met Antonio Gramsci. Starting in April 1932, he was at the prison sanitarium of Pianosa, in September 1935 in confinement in Ponza, then at the Tremiti Islands, and again at Ventotene. He got out after fourteen years, in August 1943. On October 18, the Nazis arrested him again, along with Giuseppe Saragat, and sentenced him to death. The resistance freed him on January 24, 1944. He took part in the liberation of Florence, flew to France, returned to Italy, and assisted with the liberation of Milan in April 1945. In the same year, he became secretary for the Italian Socialist Party (PSI), editor of *Avanti!*, a member of the Constituent Assembly, and a member of Parliament. Starting in 1968 he was President of the Chamber of Deputies. In 1978 he became President of the Republic. In eight years, he received 55,000 students, rejoiced in Italy's victory at the World Soccer Championships in 1982, and constantly had a pipe in his mouth ("From smokers, we can learn tolerance. I've never met anybody who protested against nonsmokers," he once said). He died in Rome on February 24, 1990, at age ninety-four. In his final years, he passed the time watching Westerns.

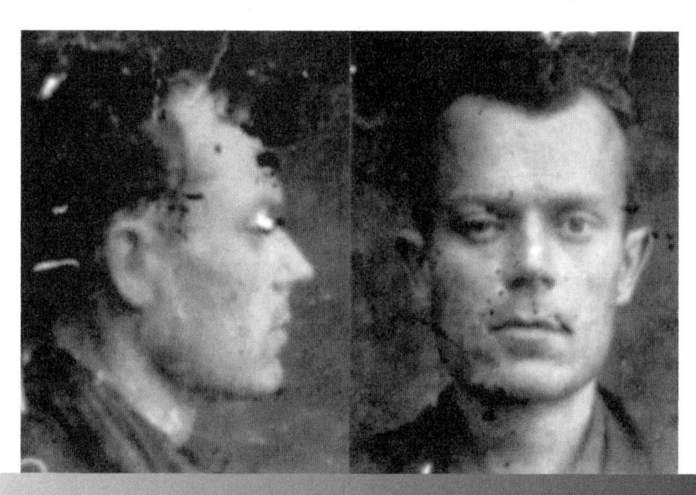

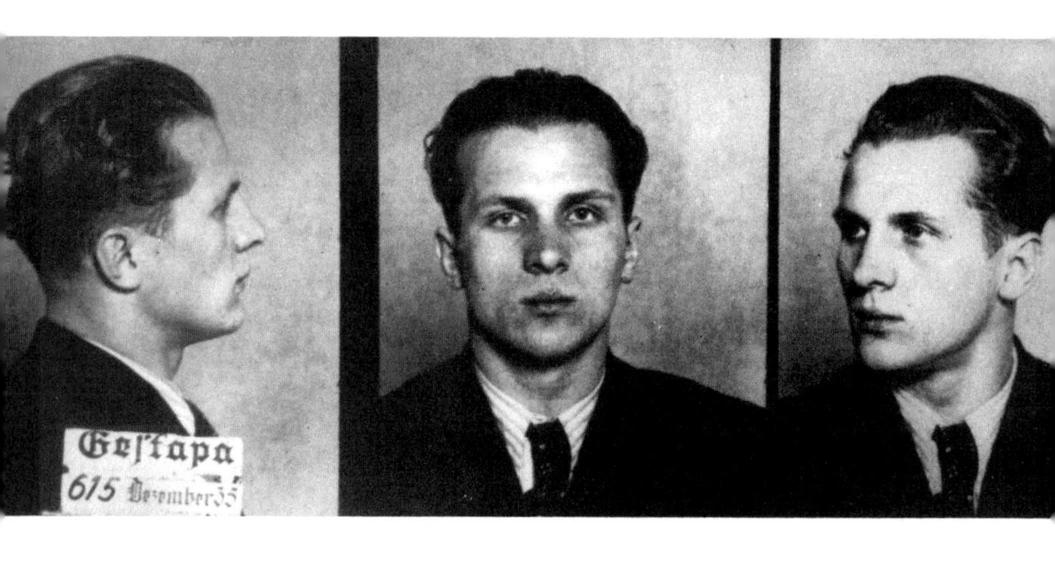

ERICH HONECKER

GERMANY, 12/1935

It happens to men, at times, that they become symbols, caricatures. For a long time, Honecker's sad attire, his melancholy ties, his boring speeches, symbolized the seriousness of the Stakhanovist worker from Eastern Germany.

Son of a Neunkirchen miner, in the region of Saar, he was born in 1912, became a Communist in 1929, and moved to Moscow. He returned to Germany in 1931 and was sentenced by the Nazis to ten years of imprisonment in 1937.

The German Democratic Republic (DDR) came into being on October 7, 1949. In 1961, it took on the task of building the Wall. In 1971, Honecker succeeded Walter Ulbricht as General Secretary of the Socialist Unity Party. Until his resignation a month before the Berlin Wall was torn down by the world and by history, he respected the border, even when it disappeared with Gorbachev's ascendance. He fled to Moscow in 1991. He was deported to Germany in July 1992 and taken to the Berlin-Moabit prison. His number was 2955/92. The charge? He had authorized soldiers to shoot anyone who tried to climb over the wall. They estimated the death toll at 192. He was released after 169 days for health reasons. He emigrated to Chile with his wife, daughter, and niece, where he died of liver cancer on May 29, 1994. At his trial he defended himself, saying: "I lived through the DDR. We have demonstrated that socialism is possible, and that it can be better than capitalism."

FIDEL CASTRO

SANTIAGO DE CUBA, 1953

Fidel Castro has earned a small place in this inventory for his invention of the "Caribbean gulag" against opponents and homosexuals. Any remaining sympathy for him is due to the wonderful letter he sent, at age twelve, to U.S. President Franklin Delano Roosevelt on November 6, 1940: "My good friend Roosevelt: I don't know very English, but I know as much as write you." After introducing himself, the future dictator of Cuba continued: "I am twelve years old, I am a boy but I think very much, but I do not think that I am writting to the President of the United States." He congratulated him on his reelection and made a request: "If you like, give me a ten dollars bill green american, in the letter, because never, I have not seen a ten dollars bill green american and I would like to have one of them." If the president had complied, maybe the United States would own another island. Fidel Castro Ruiz, born August 13, 1926, managed to overthrow dictator Fulgencio Batista on his third attempt. This photo was taken at a 1953 arrest, his second, for which he was sentenced to fifteen years. He served only one, thanks to Batista's amnesty. Figures from Fidel's own dictatorship are frightening: since 1963 some 20,000 to 73,000 people have vanished, due to death sentences, disappearances, torture, executions, and uncivilized prison conditions.

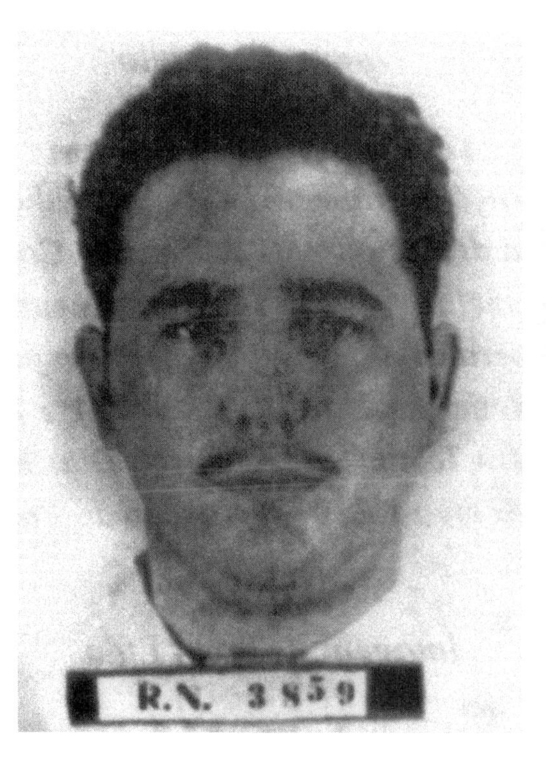

VLADIMIR ILYICH LENIN

ST. PETERSBURG, 1896

This mug shot is from 1896. Lenin was twenty-six. He stayed in jail for a year, then was sent to Siberia for another three. Lenin was born April 10, 1870, in Simbirsk (later Ulyanovsk), the third child of Ilya Nikolaevich Ulyanov, an education reformer who opened over five hundred schools, and Maria Aleksandrovna Blank Ulyanov, the daughter of a German doctor. In 1887, his older brother Aleksandr was hanged for his involvement in a plot to kill Czar Aleksander III.

Wanted by the czarist police in 1907, Lenin fled to Finland. Then he traveled—to Paris, Switzerland, and Capri, to Maxim Gorky's house—until April 16, 1917, when he returned home in time to lead the revolution. He died on January 21, 1924, at the age of fifty-four. Seven days later, on January 28, Joseph Stalin commemorated him in a speech to the cadets of the Kremlin Military School:

> I first met Lenin in December 1905 at the Bolshevik conference in Tammerfors (Finland). I was hoping to see the mountain eagle of our Party, the great man, great not only politically, but, if you will, physically, because in my imagination I had pictured Lenin as a giant, stately and imposing. What, then, was my disappointment to see a most ordinary-looking man, below average height, in no way, literally in no way, distinguishable from ordinary mortals . . .
>
> It is accepted as the usual thing for a 'great man' to come late to meetings so that the assembly may await his appearance with bated breath; and then, just before the 'great man' enters, the warning whisper goes up: 'Hush! . . . Silence! . . . He's coming.' This ritual did not seem to me superfluous, because it creates an impression, inspires respect. What, then, was my disappointment to learn that Lenin had arrived at the conference before the delegates, had settled himself somewhere in a corner, and was unassumingly carrying on a conversation, a most ordinary conversation with the most ordinary delegates at the conference. I will not conceal from you that at that time this seemed to me to be something of a violation of certain essential rules. Only later did I realize that this simplicity and modesty, this striving to remain unobserved, or, at least, not to make himself conspicuous and not to emphasize his high position, this feature was one of Lenin's strongest points as the new leader of the new masses, of the simple and ordinary masses of the 'rank and file' of humanity.

In 1922 the "great man" had sent his own testimonial to Congress, in which he wrote: "Comrade Stalin, having become Secretary-General, has unlimited authority concentrated in his hands, and I am not sure whether he will always be capable of using that authority with sufficient caution."

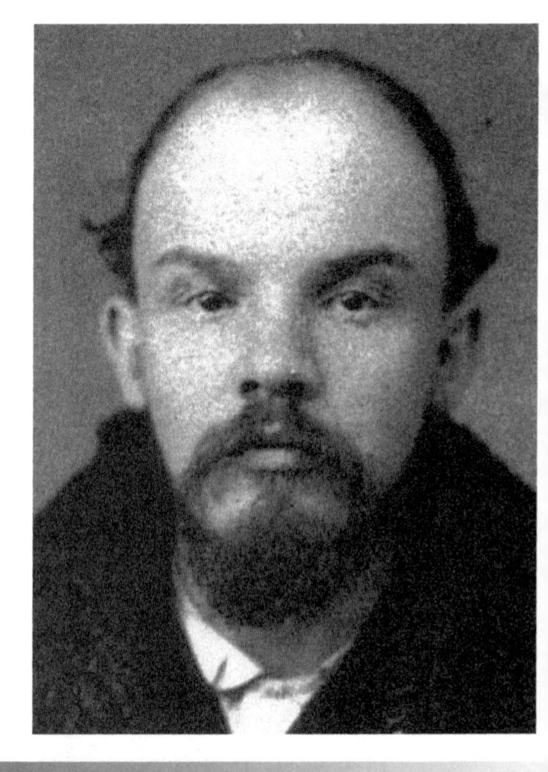

GULAG VICTIMS

USSR, 1929–56

Never has a prison society, completely occupied with surveillance and punishment, come so close to becoming a reality as it did in the USSR. Between 1929 and 1956, the very existence of a border between the inside and the outside was in doubt. The distinction between the observers and the observed disappeared or overlapped to the point of covering the entire society. The West discovered it through literature. Aleksandr Solzhenitsyn's The *Gulag Archipelago* was published in 1973. Dozens of journals and stories were to follow. Even some by Sergei Dovlatov, who experienced the other side as a guard for the Gulags, the institutions that constituted the only reality for millions of Russians.

In the spring and summer of 1950, the number of prisoners reached its peak at 2.8 million. In 1940, there were 2,040 employees of the GULag (for Glavnoye Upravleniye Ispravitelno-trudovykh Lagerey i Kolonii, Chief Administration of Correctional Labor Camps and Colonies). Abnormally high numbers, even if the *Herald Tribune* reported the number of people arrested in the United States in 2003 at 12 million and the number of long-term prison residents at 2 million.

What is unique about the Russian phenomenon and its singular development in contrast to the Nazi extermination camps, or the United States, is the idea of weaving, through labor, the prison world into the productive, economic, and geographic fabric of an enormous country. The change came about with a July 11, 1929, resolution entitled "On the Utilization of the Labor of Incarcerated Criminals." Besides installing camps in remote areas, with the idea of populating them through deportee labor, the resolution established domestic financing as a primary goal and "the exploitation of the natural resources through the utilization of prisoner labor" as the general goal of the detention system. The reasons for this reform were manifold. The approval, in 1929, of Stalin's first Five-Year Plan foreshadowed the country's forced industrialization. The strategy was to use, also to correctional ends, the compulsory labor of the detainees. The first test was the construction of the White Sea–Baltic Sea Canal, starting in 1931 and ending in 1933, which employed 115,000 prisoners (15,000 of whom died); hence the best hydraulics engineers were also arrested through sabotage. For the first time, the Chief Administration had transformed from the supplier of the labor force into its producer.

The detainees were divided into two categories: less dangerous and more dangerous. For the former, those serving one to three years, there were agricultural and industrial colonies. In order to save on surveillance costs, the latter were transported to distant, sparsely populated regions so that no one could flee to Siberia. In 1934 there were 510,000 detainees, twenty-three times more than in July 1929. But it was during the period of the Great Terror, from July 1937 to August 1938, that it became a large-scale phenomenon. If in 1936 there were 1,118 fusillades, in 1937 there were 353,074. The number of detainees soared to over 2 million—800 thousand more than the year before. Just about the same number were sent into military service from the camps and colonies during World War II to compensate for losses in the Red Army. After the war, the number of internees increased again due to the arrival of two million Soviet citizens who had repatriated or been prisoners of war abroad. At its height the Gulag held 2.8 million prisoners out of a population of 116 million. On March 5, 1953, Stalin died.

The system of detention camps was in decline; the prison utopia had failed. On October 25, 1956, the Central Committee of the Communist Party of the Soviet Unioin (CPSU) established that the further existence of the collective labor camps was "inopportune."

However, the system had slowly branched out and was deeply rooted. Out of inertia, it continued to exist to a limited extent until the collapse of the Soviet system in 1989.

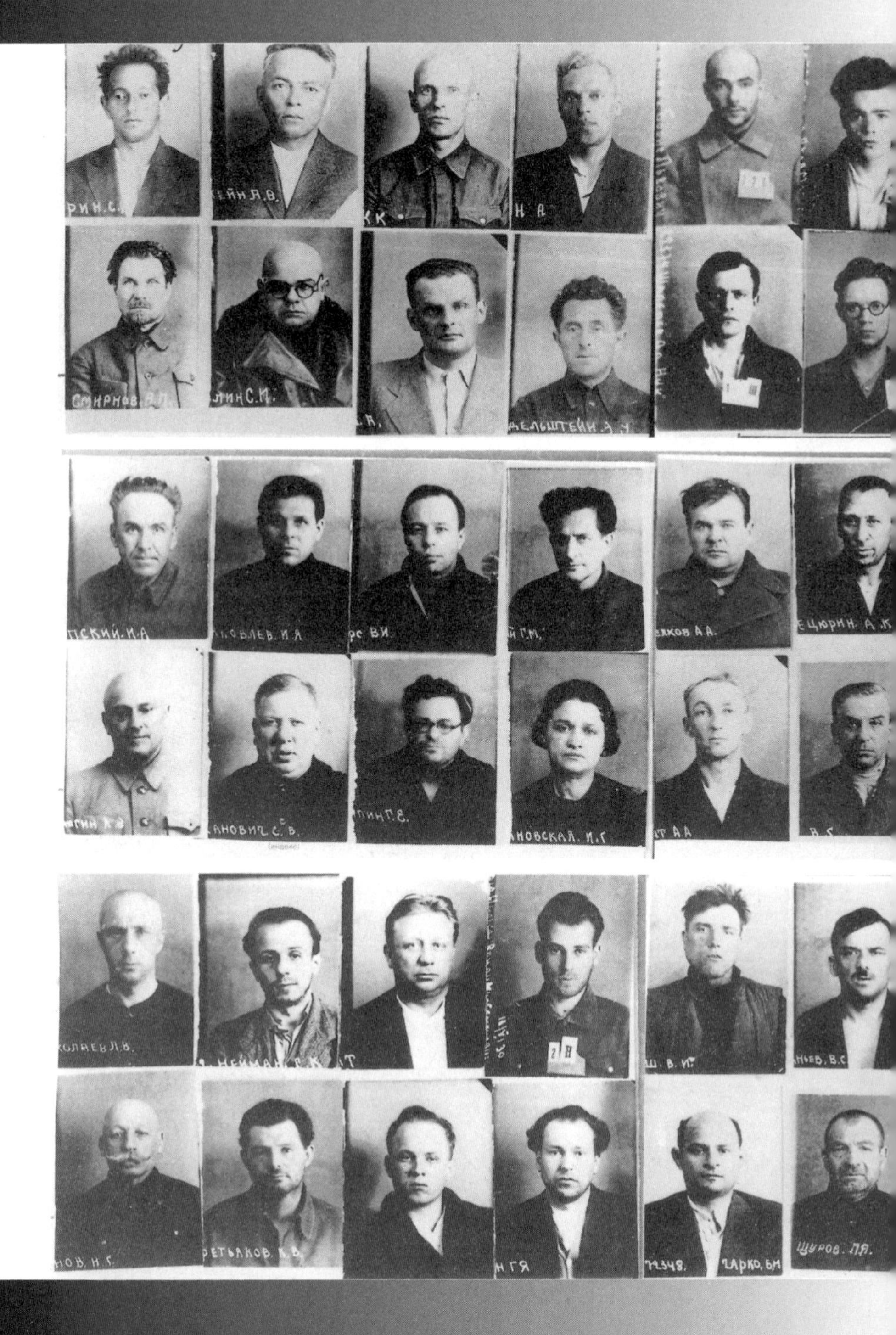
СМИРНОВ А.П.
ЕЦЮРИН А.К
ЩУРОВ П.Я.

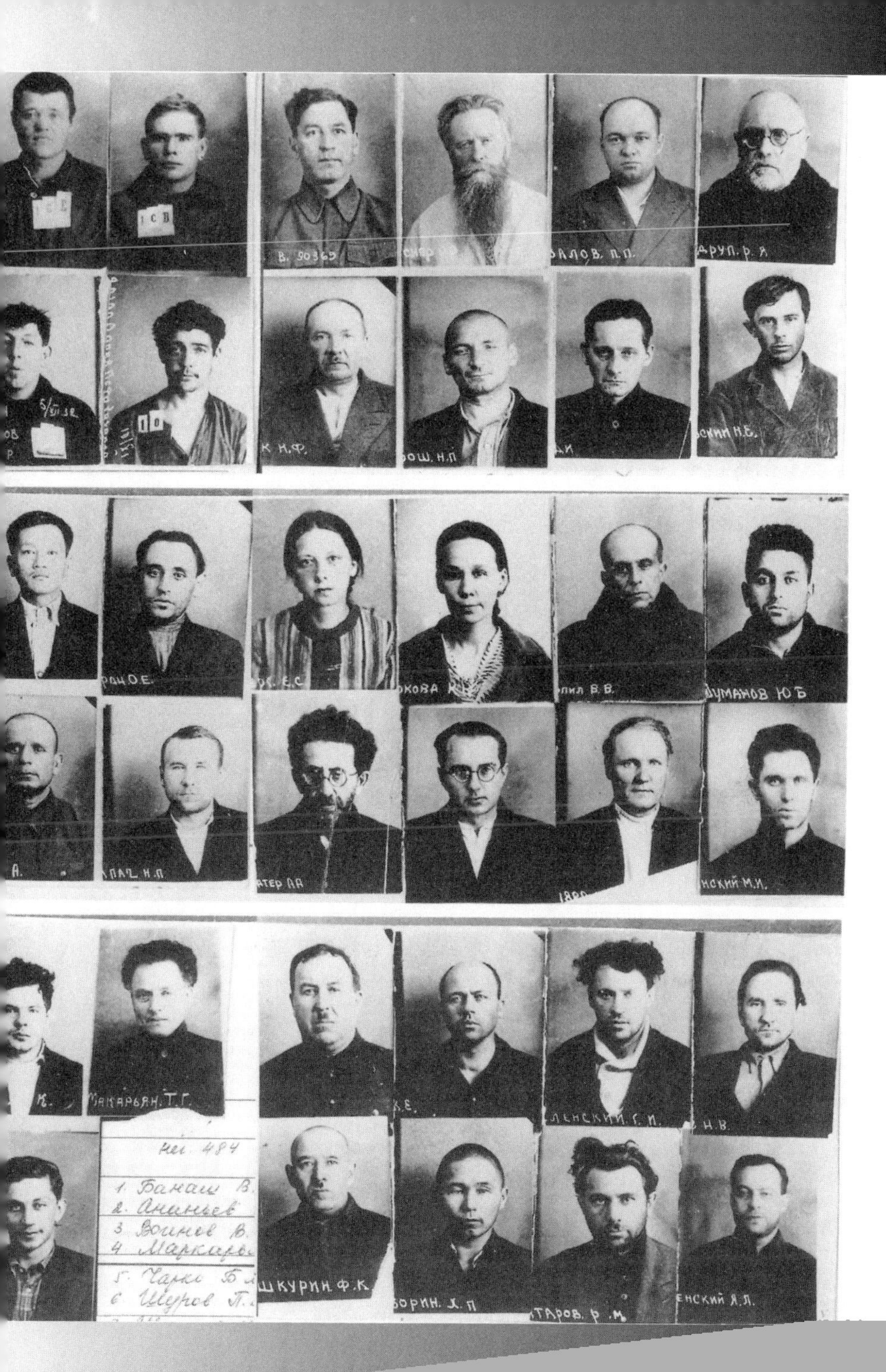

ДУМАНОВ ЮБ
МАКАРЬЯН. Т.Г.
ШКУРИН. Ф.К.

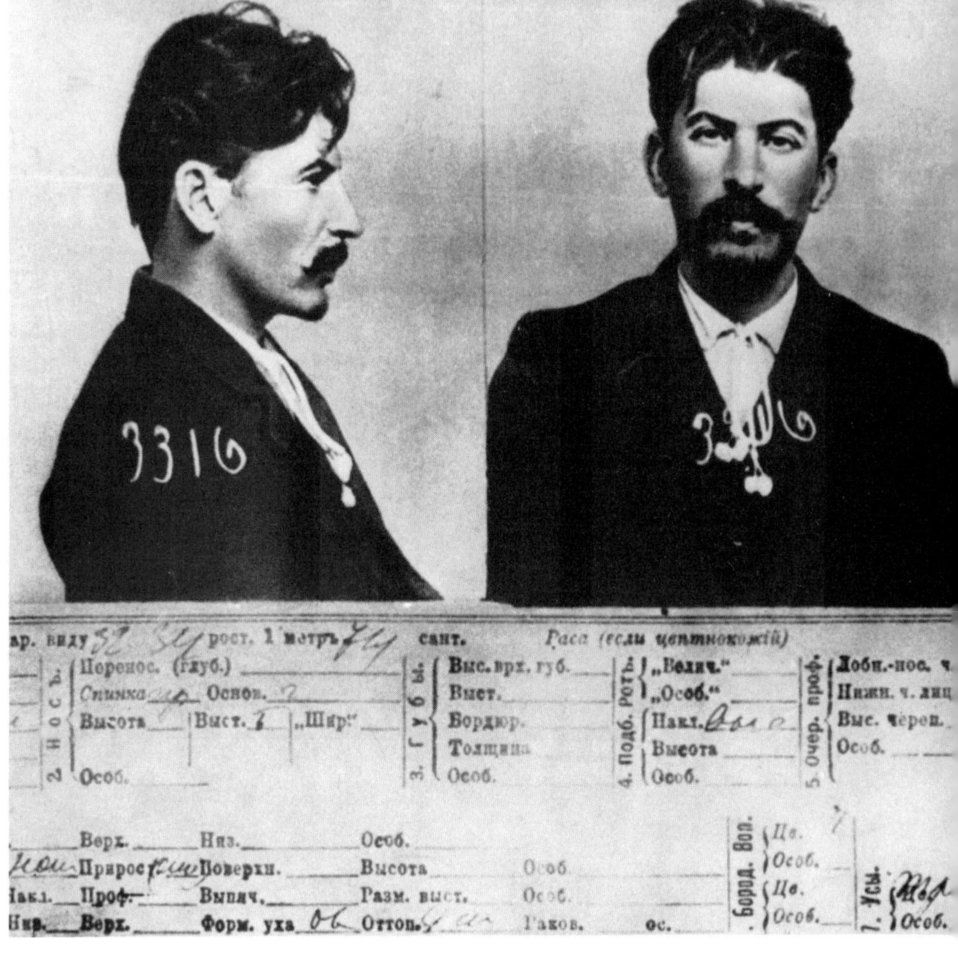

JOSEPH STALIN

1913

"Up to now the red flag still waves atop the Kremlin's towers and so we believe that Stalin is still alive. The situation is normal in the sense that one does not notice crowds gathering or Moscow residents publicly abstaining from commenting on the medical reports, obeying the directives of the party that asked all Russians to double their labor efforts to show solidarity with the work of comrade Stalin. But the churches are full and Patriarch Alexy himself has today held a second service to pray for the commander's recovery. All the Russian Jews—which number over two million—have fasted today, at the instruction of Rabbi Salomon Schiffer." It was March 5, 1953; the Swedish ambassador to Moscow thus described the anticipation of the international press. At 9:50 p.m., Moscow time, the dictator's heart stopped beating.

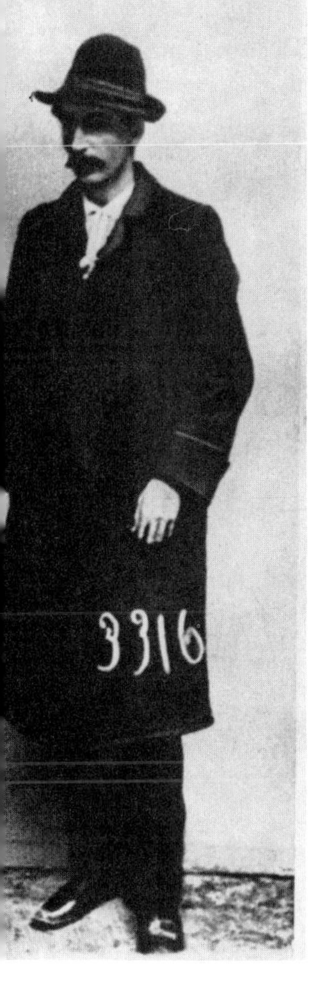

"Cerebral hemorrhage" is the official cause of death. Stalin had felt ill the night of March 1, after having eaten with Beria, Malenkov, Bulganin, and Khrushchev. In his memoirs, published in 1993, Stalin's former protégé Vyacheslav Molotov recounts that Beria later confessed to poisoning Stalin (with rat poison, according to some historians).

Iosif Vissarionovich Dzhugashvili—also known as Ivanovich, Koba, David, Nizharadze, Chizhikov, and, of course, Stalin—was born December 9, 1879, in Gori, Georgia, son of a serf and a cobbler probably from South Ossetia. He studied at the Tiflis theological seminary, but was expelled in 1899 for being a Socialist. After repeated arrests and deportations to Siberia, he entered the Central Committee of the CPSU. This mug shot, taken during that period, is even more valuable for being a full-length shot, hat included, and was intended for use by the czarist police to make the seditionary more recognizable.

Lenin died in 1924. In his Testament, he harshly criticized Stalin and other members of the Central Committee. Stalin, Kamenev, and Zinoviev controlled the party, resisting pressure from Trotsky and Bukharin. Starting in 1928, when the first Five-Year Plan was passed, Stalin had complete control of the party. But it was only with the 1936–38 purges that he gained absolute power. Most of the members of Lenin's politburo were deported, murdered, or exiled.

In 1922, after World War I and the post–1917 Revolution civil war, the USSR was the poorest nation in Europe. The industrialization tax had dropped 13% in comparison to 1914. Lenin's NEP (New Economic Policy) still left some leeway for the free market. The Five-Year Plan implemented the forced collectivization of agriculture, using forced mass labor and demanding excessive productivity from workers to build communism.

An incalculable number of human beings died of hunger, through the mass deportations and during World War II, but in a relatively short time the USSR had become an industrial, scientific, military, and ideological empire. An ideology that governed millions of people throughout the world, not only the 162 million Russians counted in the 1939 census.

Upon closer examination, the largest prison utopia in history revealed itself to be a labor utopia. The deportations were only an effect of and a tool to implement this plan. Palmiro Togliatti, secretary of the Italian Communist Party, explains this in his own way: "There does not exist a single court in the world whose composition, whose laws, whose procedure offers a complete guarantee of not only formal but essential fairness equal to what the Soviet proletarian court does, the work of a revolution that has truncated the roots of all injustices and all privileges." Not bad for a program that anticipated the ultimate end of history in a "liberation from labor": the ominous coronation of a dream that culminates in a theology of labor, combined with positivism, as a theology of the factory.

In 1956 Nikita Khrushchev criticized his predecessor in a crowded meeting. Someone shouted, "And where were you, comrade?" Khrushchev stopped talking. He looked at the audience, who had fallen silent. Then he asked, "Who said that?" No one had the courage to come forward.

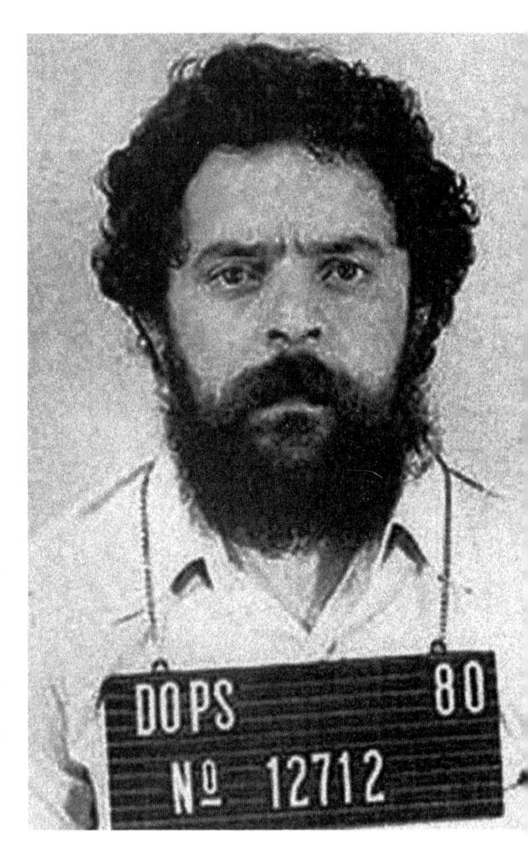

LUIZ INÁCIO "LULA" DA SILVA

SÃO BERNARDO DO CAMPO, 1980

Some of his first actions were the "Zero Hunger" program to ensure three meals a day for the poorest people, and appointing the musician Gilberto Gil the Bahia Minister of Culture. Under consideration, the tax against poverty and the national plan for agricultural reform.

Luiz Inácio "Lula" da Silva, also known as Lula, seventeenth president of Brazil, was the first worker to occupy Pedro II's post. Born in 1945 in the farming village of Garanhuns, he quit school at twelve and tried to earn money by selling peanuts and shining shoes. In the mid-sixties he found a job at a steel processing factory, and he and his brother began campaigning for workers' rights. He was arrested in 1980. He spent a month in prison and was released only because of a massive strike campaign. That same year, he gathered intellectuals, unionists, Catholics, and others from the Workers' Party, and formed the largest Socialist party in Brazilian history.

In the 2002 election, on his fourth try, he beat José Serra with 61 percent of the votes, the highest margin in the history of Brazil. For some time, he's had his share of critics. Even from the poor. And from the left. That always happens, though, when dreams come true.

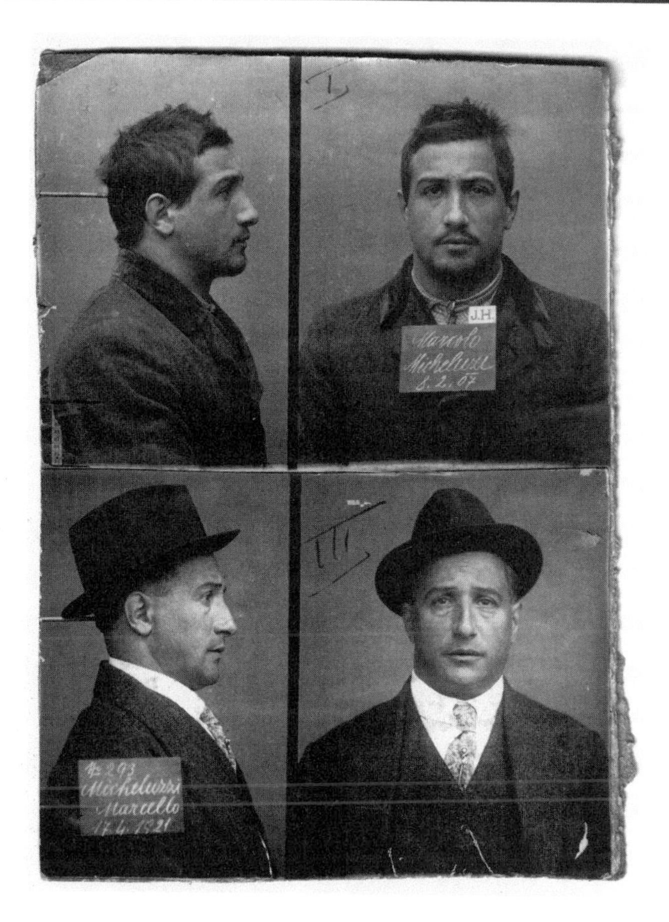

MARCELLO MICHELUZZI

1907

"Inventor of the buzz saw and burglar" is the only note on the back of Marcello Micheluzzi's file, kept at the Rome Criminology Museum. The top mug shot is marked I. The bottom one, taken fourteen years later, is marked III. It's likely that there was a II. A not infrequent event for thieves and prostitutes, whose lives became marked by the succession of police photographs.

The top photo reads "J. H. Marcolo Micheluzzi." Spelling and letters that sound strange for 1907 Italy. Finally, it's also worth noting that over his career as a professional thief, his attire improved.

JULES BONNOT

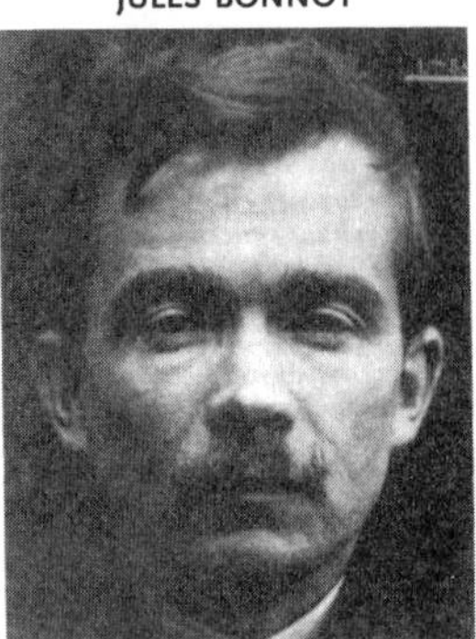

RAYMOND CALLEMIN

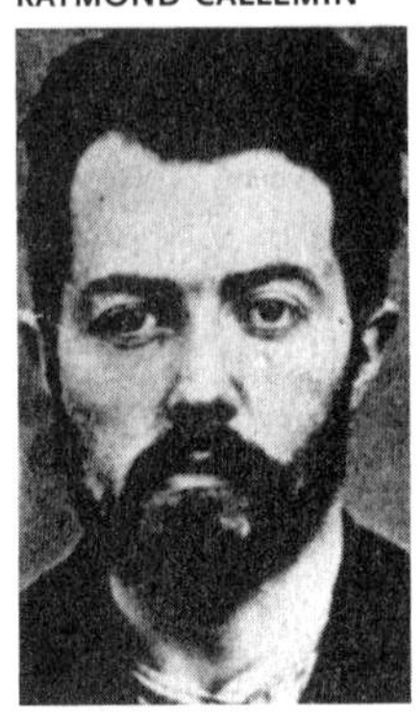

EDOUARD CAROUY

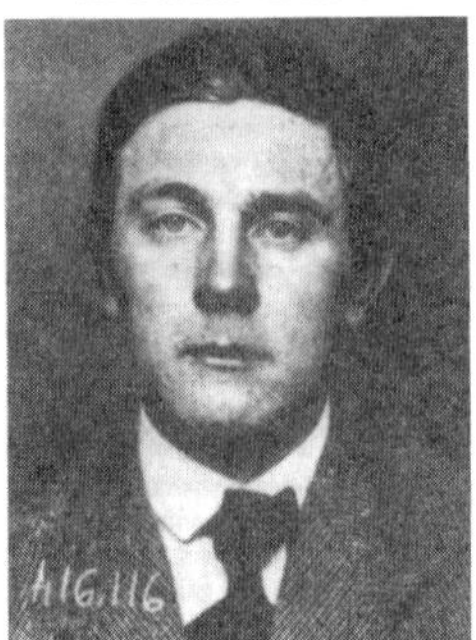

BONNOT GANG

PARIS, 1913

At the cusp of the twentieth century, at the crossroads between crime and revolution, in the still that separates film from fiction, art from the machine, the story of the Bonnot Gang emerged. From December 1911 to April 1912 they put Paris to fire and sword, while politicians and scientists were taking part in an international conference on time, to define timetables and time zones for the entire planet.

Jules Bonnot was born October 14, 1876, in Pont-de-Roide, France, near Montbéliard. At age five he lost his mother. Soon afterward his brother committed suicide and so he grew up with his father, a factory worker.

In 1901 he married a seamstress who ran off with one of his union friends, taking their child with her. Disillusioned with life, he fell in love with the Lebel musket and the engine. In Lyon, around 1910, he was the driver for Sir Arthur Conan Doyle, creator of Sherlock Holmes, or for one of his collaborators. In Paris the group centered around the magazine *l'Anarchie*, edited by Victor Kibalcic (Victor Serge) who would later serve five years; although innocent and against

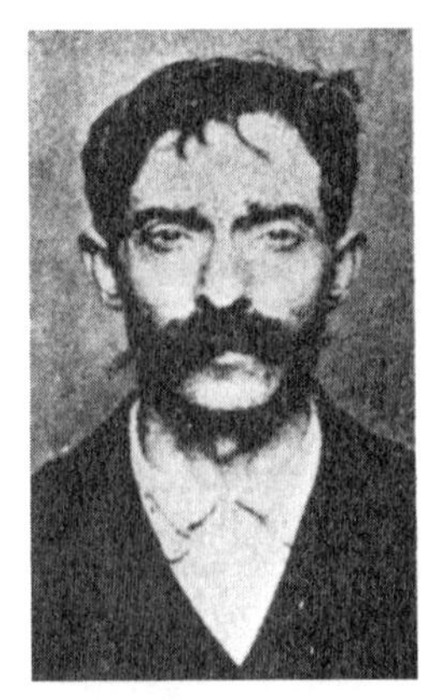

DETTWEILLER

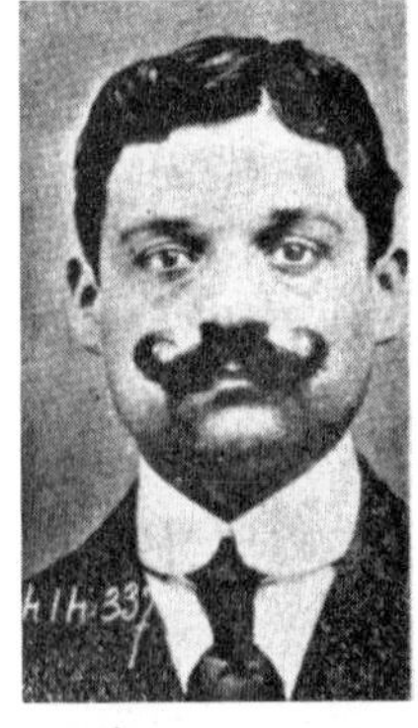

EUGÈNE DIEUDONNE

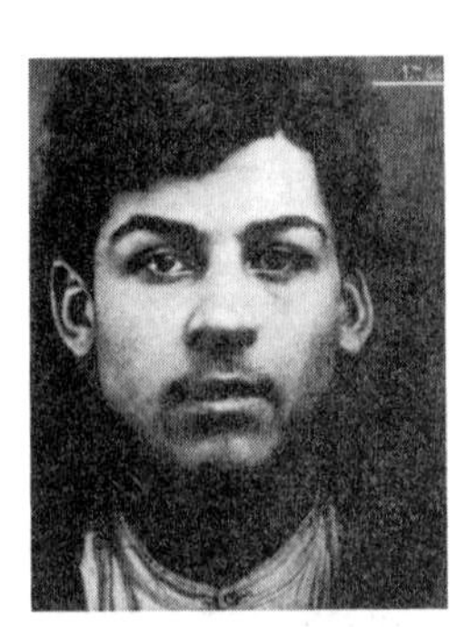

OCTAVE GARNIER

SERGE KIBALCIC

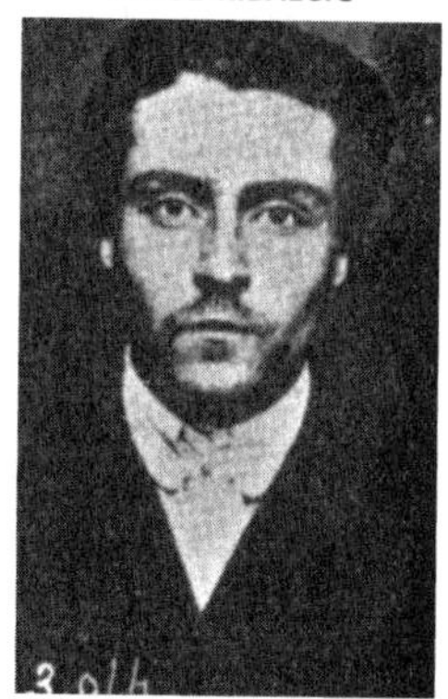

MALLET

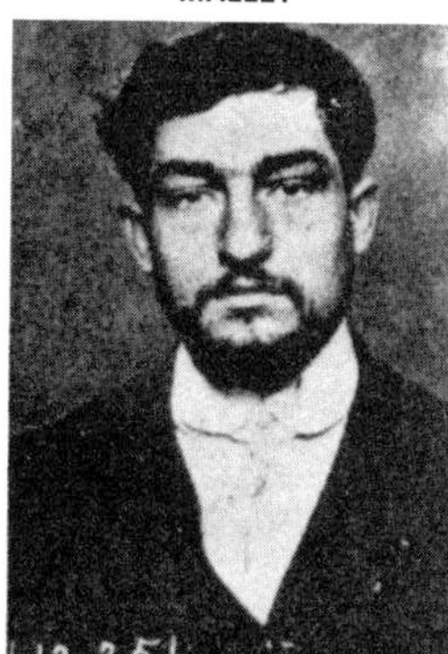

MARIUS METGE

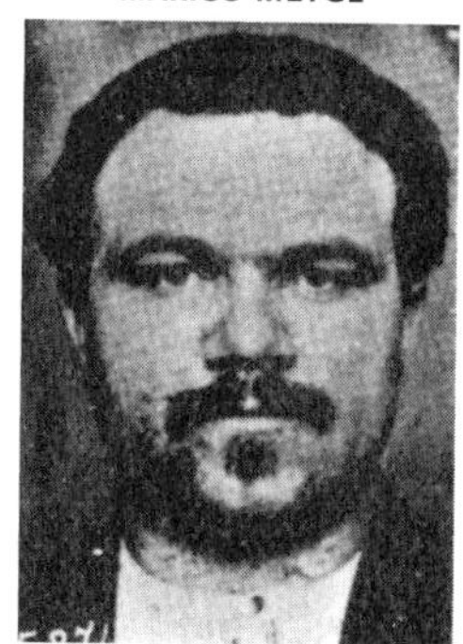

the gang's methods, he refused to name names. It was the first instance of a gang with an ideology. Anarchist enemies of the bourgeoisie, more than the aristocracy, had never been seen before.

The first robbers in history to use a getaway car appeared on Rue Ordener in Paris on December 21, 1911, at 8:20 a.m. At the wheel of the stolen Delaunay-Belleville (1909, 12 hp, bottle green) was Raymond Callemin, nicknamed *la Science*, whom Bonnot had taught to drive just one day earlier.

Jules Bonnot was finally apprehended on April 28, 1912, in a dramatic confrontation with Paris police and Republican Guards on the outskirts of Paris. After a five-hour siege, Bonnot, bullet-riddled but still alive, was captured when the little garage he had taken refuge in was dynamited. Jules's motto had been, "No matter what, no regrets." Of the twenty accused, André Soudy, Raymond Callemin, and Antoine Monnier went to the guillotine on April 1913.

The gang's story resurfaced in 1968, thanks to Philippe Fourastié's film *La bande à Bonnot* (with Jacques Brel as Callemin).

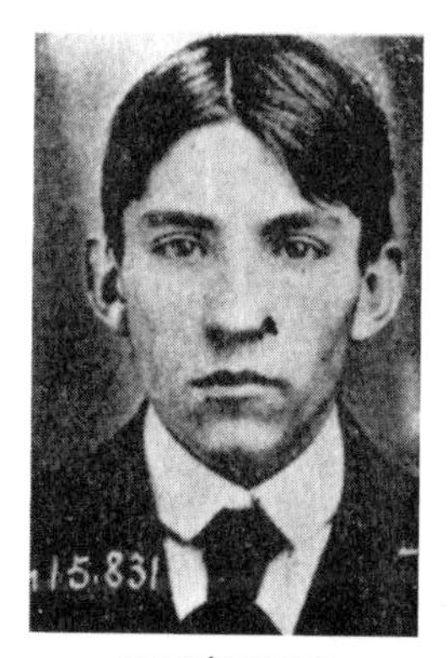

ANDRÉ SOUDY

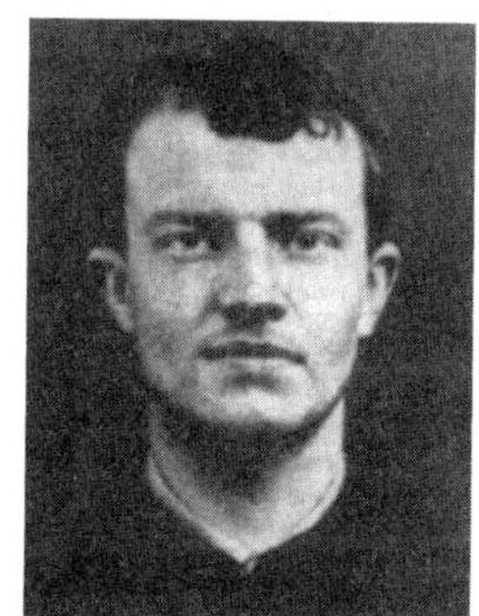

RENÉ VALET

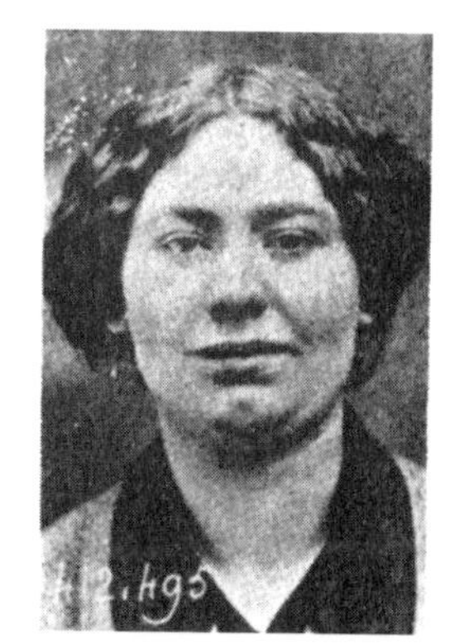

MARIE VUILLEMIN

GIUSEPPE MUSOLINO

ACQUALAGNA, ITALY, 1901

He claims that St. Joseph appeared in a dream and told him how to escape. Giuseppe Musolino was a young lumberjack from San Stefano in Aspromonte, Calabria, sentenced to twenty-one years in prison for the murder of mule driver Vincenzo Zoccali, who was gunned down in his stables on October 29, 1897. The verdict, delivered in Lucca in 1899, was unjust, and after a few months the ex-lumberjack—with St. Joseph's help—managed to break free. His brief stint as a fugitive became the legend of the brigand Musolino.

Giuseppe returned to his hometown, where his mother begged him to move to America, but he refused because he wanted to avenge the injustice he had endured. The major newspapers went out of their way to recount his heroic deeds—his vendetta that would lead to the deaths of seven people. International press like *Daily Express* and *Journal de Paris* even sent correspondents to Calabria, which was still rather backward.

The courageous, megalomaniac bandit, handsome and unlucky, poor and ruthless, won the hearts of young ladies and the poor. He epitomized the struggle of the People against the powerful. The State put a price on his head at a previously unheard of sum of 50,000 lire. A thousand *carabinieri*, police officers, and soldiers searched for him.

Then one day in 1901, in the Acqualagna countryside near Urbino, two carabinieri noticed someone quickening his pace in a suspicious manner. The long chase ended when Musolino tripped over a wire that marked a border between fields. One of the carabinieri who made the arrest was the father of Enrico Mattei, future president of ENI (National Fuel Trust). The capture did not diminish Musolino's fame; his mug shots were printed on postcards, following a tradition that had made legends out of bandits and bounty hunters in the U.S.

Giuseppe Musolino spent eleven years in the Reggio Calabria asylum. With patience and insistence, he wrangled the director's permission to take short walks around the city. Every Monday, rain or shine, Musolino drew crowds of onlookers.

He died at eighty on January 22, 1956. Six years earlier, in 1950, Italian cinemas premiered Mario Camerini's film, *Il brigante Musolino* (or *Outlaw Girl*), with Amedeo Nazzari as the brigand. A 1966 report signed by two specialists from the Aversa asylum mentions an "evident paranoid constitution" and determines that "evil was latent in him and it emerged after the psychic trauma provoked by the wrongs he experienced with his first trial."

He was the first Italian criminal to reach sex symbol status through his mug shot.

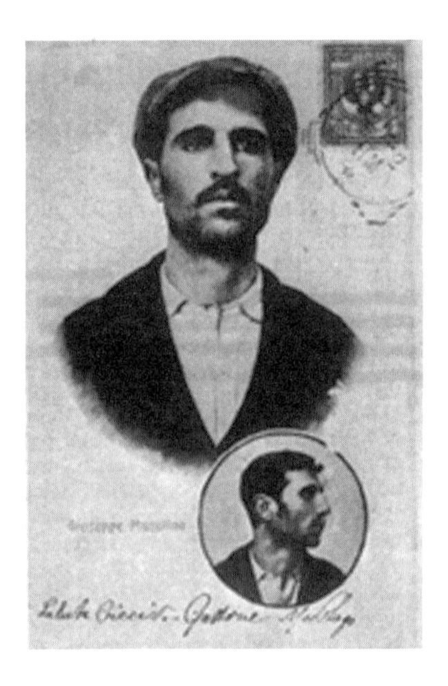

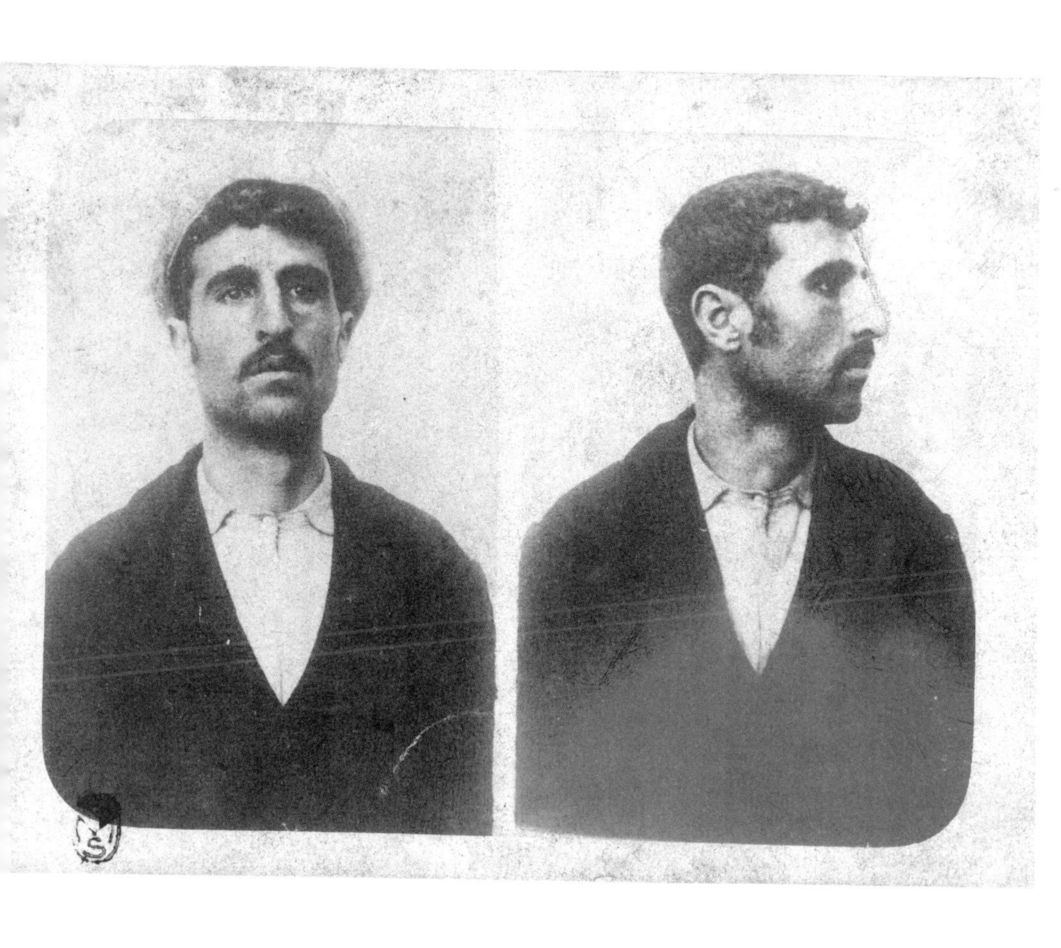

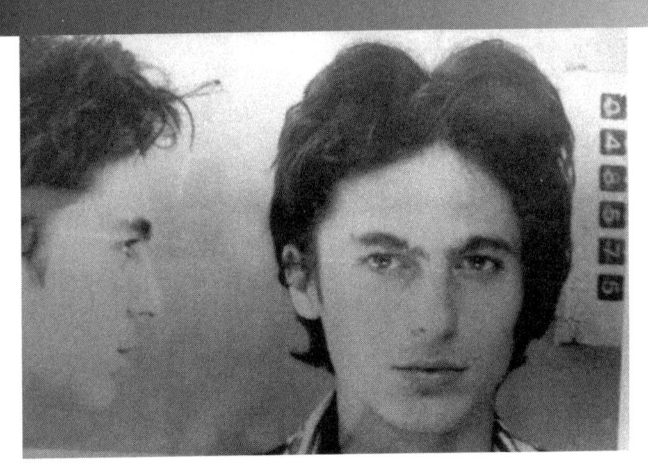

RENATO VALLANZASCA

MILAN, 02/14/1972

Il fiore del male. The flower of evil, the title of his autobiography, written with Carlo Bonini, says a lot about the character of the braggadocio of the affected Milanese crook Renato Vallanzasca. The handsome René's look was inspired by that of French gangsters in old black and white movies. His picture is reminiscent of the brigand Musolino's, the first Italian criminal marketed to female desire like a movie star. Born in Milan on February 14, 1950, Valentine's Day, by his adolescence he was the leader of a gang based in Comasina, a neighborhood on the northern outskirts of the city. His rise was meteoric. Vallanzasca was a descendent of the Milanese underworld sung about by Ornella Vanoni (a student of Giorgio Strehler) and mythologized by Giovanni Testori and Luchino Visconti in the 1960 film *Rocco and His Brothers*. But at the same time, he was already a television personality, a cross between Robin Hood and a successful soccer player. His first arrest—after a trip to Beccaria juvenile prison—occurred on February 14, 1972, his twenty-second birthday. The charge was robbery. While in jail, a son was born whom he would never see. He escaped in July 1976. In one year of freedom, he committed murder, robbery, and organized a kidnapping. When he found out that the kidnapped woman was sad because there wasn't a Christmas tree in the house, he went to the city and stole one.

His idea was to offer kidnapping victims the "good life" for the duration of their abduction—the Vallanzasca gang's trademark. In Montecatini a policeman died, in Andria a bank teller. Three more police officers, a doctor, and a traffic officer were to follow. In Dalmine, on the Milan-Bergamo highway, two agents and some of their men lost their lives. With an injured ankle, he was caught on February 15, 1977 (the day after his twenty-seventh birthday). They asked him if he declared himself a political prisoner. He responded, "Stop talking bullshit!"

On April 28 of that year, he took part in a spectacular jailbreak from Milan's San Vittore. A group of convicts, including Vallanzasca and Corrado Alunni, the leader of the Red Brigades offshoot Prima Linea, exited the prison, shooting. Almost all were immediately recaptured, including Vallanzasca. Those were the years when he befriended Francis Turatello, a Milan boss who would be a witness at his wedding. The last escape attempt occurred on July 18, 1987. As he was being transferred to a prison on the island of Asinara, he escaped through a porthole on the ship, reached Genoa, then Milan on foot, and from there, Grado. He planned to kidnap Gullit and Van Basten, the stars of Berlusconi's AC Milan soccer team. As a Rossonero fan, kidnapping a player from the Inter team violated his code of honor. He was caught on August 7 and sentenced to serve four life sentences and 260 years.

VINCENZO PERUGIA

01/25/1909

The thief of the *Mona Lisa* spent the night of Sunday, August 20, 1911, hidden in a Louvre closet. He emerged Monday morning when the museum was closed. He removed the *Gioconda* canvas from its frame, pocketed it, and left. A few months earlier, the Louvre had decided to place its masterpieces under glass. Perugia himself had constructed the display case for Leonardo's painting. The police questioned him. They even questioned Pablo Picasso, but for twenty-seven months the artwork disappeared entirely.

They caught him when he tried to sell the painting to the Uffizi Gallery in Florence. During the trial he became a hero. He claimed that he had acted out of patriotism, to restore the work to its homeland. He didn't know, or pretended not to know, that it was Leonardo himself who sold it to France for 4,000 gold coins.

In Italy, he became a celebrity. Women wrote him love letters, men sent him bottles of wine and olive oil. Ultimately, the judge declared him insane, non compos mentis, so he was given the minimum sentence and spent less than a year in jail. The truth was that Vincenzo Perugia was hopelessly in love with a woman who lived five hundred years before him. A type of relationship that has certain undeniable advantages.

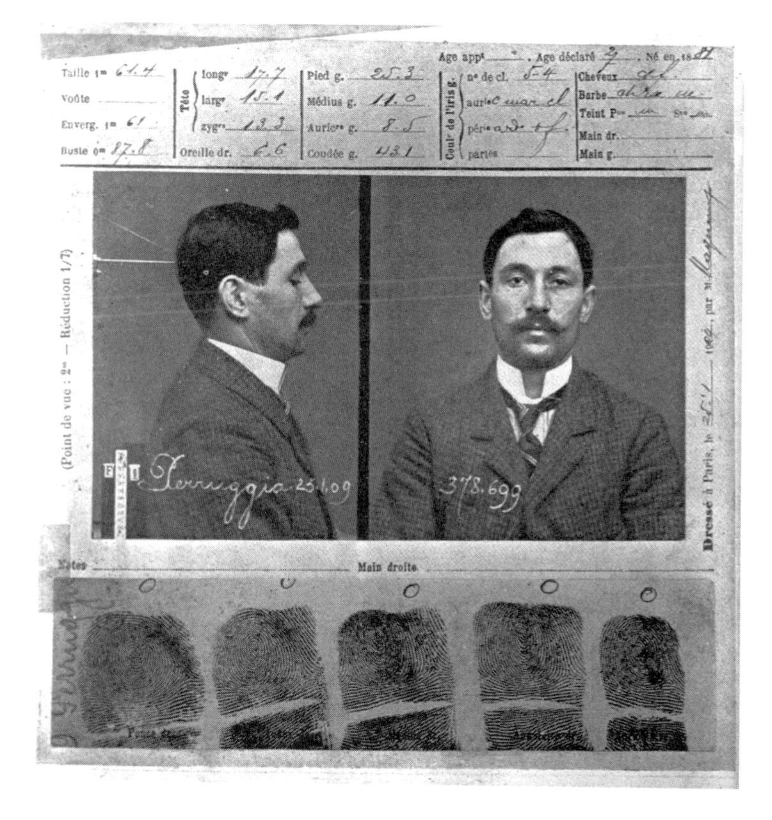

THIRTEEN MOST WANTED MEN

NEW YORK CITY, 1964

Among the ruins extracted from the refuse of the twentieth century and elevated to art by Andy Warhol, mug shots are right up there with the Campbell's soup can and movie stars.

Philip Johnson, architect of the New York State Pavilion at the 1964 World Fair, assigned Robert Rauschenberg, Roy Lichtenstein, Robert Indiana, John Chamberlain, and Andy Warhol to decorate the exterior. Warhol responded with *Thirteen Most Wanted Men*, a work composed of giant posters of those most sought-after in the FBI's annual ranking. Many were Italian, and in fear of offending the sensibilities of the Italian-American community, the government pushed for the installation's removal.

Andy Warhol counterproposed a series of twenty-five sneering portraits of Robert Moses, the fair's director. The original work remained in place, but was covered by a layer of silver varnish.

The artist declared: "My image is a statement of the symbols of the harsh, impersonal products and brash materialistic objects on which America is built today." The mug shot occupies a space among such objects. No one is denied their fifteen minutes of fame.

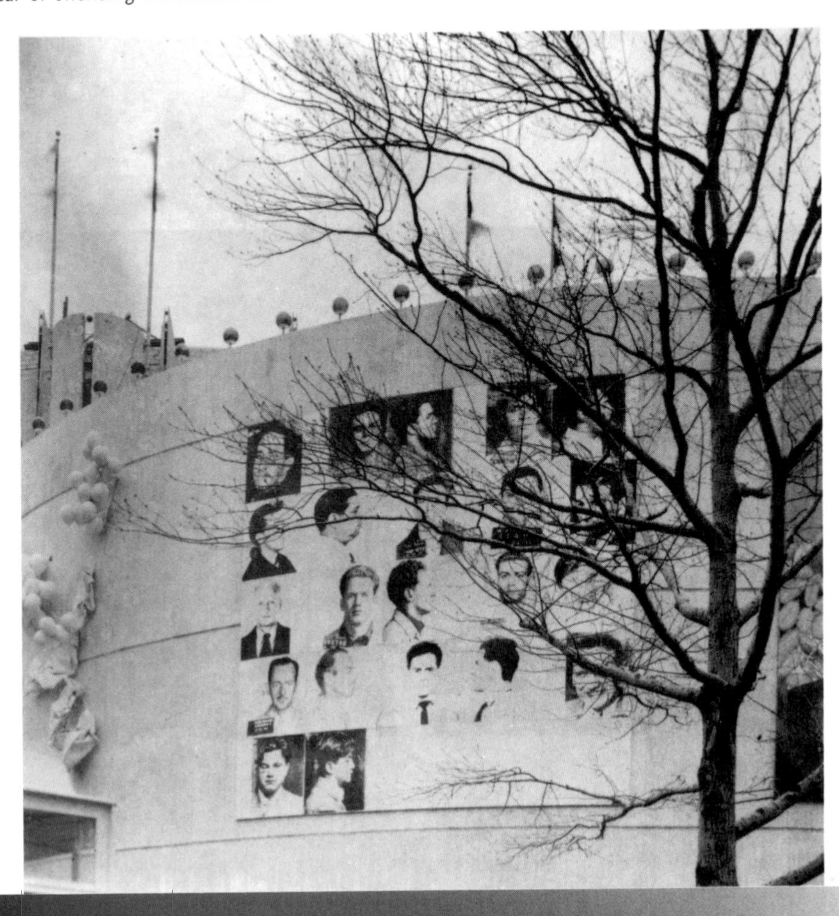

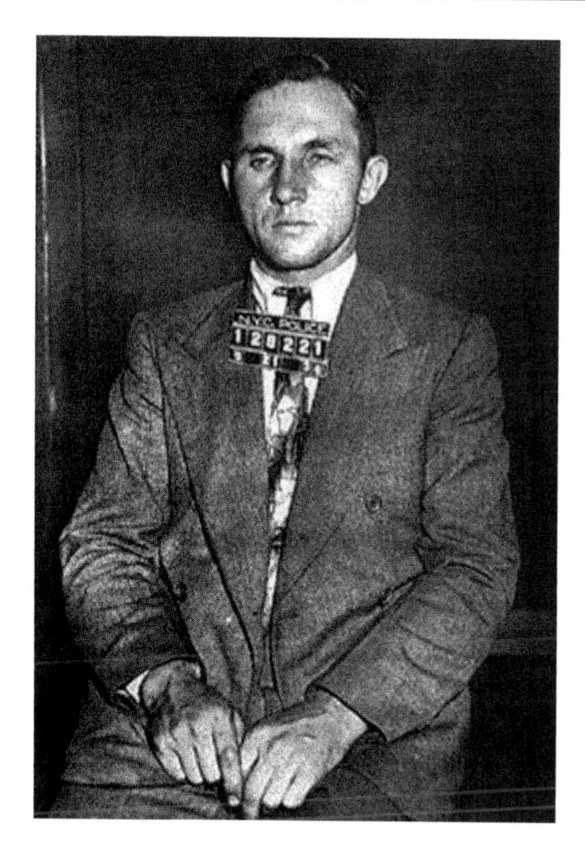

BRUNO RICHARD HAUPTMANN

NEW YORK CITY, 09/21/1934

"Dear Sir! Have 50000$ redy. 25000$ in 20$ bills 15000$ in 10$ bills and 10000$ in 5$ bills. After 2–4 days we will inform you were to deliver the money. We warn you for making anyding public or for notify the police the child is in gut care." The message left in the room of a twenty-month old who was kidnapped on the evening of March 1, 1932, was in broken English, with a clear Germanic influence. The baby was the son of Charles Lindbergh, the first person to fly across the Atlantic, a Nazi sympathizer and pre-war American icon. The kidnapping touched everyone, even Al Capone, who offered ten million dollars for the ransom.

On May 12, 1932, the tiny corpse was found in a New Jersey forest near Lindbergh's house. His head was crushed, perhaps by falling from a homemade extension ladder Hauptmann had used for the kidnapping. Grilled by the police, Lindbergh's maid committed suicide.

Hauptmann was captured in September 1934. He was a timid, reserved German carpenter. The blue Dodge and the spent banknotes from the ransom condemned him. He claimed to have gotten them from a German emigrant friend of his, who had recently passed away. On April 3, 1936, Hauptmann died on the chair. Journalist H. L. Mencken noted, "It's the greatest story since the Resurrection."

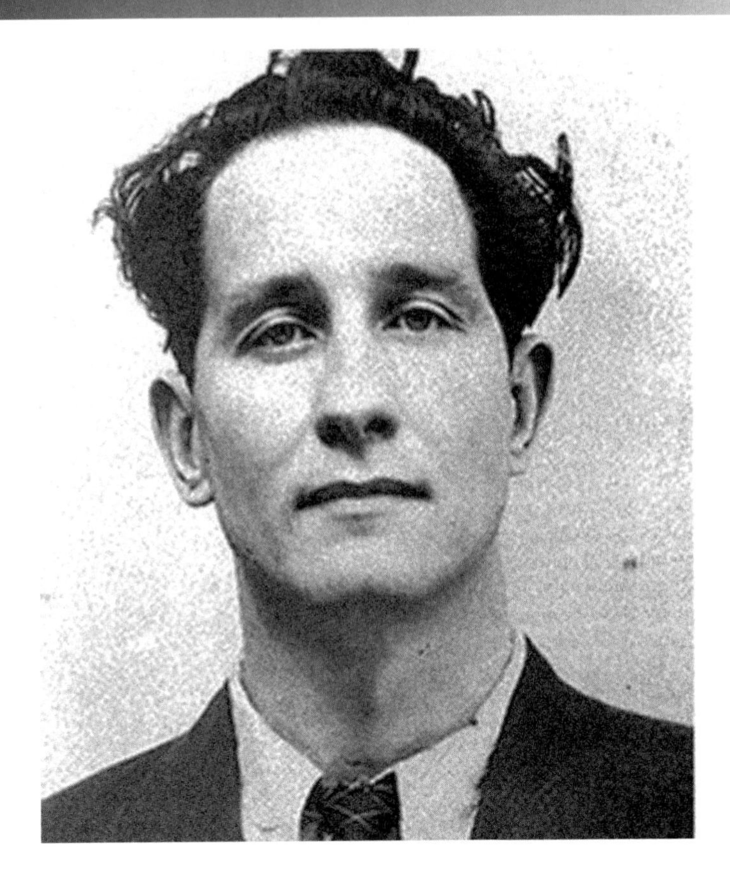

RONNIE BIGGS

WANDSWORTH, GREAT BRITIAN, 1963

3:03 a.m., August 8, 1963. Outside Cheddington, in Buckinghamshire, Great Britain, a group of robbers disguised as railroad workers waited for the mail train from Glasgow. Due to a false signal rigged by the thieves, the train stopped. The driver, struck in the head, remained an invalid forever. The robbers took 2.6 million pounds, (today equivalent to about forty million). And this, in short, is "The Great Train Robbery," the biggest in UK history.

The approximately twenty people who made up the gang were nabbed shortly thereafter because they left their fingerprints on the actual banknotes with which, pretending to be millionaires to amuse themselves, they played Monopoly. Almost all managed to escape before the sentencing.

Ronnie Biggs, the youngest of the group, fled in 1965 and in 1970 settled in Brazil. In 1978, he cut a track with Steve Jones and Paul Cook of the Sex Pistols, "No One Is Innocent."

By the time he returned to London in 2001, he was an old man in a wheelchair wearing a panama hat. Accompanied by his son Michael (a musician so famous in Brazil that he opened for Ricky Martin), he told the BBC: "My last wish is to walk into a Margate pub as an Englishman and buy a pint of bitter." He has twenty-five years left to serve.

CHARLES PONZI

BOSTON, MASSACHUSETTS, 08/13/1920

"Fifty per cent profit in forty-five days," was the promise of Charles Ponzi—born in Italy in 1882, educated in Parma, and emigrated to the United States in 1902 with $2.50 in his pocket—that would have tempted a billionaire. By 1920, Ponzi gathered millions of dollars from over ten thousand individual investors in perhaps the earliest version of the pyramid scheme.

A bankruptcy judge at the time explained the phenomenon: "It's just another instance of robbing Peter to pay Paul." When Ponzi went bankrupt, he was given the maximum penalty—five years. With his wife in tears, the judge pronounced, "The defendant conceived a scheme which on his counsel's admission did defraud men and women. It will not do to have the public, the world, understand that such a scheme as his through the United States' instrumentality could be carried out without receiving substantial punishment." Ponzi passed a piece of paper to reporters on which he had written "sic transit gloria mundi" ("Thus passes worldly glory").

He died in poverty in 1949 in Rio de Janeiro, leaving behind seventy-five dollars, enough for a modest funeral service.

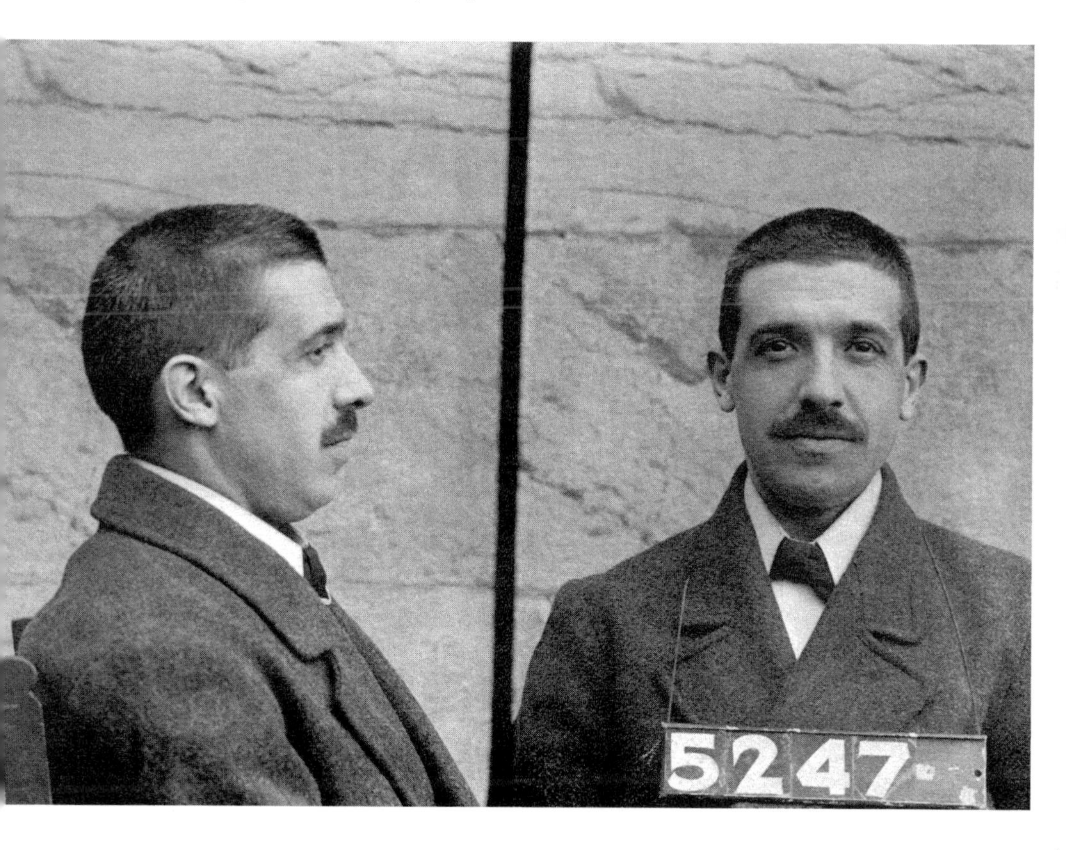

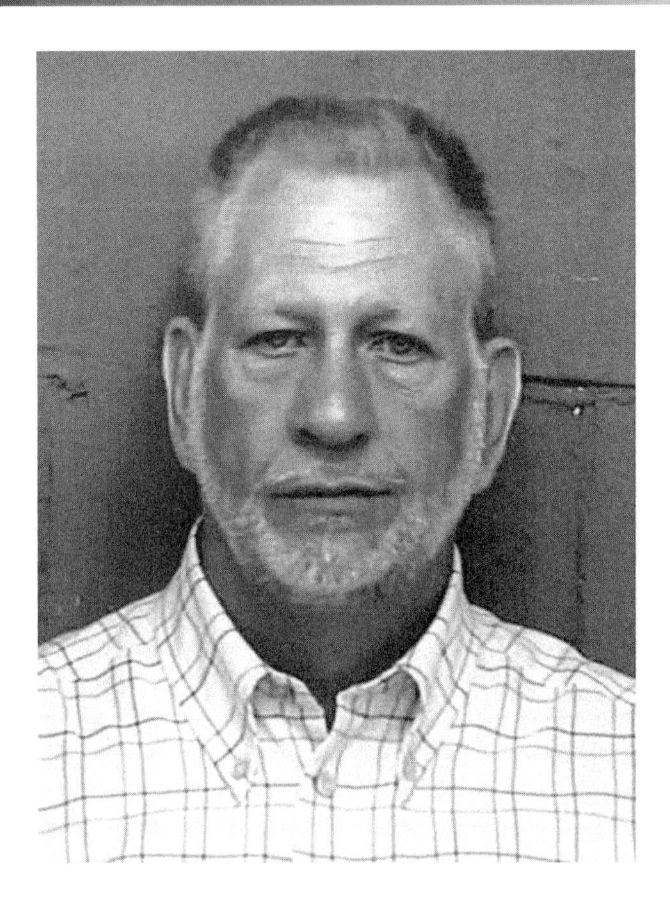

BERNARD EBBERS

His is the story of a self-made man. High school basketball coach, motel magnate, car salesman, milkman, bouncer, prophet, bard of the miracles of the new economy, and finally, a conman, for the considerable sum of eleven billion dollars.

Bernie Ebbers was involved in one of the most talked-about financial scandals in U.S. history, second only—in terms of consequences—to the Enron case: 17,000 layoffs, 41 billion dollars in debt, 4 trillion dollars up in smoke in 18 months because market shares fell. In 2003 he was accused of tampering with accounts at WorldCom, which he founded and ran, to boost its stock value, until he caused a frightening gap in its funds.

At the trial, Ebbers took the stand and denied all accusations. He denied the charge of fraud, and claimed that if there had been errors in judgment and wrongful conduct, it was all done in good faith without the intention of harm. However, chief financial officer Scott Sullivan, pled guilty and testified against Ebbers as part of his plea bargain with prosecutors. In July 2005 Ebbers was sentenced to a 25-year term.

DAVID HAMPTON

NEW YORK CITY, 1985

Going outside the lines. Evading identity. October 1983. The young man who inspired Fred Schepisi's film *Six Degrees of Separation* starring Will Smith spent twenty-one months in prison for attempted robbery. In the months leading up to the arrest, he got himself adopted by the New York jet set, claiming he was the son of black actor Sidney Poitier. His criminal record listed six other arrests.

David's real father was a lawyer from Buffalo, New York. David had a wild imagination and a life that seemed dull. So he kept reinventing it. In 1992 he decided that John Guare, author of the play and the screenplay inspired by his life, owed him something. So he decided to sue him for $100 million, but lost. Then he left this message on Guare's answering machine: "I would strongly advise you that you give me some money or you can start counting your days." He was charged with harassment.

He died in poverty at thirty-nine from AIDS-related complications at Beth Israel Hospital in New York City. A friend remembered him, saying: "David took a great joy in living the life he lived. It was performance art on the world's smallest possible stage, usually involving an audience of only one or two."

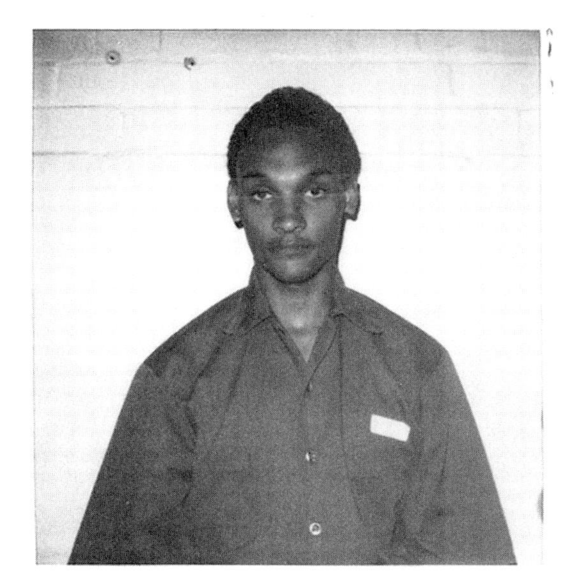

- Hampton 85-B-0075

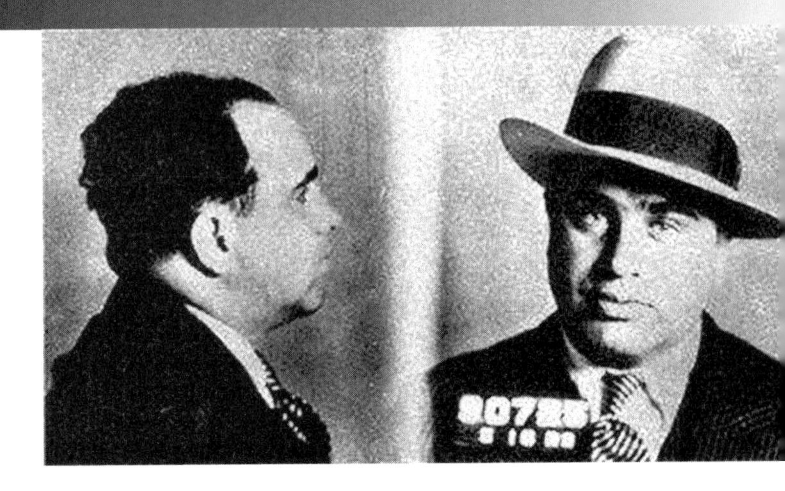

AL CAPONE

Stowed away among the 43,000 Italians arriving in New York in 1894, were Gabriele, barber, and Teresina Raiola, seamstress, who had both embarked at the lively city Castellammare di Stabia, near Naples. Alphonse, their fourth child, the first born in America, came into the world on January 17, 1899.

As a kid he started out in a couple of gangs, then got into more serious affairs. In 1921 he moved to Chicago and his ascent began. During the Depression his restaurant The Free Lunch fed crowds of poor people every day at no charge. The combined income, including all his side businesses, was around $100 million a year. The whole city was on his payroll: police officers, journalists, judges, gravediggers, prostitutes, and petty criminals. Even Jacob Rubenstein, Ruby, future assassin of John Kennedy's assassin. After various trials that went nowhere, in 1931 he was sentenced to ten years in prison for tax evasion. He died a free man on Palm Island, Florida, on January 25, 1947, from syphilis-related apoplexy. "Scarface" was photographed, inside and out, more than a Hollywood star. In all his mug shots, he has an indifferent, amused look. In the profile shot below, the frame cuts him off. He was 5 feet 10 inches tall and 220 pounds of pure American dream.

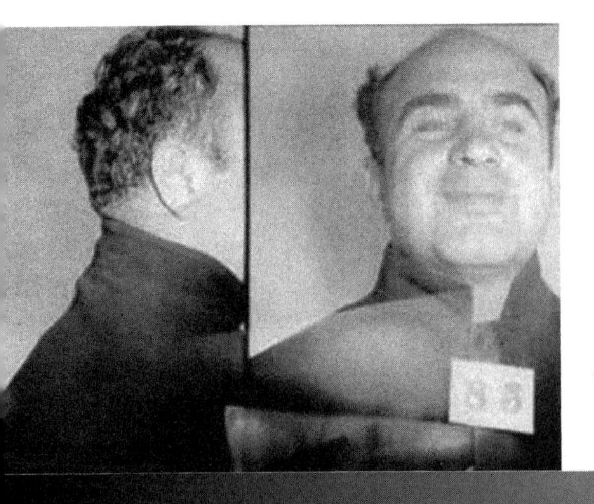

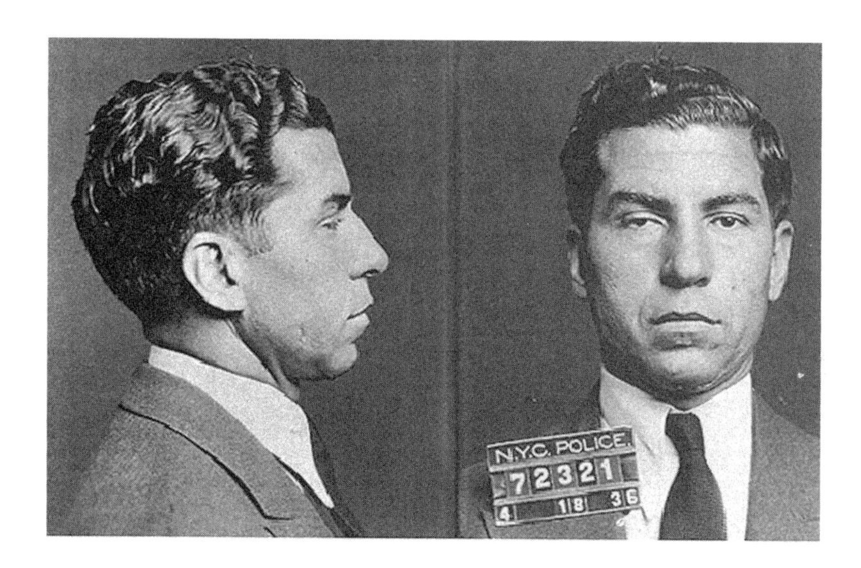

LUCKY LUCIANO

NEW YORK CITY, 04/18/1936

Salvatore was nine years old when his father, a sulfur miner from Lercara Friddi, near Palermo, emigrated to New York. It was 1906 and the boy immediately understood that the only way to make America keep its promises was to take them by force. He was arrested one year after his arrival, in 1907, for shoplifting. At school he unsuccessfully tried to extort money from a Jewish classmate, Meyer Lansky. Together they would reform organized crime, changing it from child's play to a modern industry, carving their names into the history of the twentieth century.

In New York, Salvatore became Charles and finally—after surviving a 1929 attack during which his attackers slit his throat, beat him with an ice pick, and threw him in front of a moving car—"Lucky" Luciano. He dressed like a movie star, hung out with crooner and actor Frank Sinatra, and lived in a suite at the Waldorf Astoria. After warring with, and eliminating, bosses Giuseppe Masseria and Salvatore Maranzano, Lucky Luciano and Lansky reinvented the mafia, adopting hierarchies, sanitary methods, meritocratic criteria, and the worldly air of big American corporations. In June 1936, he was sentenced to fifty years in prison. He got out, thanks to Hitler, because after Pearl Harbor the FBI asked him to help find German submarines off of New York. On February 10, 1946, at 8:50 a.m., he left the U.S. for Italy, where he would live until his death.

He died from a heart attack at the Naples airport on January 26, 1962. The next day, the *Sunday Times* printed: "Reports circulated here that the onetime vice-king of New York may have tried suicide to avoid his impending arrest in a crackdown on an international narcotics ring." He was buried at St. John's Cemetery in New York.

MEYER LANSKY

NEW YORK CITY, 1930s

The life of Majer Suchowliński, a slight Russian Jew who landed in New York as a baby, practically has its own film genre, considering how often it has been depicted. Meyer Lansky inspired Sergio Leone's film *Once Upon a Time in America*, as well as the character of Hyman Roth in Francis Ford Coppola's *The Godfather II*. Lansky's biography seamlessly blends truth and legend. From his partnership with Lucky Luciano, who failed to extort money from him when they were schoolmates and therefore had to respect his boldness, to his friendship with Bugsy Siegel, future creator of the city (and the economy) of Las Vegas.

Meyer Lansky was the man who, with Lucky Luke, transformed the mafia from small-time racketeering into an organized industry according to the pattern of modern capitalism. Someone who learned his trade observing how the wealthy behaved. He dressed like an office worker, lived in a normal house, stayed away from the scene. But gambling, prostitution, and American business in Cuba all went through him. Charged with tax evasion in the seventies, he fled to Israel. He came back to the U.S. and served a little time.

He died of lung cancer on January 15, 1983, in Florida, leaving an estate worth over $400 million dollars.

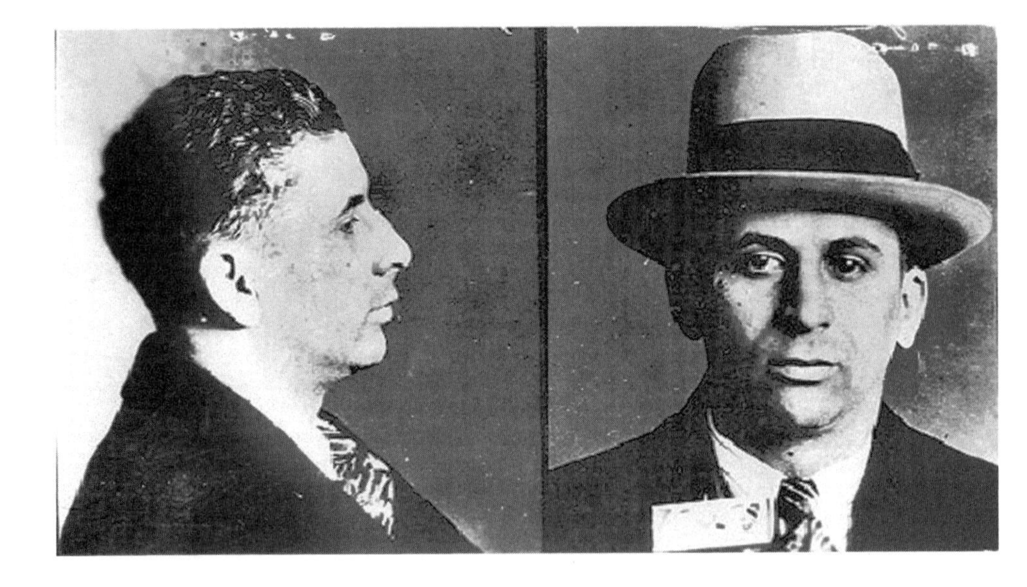

BUGSY SIEGEL

NEW YORK CITY, 04/12/1928

This and the previous mug shot portray two friends and business partners. They were taken during the same period, probably for the same reasons. Meyer Lansky and Bugsy Siegel were in their twenties and were established professionals. But their paths were separate. It was written all over their clothes.

Lansky was a professional. He wasn't contemptuous or defiant. He serenely accepted jail as a possibility. His attire was discreet. Siegel's appearance, however, issues a challenge. Viewed from the front, he's arrogant. In profile, a loser. The brim of his fedora askance. A gangster who would never be anything but. His life, too, like Lansky's, would be pillaged by cinema.

If Lansky is the one who considered violence a means to an end, Bugsy Siegel was the impulsive one, and he would die young. He was killed in 1947, despite Lansky's protection. His epitaph is recited by Hyman Roth in *The Godfather II*: "There was this kid I grew up with . . . As much as anyone, I loved him—and trusted him. Later on he had an idea—to build a city out of a desert stop-over for GIs on the way to the West Coast. That kid's name was Moe Green—and the city he invented was Las Vegas. This was a great man—a man of vision and guts. And there isn't even a plaque—or a signpost—or a statue of him in that town."

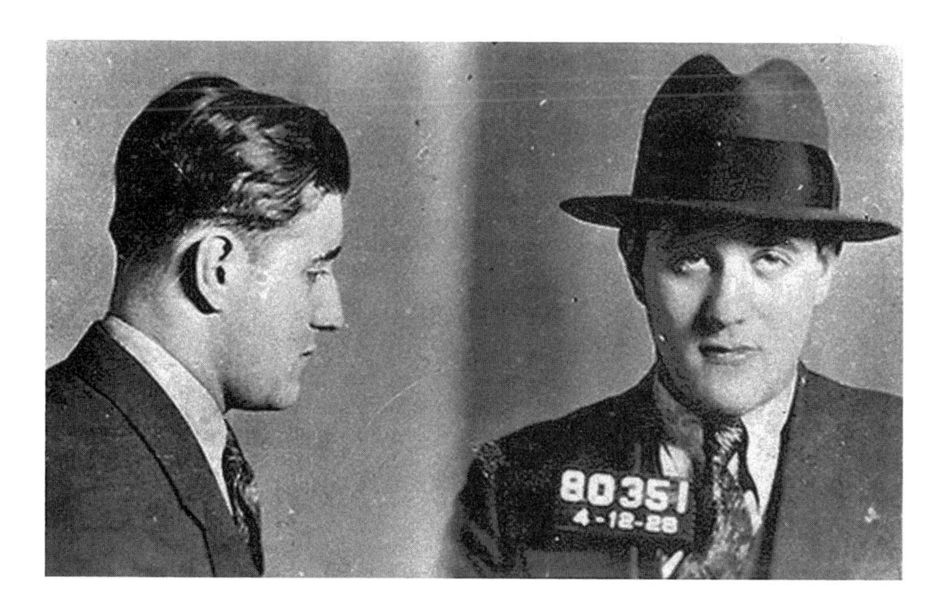

CARLO GAMBINO

NEW YORK CITY, 11/14/1957

The first convention of *cosa nostra* that journalists took full notice of occurred on Thursday, November 14, 1957. The bust went down at Joseph Barbara's eighteen-room mansion in Apalachin, New York, where fifty-eight of the most powerful mafiosi of the time held meetings to discuss the succession of Albert Anastasia (who had just been killed at a barbershop). When the police arrived, everyone was crowded around the barbecue pit. Some fifty escaped in the woods, and it took eight hours to identify all the others. No one was armed. However, the police confiscated about $300,000 in cash. The guests had come from New Jersey, New York, Colorado, Texas, Ohio, California, Puerto Rico, and Cuba. Some even came from Italy. Among the names of those arrested are Vito Genovese and Carlo Gambino, perhaps the most intelligent, the most "political" of the bosses of the five New York families.

Cosa nostra made another appearance in Washington, in Fall 1963, when Joe Valachi, the first big mafia informant, testified before the commission presided over by John McClellan, Democratic senator of Arkansas. Valachi described the initiation process, rites, and rules (never get involved with the wife, sister, or daughter of another member); he recounted mafia wars, relations with the Irish, and the "bizniz" in detail. But most importantly, he identified Carlo Gambino, Joseph Magliocco, Joseph Bonanno, Thomas Lucchese, and Vito Genovese as the heads of the five families who controlled *cosa nostra* in New York. During the proceedings, the lawyers' curiosity opened the way for description of minutia. As if America were discovering how Italian-Americans lived, what they ate, and how they spoke. At a certain point, there was talk of one Terranova, known as "the Artichoke King." McClellan asked, "Are artichokes that important?" Valachi replied, "The artichoke is something that any Italian must always keep on the table for dessert."

That day, the *New York Times* reported the following regarding Gambino: "Born in Italy in 1902 . . . Other witnesses at a State Investigation Commission inquiry testified Gambino (gam-BEE-no) invited them to the Apalachin meeting in November, 1957, for barbecue and because he wanted to compare cardiac notes with the late Joseph Barbara, fellow sufferer of heart disease, on whose estate meeting was held . . . Lives at 2230 Ocean Parkway in Brooklyn."

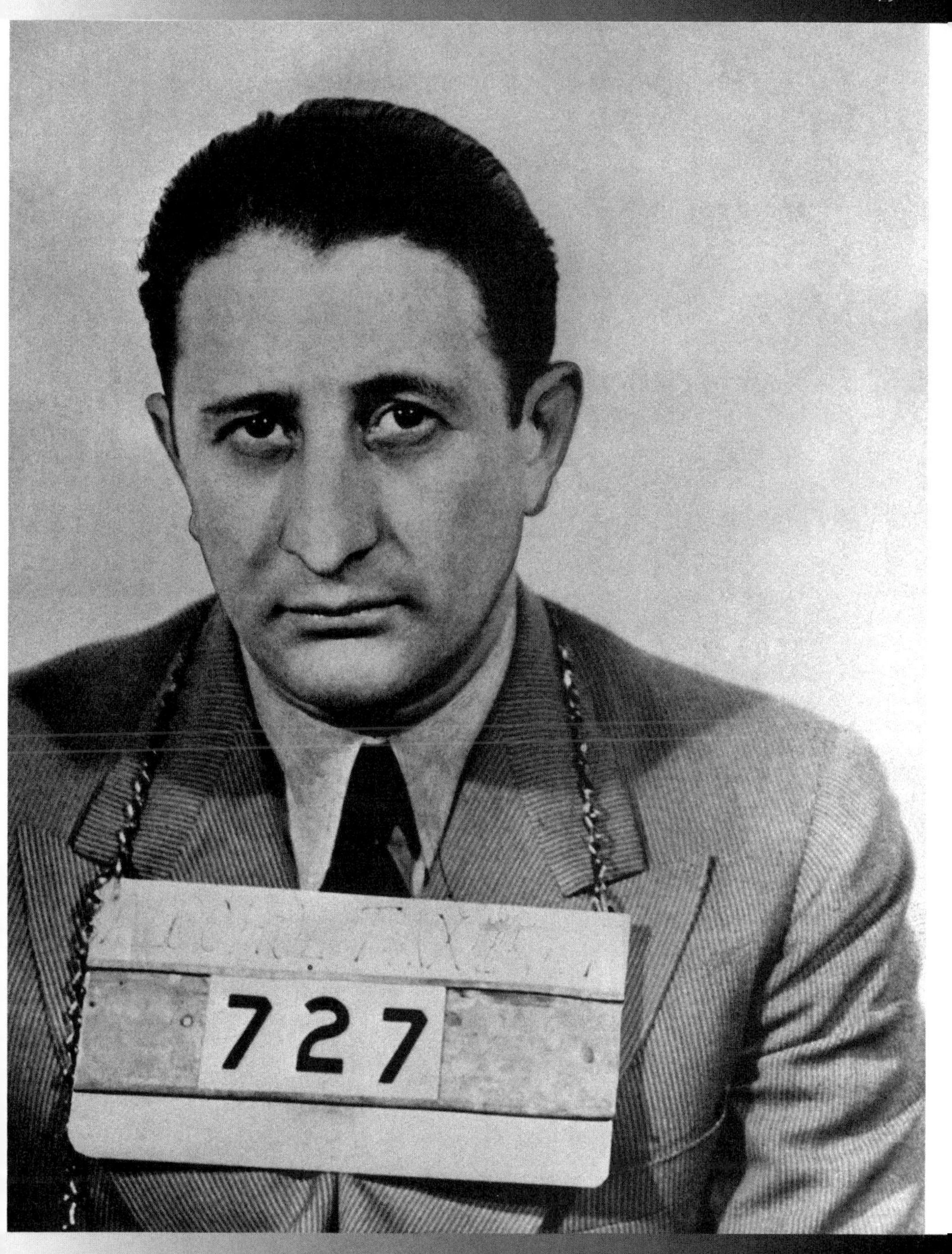
727

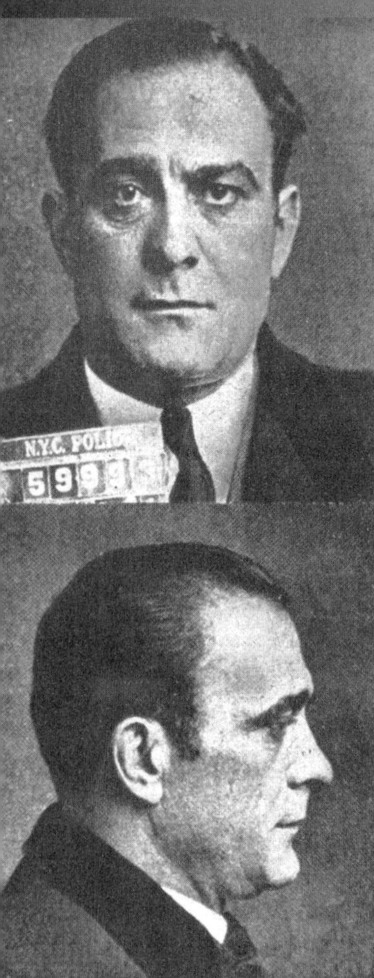

VITO GENOVESE

SPRINGFIELD, MONTANA, 07/7/1969

In one photograph of Vito Genovese he's smiling. He's wearing an American army uniform, with one hand in his pocket and the other on outlaw Salvatore Giuliano's shoulder. Leonarda Sciascia wrote: "Vito Genovese, wanted in America for manslaughter, found himself in Sicily in 1943–44 as an interpreter for the Allied Military Government. A policeman named Dickey was on his trail and managed to find him. With the help of two English soldiers (English, mind you, not American) he was arrested; they found letters of credence on him signed by American officials, which called Genovese 'deeply honest, trustworthy, loyal, and certainly reliable for service.'"

Born in Rosiglino, near Naples, in 1897, he emigrated to New York in 1912 where he started working for Lucky Luciano. To avoid going to trial, he returned to Italy in 1937. In Sicily, he met Benito Mussolini and, according to some, procured cocaine for Galeazzo Ciano, Mussolini's foreign minister and son-in-law. Then he actively collaborated, like many mafiosi, on the Allied landing. He came back to the U.S. with the intention of taking power. Luciano, Lansky, and other bosses of the time plotted against Genovese by setting up a lucrative drug deal and paying the dealer to testify against him. He died in 1969, after ten years in prison. With him, *cosa nostra* had entered the drug trade.

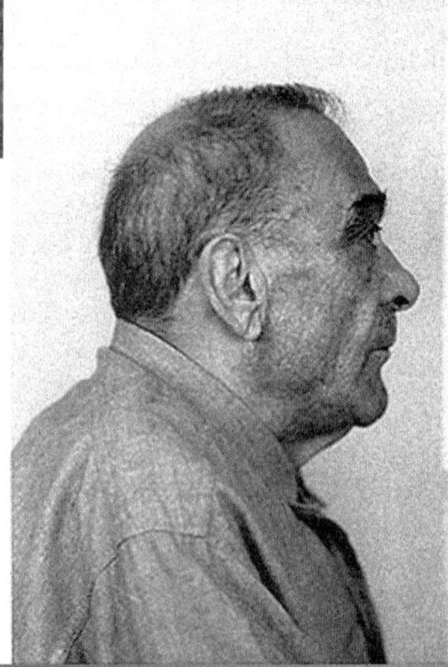

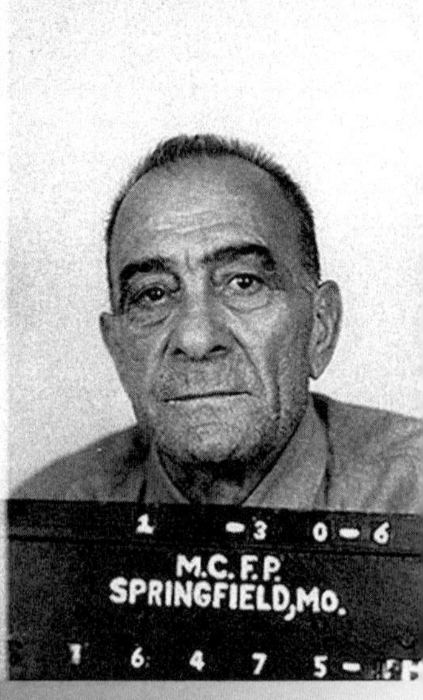

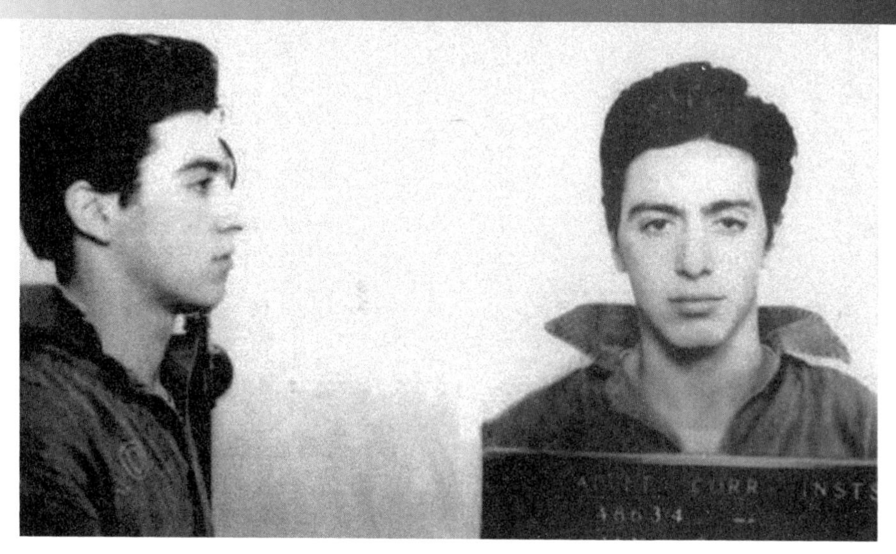

AL PACINO

WOONSOCKET, RHODE ISLAND,

01/07/1961

Among the many characters Alfredo James Pacino has given life and breath to, he hasn't played the young man on the mean streets very often. To imagine the actor's younger days it helps to recall two of his best characters: Lefty Ruggiero, the middle-aged, small-time crook trying to get by in Mike Newell's *Donnie Brasco*, and Carlito Brigante, the protagonist of Brian De Palma's *Carlito's Way*.

The young man was arrested in Woonsocket, just outside Providence, Rhode Island. On the night of January 7, 1961, a patrolling officer stopped to check a suspicious vehicle. Inside he found the twenty-one-year-old Al and two friends with a full set of black masks and gloves. The officer joked, "Don't tell me you're coming from a Halloween party." Unfortunately, it was January, and the search revealed a .38 caliber pistol. As the officer recalls, Pacino was very helpful during questioning. He explained that they were all actors and that he and a friend, Cohen, had taken the bus up from New York to visit another friend, Calcagni, whom he had met in the service.

Unable to pay the two-thousand-dollar bail, the three passengers spent three days and three nights in jail.

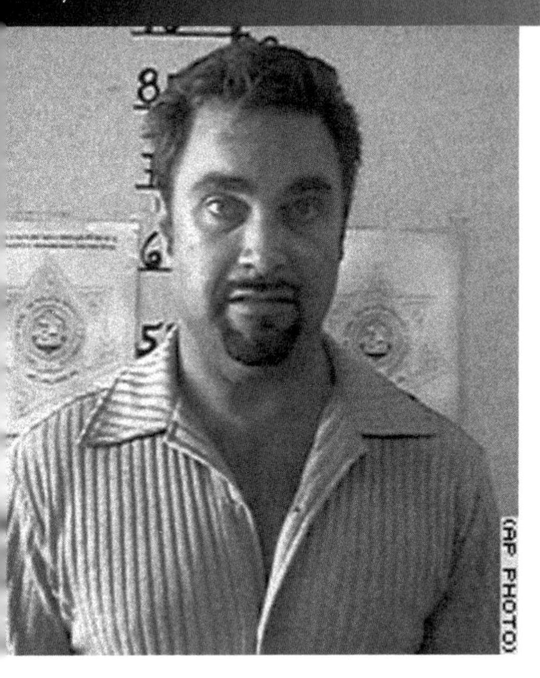

(AP PHOTO)

ANDREW LUSTER

PUERTO VALLARTA, MEXICO, 06/18/2003

"That's exactly what I like in my room: a passed-out, beautiful girl," Andrew Luster said in one of the videos that led to his conviction. Max Factor's great-grandson was sentenced to 124 years in prison for drugging and raping three women. He himself supplied proof of the accusations: home videos that show him having sex with women who are visibly unconscious, and a notebook with a list of his victims and prosecutors he wants to get even with under the heading "payback." In this notebook, found after the arrest, he claims that ruining a "good man's life" is unforgivable.

DOG CHAPMAN

PUERTO VALLARTA, MEXICO, 06/18/2003

He's the latest incarnation of the bounty hunter, a category precious to the beginnings of criminal photography. Duane Lee Chapman, a.k.a. Dog, an ex-con turned bounty hunter, started trailing Andrew Luster on January 5, 2003. The search lasted 165 days. He said, "I'm a bounty hunter, this is the number one fugitive in America, and I'm on his ass. This one has become personal." He caught Luster in Mexico, but was arrested himself on June 18, along with his two sons, his brother, and two members of his TV crew. The charges: criminal association and illegal deprivation of liberty. He had captured Luster without first getting permission from the local authorities. The million-dollar bounty went up in smoke.

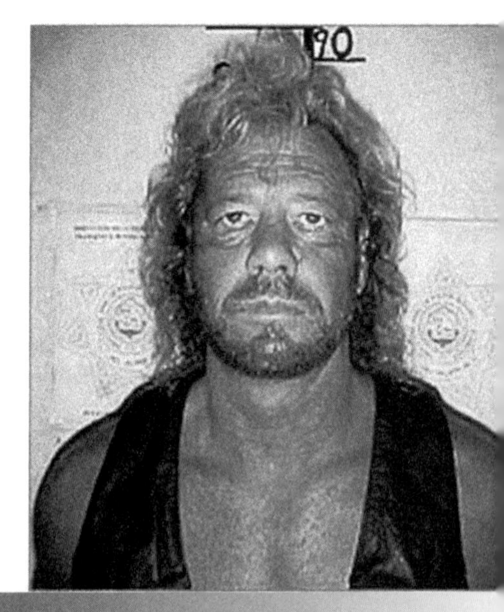

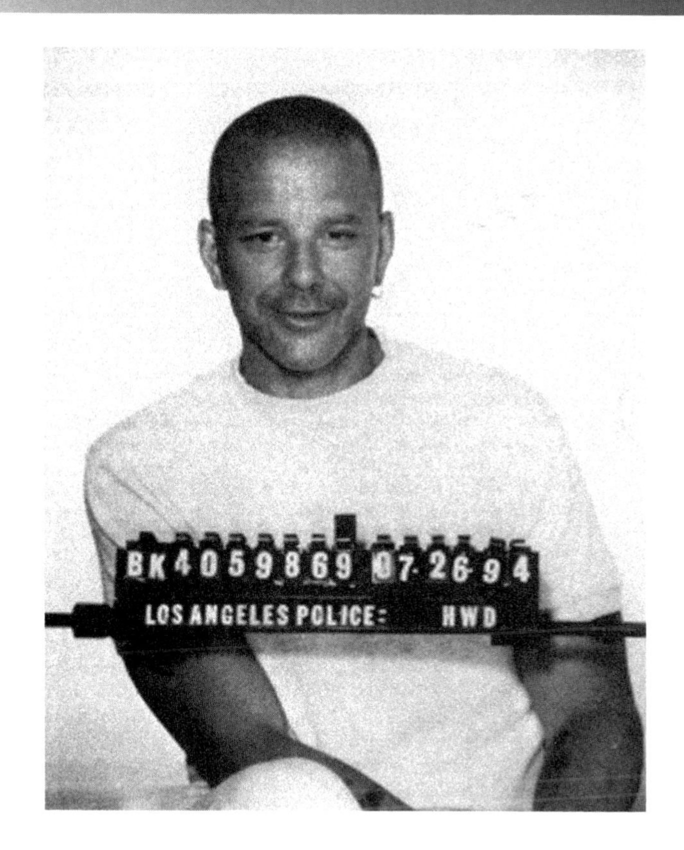

MICKEY ROURKE

LOS ANGELES, CALIFORNIA, 07/26/1994

He punched and kicked Carré Otis, his beautiful companion, during an argument. The charge was dropped almost immediately because she stopped cooperating and retracted the claim. Theirs was an intense and obsessive love affair. In an interview published a year after their separation, Otis confessed that she was still obsessed with the sight of his penis, a sort of totem of flesh.

Philip Andre Rourke Jr. was born in Schenectady, New York, on September 16, 1956. He wanted to become a boxer, but ended up studying at the Lee Strasberg institute. During his career he acted alongside many of the greats: he was great in Francis Ford Coppola's *Rumble Fish*, had a small part in the masterpiece *Heaven's Gate*, and was the protagonist in *Year of the Dragon* directed by Michael Cimino. His big break was Adrian Lyne's *9 1/2 Weeks*. A movie he loathed.

From 1991 to 1995 he went back to boxing, even fighting former middle-weight champion Carlos Monzón, who knocked him out on the first hook. His face, ravaged by boxing and alcohol, led him to plastic surgery. He collaborated with David Bowie on his album *Never Let Me Down*.

He is a great talent and has lived hard. But many people don't give him enough credit.

ROBERT DOWNEY JR.

CALIFORNIA, 08/25/1999

Even going to jail and posing for the police can become a habit. His first arrest was in 1996, for possession of heroin, crack, cocaine, and a .357 Magnum. He was sentenced to three years probation and periodic drug tests, which he often tended to skip.

In 1997 he did six months in prison. In 1999, a year. He got out in August 2000. In November, another arrest for cocaine and valium. In April 2001, after the umpteenth arrest, the producers of the sitcom *Ally McBeal*, for which Downey had won a Golden Globe, dropped him from the series. "It's like I have a shotgun in my mouth, and I've got my finger on the trigger," he explained to the judge in 1999, "and I like the taste of the gunmetal."

Born in New York on April 4, 1965, be debuted at five as a puppy in *Pound*, directed by his father. He grew up in Greenwich Village, in the New York avant-garde environment of the early seventies. He attended, but didn't graduate, Santa Monica High School with Sean Penn and Rob Lowe. A teacher remembers that he stood out for his talent, depth, and vulnerability. He dated actress Sarah Jessica Parker for seven years. He was famous for his roles as a drug addict in *Less Than Zero* (from the novel by Bret Easton Ellis) and as Charlie Chaplin in Richard Attenborough's *Chaplin*.

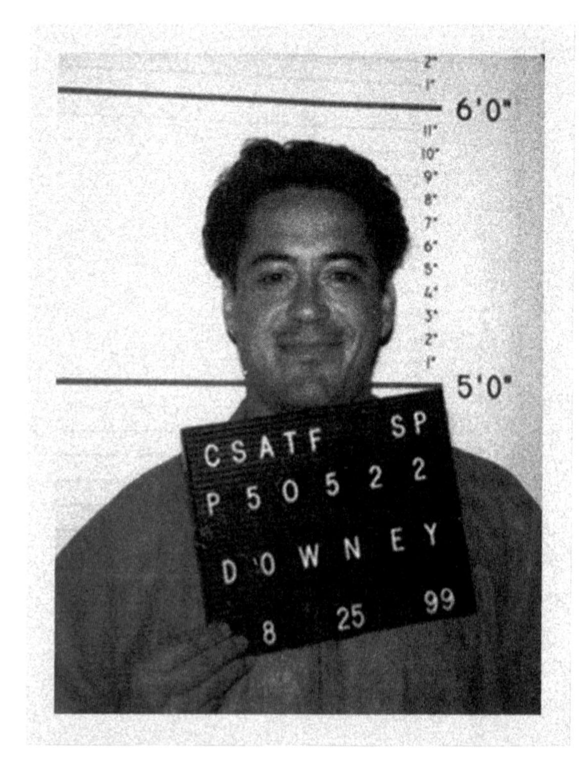

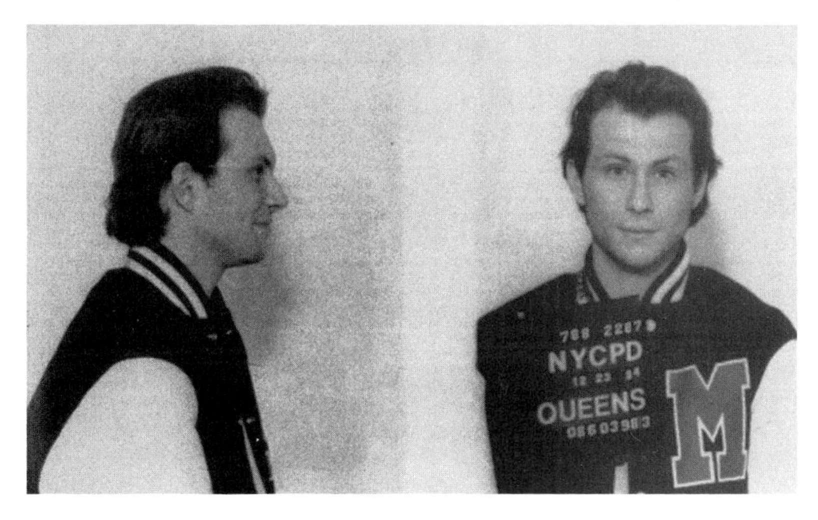

CHRISTIAN SLATER

NEW YORK CITY, 12/23/1994

A young, successful actor is stopped at the JFK airport in New York when he tries to board an airplane with a gun. His penalty is commuted to three days of community service with homeless children. Christian Michael Leonard Hawkins was born in New York on August 18, 1969. His mother, Mary Jo Slater, was a casting director. His father, Michael Hawkins, however, was an actor. His record lists four arrests: one in 1989, one in 1994 (pictured), one in 1997, and one in 2005. *Star Trek* is to blame for the shape of his eyebrows: one Halloween, when he was young, they were shaved to look like Spock's. They never grew back normally.

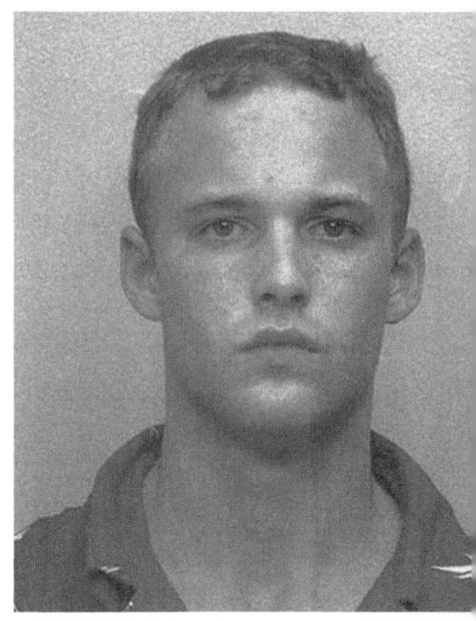

BRAD RENFRO

FORT LAUDERDALE, FLORIDA, 08/2000

"Brad you're so fine / I wanna make you mine / But I don't wanna cross the line / Before you give me the sign," by "Praisy." On the fan website for Brad Renfro, the boy in the 1994 film *The Client*, girls engage in a sort of literary "contest." He does everything a star does, mug shots included. He was born in 1982 in Knoxville, Tennessee. At school he did little and did it poorly. Arrested the first time in 1998 for possession of cocaine and marijuana, on August 28, 2000, he and a friend tried to steal a yacht in Ft. Lauderdale, Florida. But he forgot to untie it from the dock, damaging the pier and the boat.

YASMINE BLEETH

DETROIT, MICHIGAN, 09/12/2001

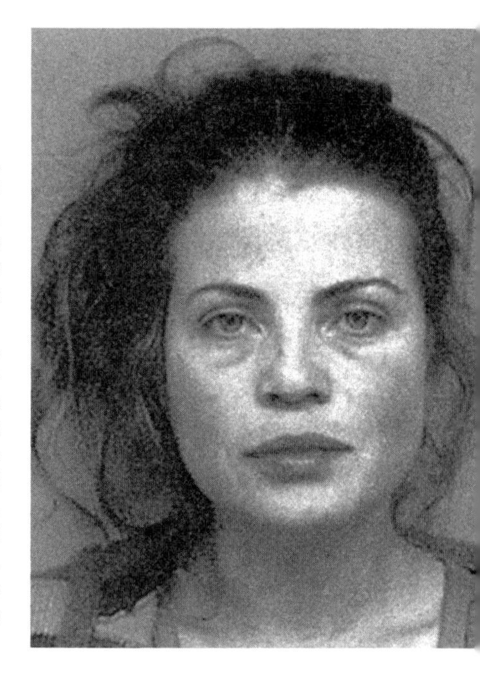

"I was driving under the influence of narcotics. Cocaine, your honor." From the same beautiful mouth of Caroline Holden, one of the most popular characters on *Baywatch*, a favorite with American guys, and therefore, all the Western world. The admission of guilt, made before judge Karen Ford Hood on December 1, 2001, turned up on American televisions and newspapers.

The act took place on the night of September 12, 2001. Bleeth and her boyfriend had gone to visit his parents in Detroit. The September 11 attacks and the airspace closures had impeded their return to Los Angeles. In Romulus, near the Detroit airport, the actress drove into the traffic divider. Under the driver's seat, the police found four syringes, some of which tested positive for cocaine. She was sentenced to two years with parole, one hundred hours of community service, and regular drug testing. Yasmine made her debut in a commercial for Johnson & Johnson "no more tears" baby shampoo when she was six months old.

VINCE VAUGHN

WILMINGTON, NC, 04/2001

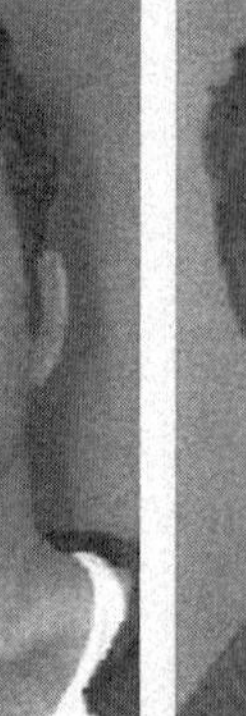

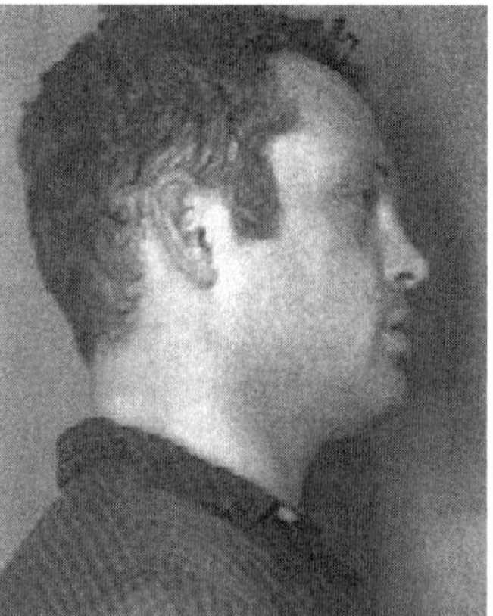

The charge was causing a bar brawl. Vaughn couldn't have played it better if he was in a traditional fistfight scene. He was given a $250 fine and ordered never to set foot in the Wilmington, North Carolina, bar again, and to enter a detoxification program.

Vince Vaughn, born in 1970 in Minneapolis, rose to stardom with *Swingers*, appeared in *Jurassic Park*, was Norman Bates in the pointless remake of Sir Alfred Hitchcock's *Psycho*, and starred in the blockbusters *Old School* and *Dodgeball*.

JOSHUA JACKSON

RALEIGH, CALIFORNIA, 11/09/2002

His mother Fiona was a casting director, so he appeared in some movies as a baby. The newborn in *The Changeling* with George C. Scott, for example. Later, mom had second thoughts, but Joshy really wanted to become an actor.

His consensual debut happened at age eleven in a commercial for Keebler chips. But his big break came in 1998 with the show *Dawson's Creek*.

In 2002, in Raleigh, California, he was arrested for assaulting a security guard during a Carolina Hurricanes hockey game.

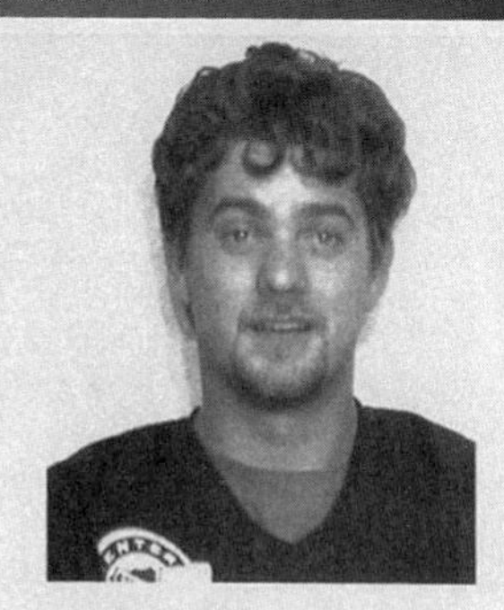

NAME: LAST: JACKSON______ FIRST: JOSHUA________ MIDDLE: ____________
ADDR: [redacted] __ CHESTNUT________________________ ST__ APT: ___
CITY: WILMINGTON________ ST: NC ZIP: 284
ARRESTING AGENCY: RPD-Raleigh Police Dept.__________ ALCOHOL PERCENT: 00.000
CHARGE 1: ASSAULT AFFRAY 14-33______________ COUNTS: 001
CHARGE 2: INTOXICATED & DISRUPTIVE 14-444____ COUNTS: 001
RACE...: White__________ SEX...: Male__________ DOB...: 06/11/78
SSN...: [redacted] HEIGHT: 602 WEIGHT: 180
ETHNIC: NON-HISPANIC___ EYES..: BLUE__________ HAIR..: BROWN__________
COMPLX: Fair__________ BODY MARKS: ______________________________
ALIAS LAST: ______________ FIRST: ______________ MIDDLE: ____________
OCCUPATION: ACTOR______________________ EMPLOYER: NETWORK TV SERIES_____
NEAREST RELATIVE: NONE________________________________
HOME PHONE #...: 919/000-0000 BUSINESS PHONE #: 919/000-0000
ARREST DATE/TIME: 11/09/02 2215 BOOKING DATE/TIME: 11/09/02 2339
COURT DATE/TIME: __/__/__ ____ RELEASE DATE/TIME: 00/00/00 0000
ID #...: 233170____ BOND AMT: __________.__
FBI #...: ______________ STATE #.: ______________

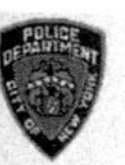

New York City Police Department

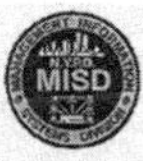

Mugshot Pedigree

NAME: ILER, ROBERT

NYSID # : 1163063H
Arrest # : M01065219-N
Arrest Date : 07/04/2001
Top Charge : PL 1601001
Date of Birth : 03/02/1985
Age at Offense : 16
Social Security # : [redacted]
PCT of Arrest : 019
Source : LIVE

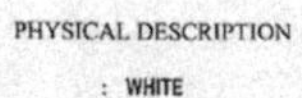

PHYSICAL DESCRIPTION

Race : WHITE
Sex : MALE
Height : 5'7"
Weight : 135
Hair Length : SHORT
Hair Color : LT BROWN
Hair Type : STRAIGHT
Skin Tone : CLEAR
Eye Color : BLUE

Scars, Marks Tatoos
Desc : SCAR
Location : FACE
Bodyside :
:
Alias 1 :
Alias 2 :
Alias 3 :
Alias 4 :

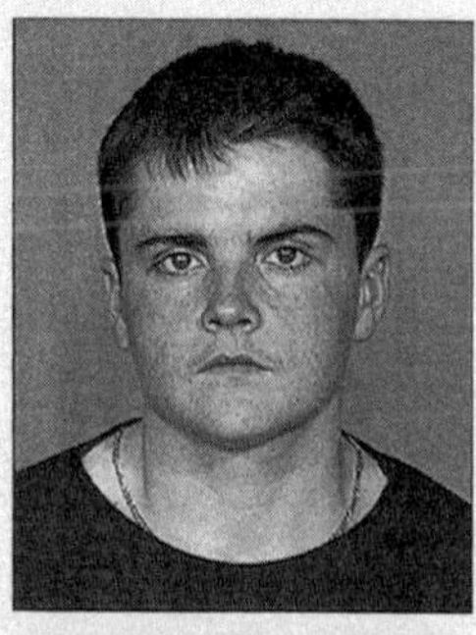

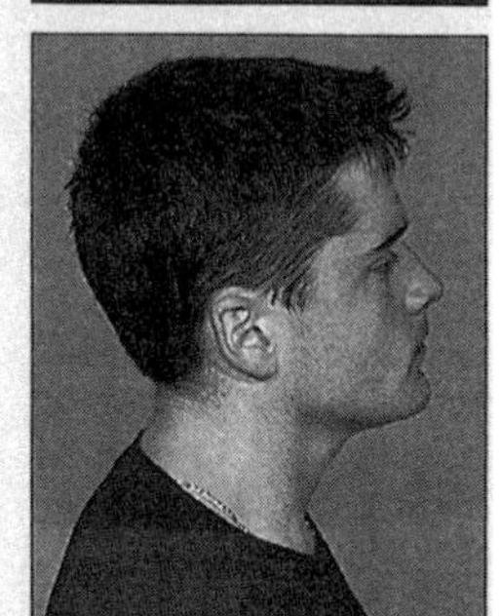

ROBERT ILER

NEW YORK CITY, 07/04/2001

Another child debut. Another debut in commercials. Robert Iler came out at age six in a Pizza Hut ad. This was followed by a forgettable movie, an appearance on *Saturday Night Live*, and other commercials (such as IBM, AT&T, ESPN). He gained fame as a pot-smoking mobster kid in the series *The Sopranos*. Born in New York on March 2, 1985, he was arrested in Manhattan on July 4, 2001, at sixteen, along with three friends.

The boys claimed innocence of the charge, which was marijuana possession and the theft of forty dollars from two Brazilian tourists passing through the Upper East Side. Iler later copped a plea bargain.

HUGH GRANT, DIVINE BROWN

LOS ANGELES, CALIFORNIA 06/27/1995

Hugh Grant was born in London on September 9, 1960. He started acting at the University of Oxford. His first major movie appearance dates back to 1987 in James Ivory's *Maurice*. His big break came in 1994 with *Four Weddings and a Funeral*. The following year he was arrested for picking up a prostitute in Hollywood. It seemed like he was finished. Then he made a comeback in 1999 with *Notting Hill*, costarring Julia Roberts.

She, the prostitute, is named Estella Marie Thompson, known on the street as Divine Brown. At the time of the incident she was twenty-three. She worked Hollywood's Sunset Boulevard. She got into a white BMW at 1:30 a.m. "They were later observed to be engaged in an act of lewd conduct," stated officer Lori Taylor, declining to specify which act.

After the arrest, or thanks to the arrest, she earned (and squandered) 1.6 million dollars. Today she makes her living in a licensed brothel in Nevada. In 1996 she made a film directed by porn star Ron Jeremy called *Sunset and Divine: The British Experience* (a.k.a. *Nine Minutes*). She was probably the first prostitute to have gotten something out of it.

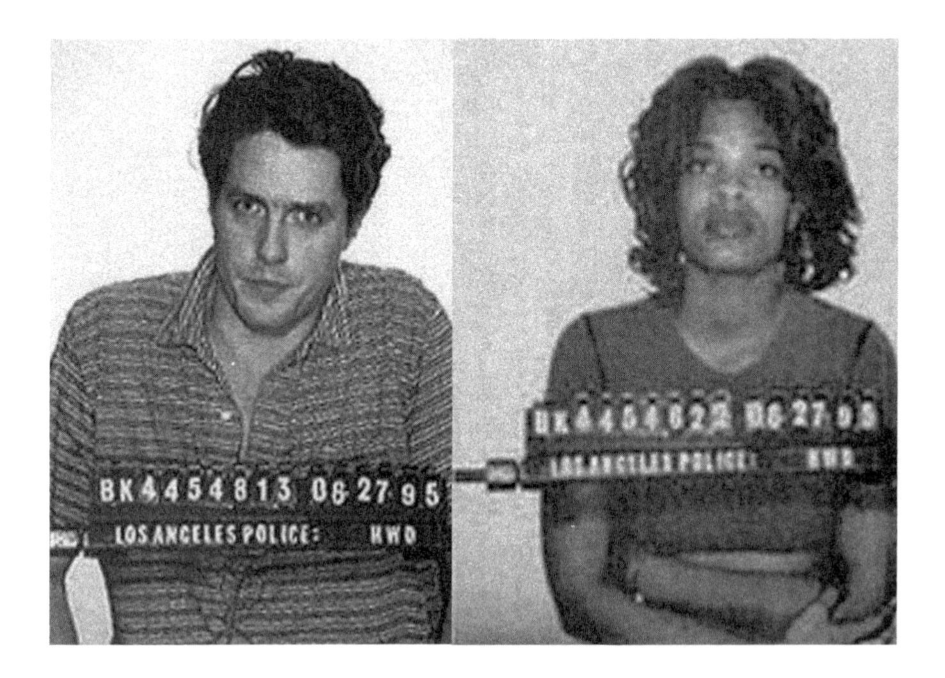

DANA PLATO

LAS VEGAS, NEVADA, 01/1992

What an ugly end for sweet Kimberly, Arnold's stepsister in *Diff'rent Strokes*. The show was so famous that Nancy Reagan agreed to appear in an episode to warn kids against drugs.

Dana was born in 1964 in Maywood, California. Her mother, who was sixteen and already had a little boy, decided to give her up for adoption. She debuted at age seven in a Kentucky Fried Chicken commercial. She appeared in over a hundred ads. For Dole fruit cocktail she had to eat eighty-two bananas in one day. From 1978 to 1984, for $22,000 an episode, she was Kimberly. They fired her when she got pregnant by a guitarist, but she returned for the final season.

Her first arrest was for stealing $164 in a video store she had entered wearing a blond wig. She would later say, "If I hadn't gotten caught, it could have been the worst thing that happened to me because I could have died of a drug overdose." The second (pictured below) occurred in January 1992. This one was for faking a Valium prescription. Numerous other arrests ensued. She reappeared, identifying as a lesbian, in some B pornos.

May 7, 1999, was her last interview. She claimed that she had been clean for ten years. She died the next day, without leaving a note, from an overdose of Valium and Loritab, which the coroners deemed intentional.

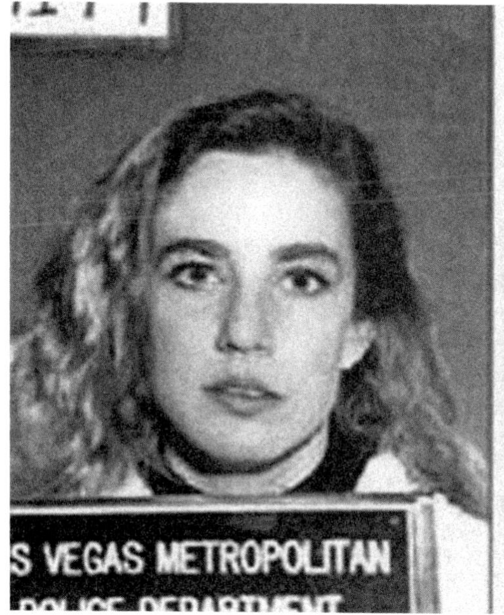

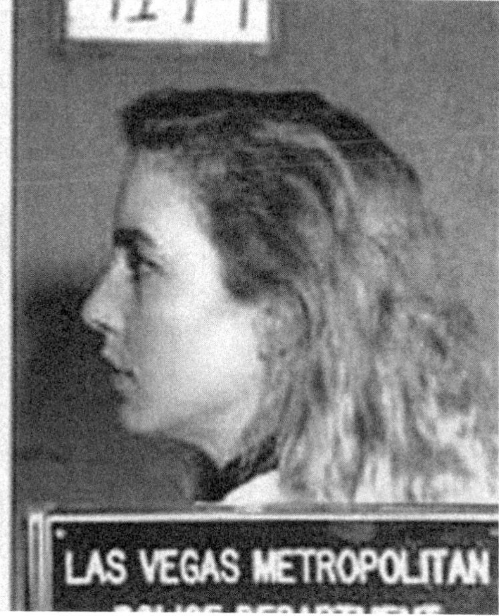

NICK NOLTE

MALIBU, CALIFORNIA, 09/12/2002

On *Larry King Live*, May 10, 2003, the special guest is actor Nick Nolte.

King: Tonight, Nick Nolte here to tell us how he went from Hollywood heartthrob to this. What really happened when he was caught in the photo that shocked the nation? And, why his driving under the influence bust was the best thing that ever happened to him in his long battle with addiction.

Nolte: I know the first thing I said in my own mind when the lights went out. I said the jig is up. I was much relieved . . .

King: And that was what happened in September?

Nolte: September, oh September the 11th, yes, when . . .

King: Because the last time you were on the show you told me you had been sober for, did I get it right, fifteen years? . . .

Nolte: And, the day on September 11, everybody was waiting for some terrorist act and nothing happened so I was the biggest news of the day.

Nicholas King Nolte was born February 18, 1941, in Omaha, Nebraska. This interview is one of the very rare cases in which an offender and an interviewer comment together on a mug shot.

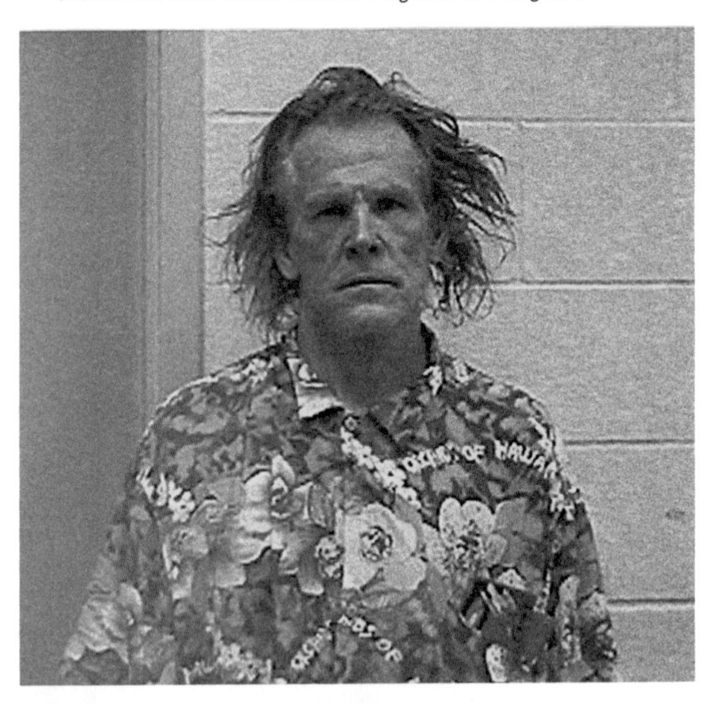

LARRY KING

MIAMI, FLORIDA, 12/20/1971

The interrogation took place at the office of the administrative assistant state attorney, Seymour Gelber, on the sixth floor of the Metropolitan Dade County Justice Building in Miami, Florida, on Wednesday, September 15, 1971, at 10:30 a.m. Also present was Louis Wolfson, owner of Channel 4 TV and the Miami Seaquarium.

State of Florida vs. Larry King. Case No. 71-10512:

Gelber: Mr. Wolfson, you have had occasion to be involved with Larry King in a matter in which certain monies were to be transmitted to Mr. Garrison, who is the present district attorney in New Orleans, Louisiana, is that true?

Wolfson: Yes, sir.

Gelber: What I would like you to do is to recall in the best fashion you can the circumstances surrounding that transaction, and give me the date, or as close to the dates as you can when these events occurred.

Wolfson: I met with Mr. Jim Garrison, Larry King, Richard Gerstein, David Goodhart, here in Miami Beach. We discussed the assassination of former president Kennedy, and out of this discussion he indicated that it would take $25,000 to finish his investigation.

Gelber: Do you have any recollection as to the date of that?

Wolfson: Yes, I think it was the latter part of 1968. I agreed to give this money for this purpose to Larry King and Richard Gerstein, who in turn assured me that it will be given to Jim Garrison . . . After this first $5,000, I continued to give King or Gerstein–I think I gave Gerstein on one occasion part of this money–a total of $20,000 making a total of $25,000, and I completely divorced myself from any contact with Gerstein about the matter, and Garrison about the matter, until 1969, early part of 1969. I got concerned about Larry King's activities and I had some doubts of his honesty.

Larry was arrested in Miami on December 20, 1971, but the case was dismissed due to the statute of limitations.

The future great CNN interviewer was born as Lawrence Harvey Zieger on November 19, 1933 in Brooklyn, the son of two Russian immigrants. After a childhood of poverty, he had a thousand different jobs, such as UPS delivery man, before moving to Miami to pursue his dream of working for the radio. In 1983 he was noticed by Ted Turner, CNN magnate. In the early nineties, *Larry King Live* was the channel's top program, which over the years ended up airing interviews with basically everyone.

A host who is shorter than all the women he has ever loved, married, and dated, including a former Playboy bunny, Alene Akins, and actress Angie Dickinson.

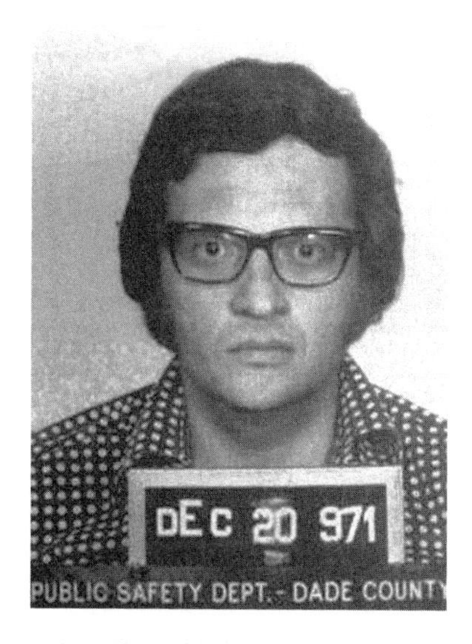

BILL GATES

ALBUQUERQUE, NEW MEXICO, 12/13/1977

This mug shot would delight many devotees of Apple and admirers of Linux. But it is still difficult to think that a man listed by *Forbes Magazine* in 2004 as the "#1 Richest Man in America," with a net worth of $48 billion, could have encountered the nuisances of an ordinary American life in his youth. It just so happened that the young William Henry Gates III, a.k.a. Bill, future emperor of Microsoft, in 1977 at age twenty-two, was arrested in New Mexico for a traffic violation.

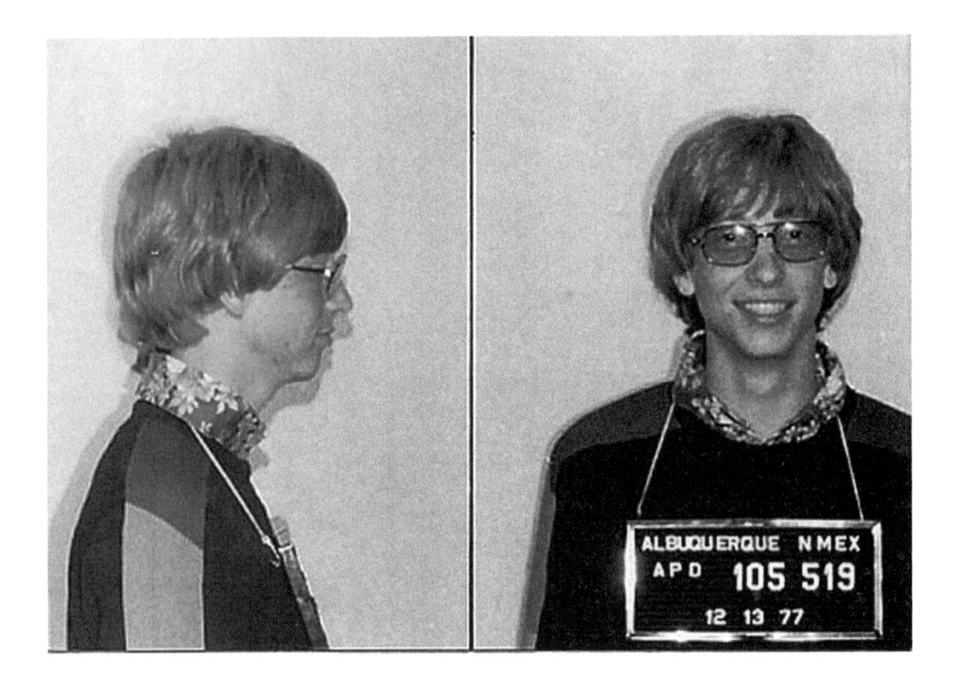

MICHAEL JACKSON

SANTA BARBARA, CALIFORNIA, 11/20/2003

The following excerpt about his penchant for sharing a bed with young boys is taken from a 2003 interview with Martin Bashir, the English journalist made famous for getting Lady Diana to admit that she was unfaithful to Charles:

Bashir: But is that right, Michael?

Jackson: It's very right. It's very loving, that's what the world needs now, more love more heart?

Bashir: The world needs a man who's forty-four who's sleeping in a bed with children?

Jackson: No, you're making it—no, no you're making it all wrong . . .

Bashir: Well, tell me, help me . . .

Jackson: Because what's wrong with sharing a love? You don't sleep with your kids? Or some other kid who needs love who didn't have a good childhood?

Bashir: No, no, I don't. I would never dream . . .

Michael Jackson was born in Gary, Indiana, on August 29, 1958, the seventh of nine children. His parents are Jehovah's Witnesses, who go door-to-door preaching their prophecies and distributing pamphlets. His mother and father were so orthodox that when his younger sister LaToya refused to go to a meeting, Michael was instructed to ignore her. He left the religion in 1987. In 1969, the Jackson Five, composed of Michael and his four brothers, got a deal with Motown. Michael was a cute black kid, with curly hair and a flat nose, who sang and danced the blackest music there was. He attained solo success in 1982 with *Thriller*, which has sold over 40 million copies. The first molestation charge came in 1993. Jackson forked over millions of dollars to avoid a trial. He was accused of molestation again in 2003. One month later, he was charged with seven counts of child molestation and two of administering an intoxicating agent for the purpose of committing a felony.

As he awaited the verdict, Michael Jackson radiated a monstrous beauty. He is a great dancer, terrified of time—of the time that flows over his face, that his African origins have carved in his body. He seems to be obsessed with erasing those traces. A black man born black who, piece by plastic piece, has tried to become white. A man born a man who wants to transform himself into a puppet. A grown man who, child after child, tries to suck away a little bit of childhood wherever he can.

Santa Barbara County Sheriff's Dept.

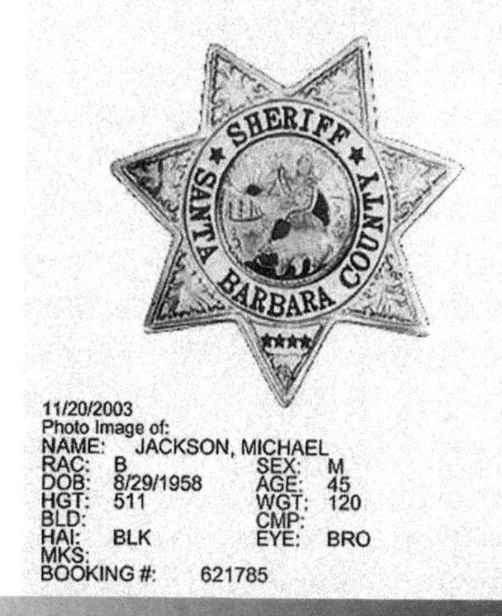

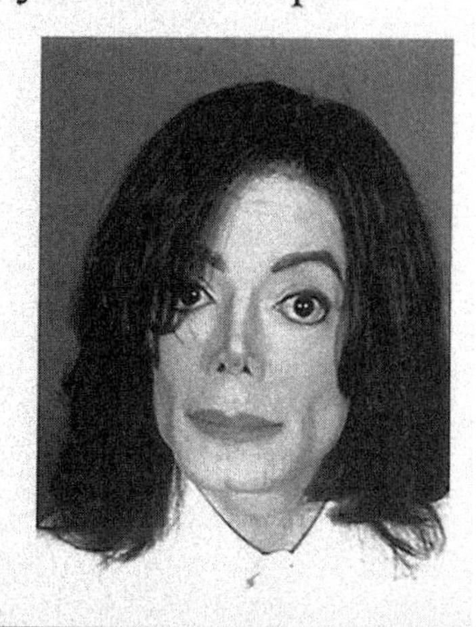

DAVID CROSBY

DALLAS, TEXAS, 04/13/1982

His father Floyd was a director of B movies (like *Sex and the College Girl*, 1964) with a heavy past on his shoulders. In 1930 he was the cinematographer for Friedrich Murnau's *Tabu*, and in 1952 for Fred Zinnemann's *High Noon*.

David Van Cortland Crosby was born in Los Angeles in 1941. In 1963 he started The Byrds; four years later The Byrds kicked him out. In 1968 the trio Crosby, Stills, and Nash appeared, to which, years later, Young was added.

His first arrest, shown in the photo, occurred on April 13, 1982, when he was arrested for driving under the influence of cocaine and possession of a .45 caliber pistol. He was sentenced in 1985, but released in August 1986 when his conviction was overturned on appeal. In 1988, he published an autobiography, *Long Time Gone*. In 1994 he had a liver transplant. He saw his son James for the first time, already thirty years old, in February 1995. Three months later, he had another son: Django. He married in 1997. In 2000, lesbian singer Melissa Etheridge revealed that David Crosby was the sperm donor that enabled her and her partner to have two children.

His last arrest (for possession of marijuana and another .45) occurred in February 2004. He wrote "Suite: Judy Blue Eyes."

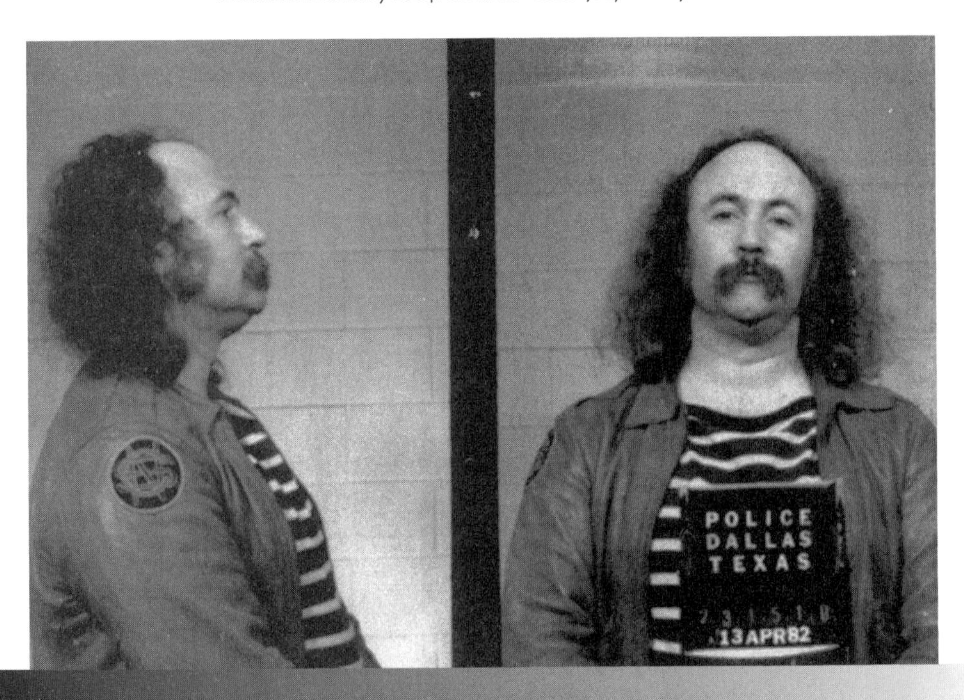

MICK JAGGER

BOSTON, MASSACHUSETTS, 07/18/1972

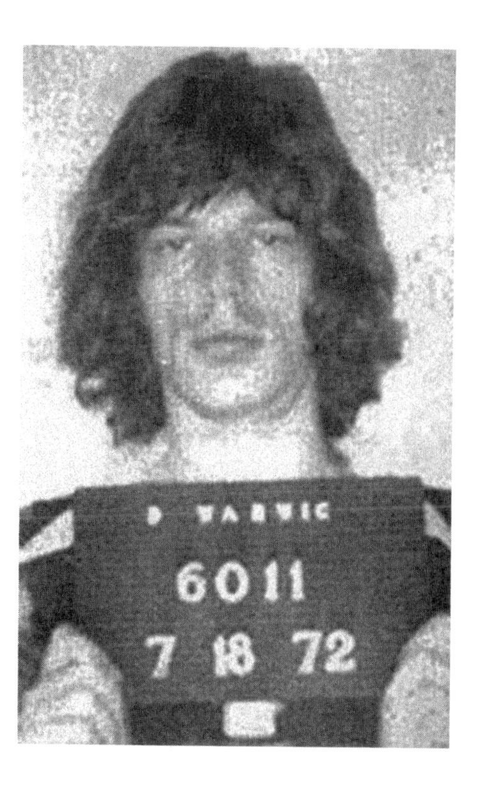

"Heroin, marijuana, amphetamine, and methamphetamine," reads the inspection list that on February 12, 1967, led to the arrest of Mick Jagger and Keith Richards, both twenty-four, the lead singer and guitarist for the Rolling Stones, the band that sang about drugs more than all the rest, especially about heroin as an angel. Richards was sentenced to a year and Jagger to three months, but Richard's conviction was quashed on appeal. Jagger's was reduced to a conditional discharge.

This photo depicts Jagger's second arrest, which took place on July 18, 1972, before a concert in Boston. Jagger and Richards were charged with another of the rock star's canonical charges: resisting and verbally assaulting an officer.

SID VICIOUS

NEW YORK CITY, 10/12/1978

Music doesn't change. The seventies were ushered in by the deaths of Jimi Hendrix and Janis Joplin in 1970, and ended in early 1979 with the overdose of Sid Vicious, the primary suspect in his girlfriend's death four months prior. Out of the psychedelic mythology of rock arose the punk nihilism of the Sex Pistols, for whom Vicious was the bassist and undisputed leader.

From Indictment No. 4529/78, People v. Ritchie a.k.a. Vicious, written up by the New York police and dated October 18, 1978:

> To the first police officers he said in substance that: He didn't know what happened—he wasn't there; He discovered the body about 10:30 a.m.; He wished they would shoot him or kill him . . . To the detectives he said in substance that: He and the deceased had taken tuinal that night and he went to sleep about 1 a.m . . . Nancy was sitting on the edge of the bed flicking a knife. They had had an argument.
>
> He claimed when he woke up in the morning the bed was wet with blood. He thought he had "pee'd" himself. He found the deceased in the bathroom sitting on the floor (same position as found by the police). She was breathing. She had a stab wound in her stomach.
>
> He left her. He went out to get her methadone—at Lafayette Street. When he returned she was full of blood. He washed off the knife and attempted to wash her off. When he could not wash the blood off her he called for help. He did not know what happened to her. He had slept the entire night through. At various times he said "my baby is dead" or words to that effect . . .
>
> The defendant also said that he did not remember what their argument was about and that she hit him and he hit her on top of the head and knocked her onto the bed—but he did not knock her unconscious. He said "I stabbed her but I didn't mean to kill her. I loved her, but she treated me like shit."
>
> At other times the defendant said the deceased must have fallen on the knife and that she must have dragged herself into the bathroom.
>
> When asked why he left the deceased in the bathroom, wounded, and went out to get his methadone he said "Oh! I am a dog."

Sid Vicious was arrested in October 1978, accused of killing his girlfriend Nancy Spungen in a room in New York's Chelsea Hotel. Four months later, at twenty-one, Sid Vicious committed suicide by overdosing on heroin. The death of Nancy Spungen is still not completely resolved.

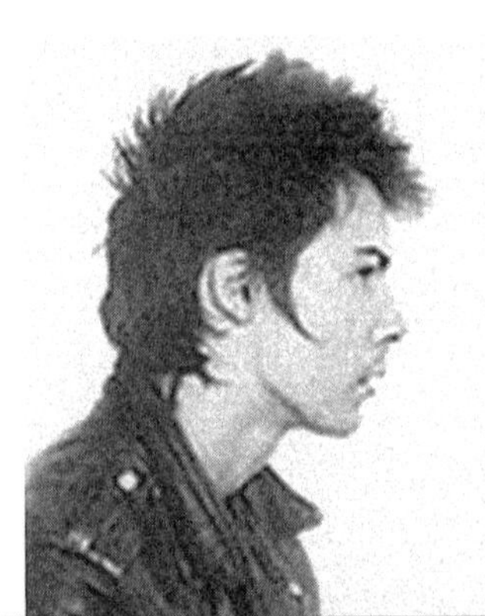

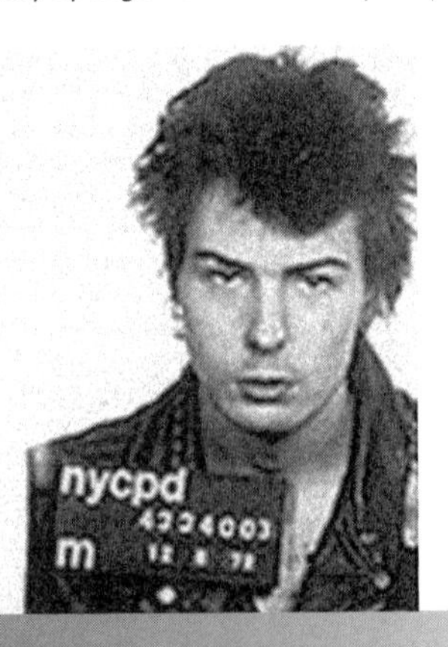

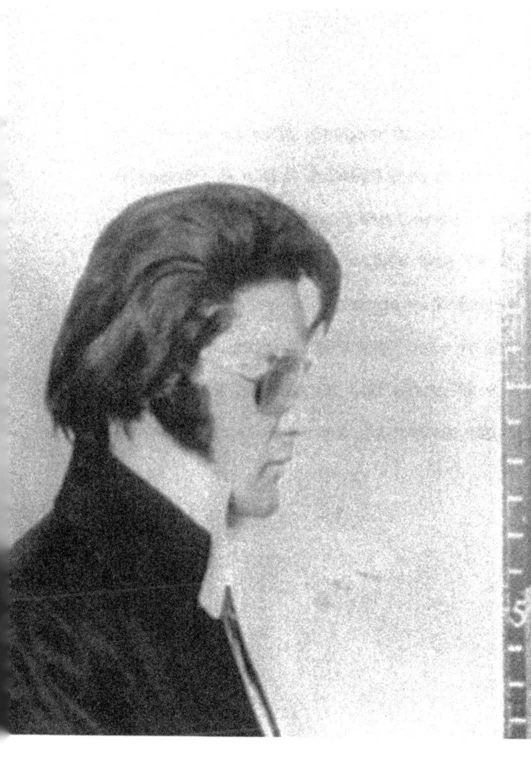

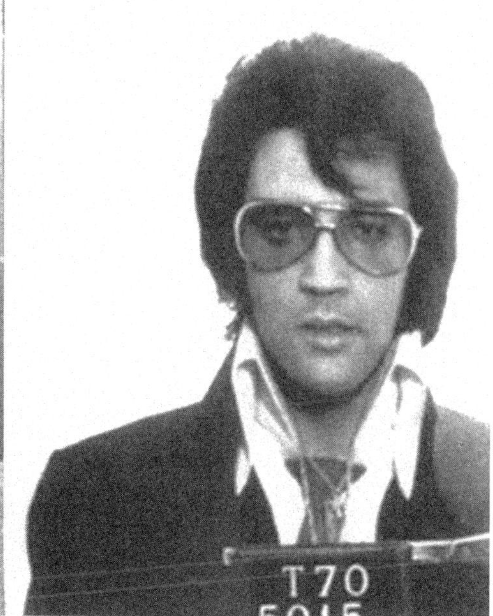

ELVIS PRESLEY

WASHINGTON, D.C., 1970

Year: 1970. The King is thirty-five. The King is crazy about pharmaceuticals, guns, and badges. During a visit to the White House, he asks President Richard Nixon for a gift for his personal collection: a "specially prepared" badge from the Bureau of Narcotics and Dangerous Drugs. His mug shot should have been taken that day, for that reason alone.

Born penniless in Tupelo, Mississippi, on January 8, 1935, Elvis Aaron Presley had a twin who died at birth, Jessie Garon. When he showed up at Sun Studios in Memphis, Tennessee, to record a song for his mother Gladys's birthday present, the studio head took notice.

Musicians asked him what kind of music he liked to sing. He responded, "I sing all kinds." He wasn't lying. He was the first singer to mix country and blues, pioneering the tendency toward musical contamination that made pop music history. He was also the first teen idol. From 1958, when he enlisted in the army, to 1964, when the Beatles came onto the scene, he dominated the American charts. He died on August 16, 1977, at his Graceland estate.

FRANK SINATRA

HACKENSACK, NEW JERSEY, 11/27/1938

"Frank Sinatra, Arrest 42799, Bergen County Sheriff's Office, Hackensack, New Jersey was arrested on November 26, 1938 charged with Seduction."

The 1,300-page FBI file on Sinatra goes on to explain that on November 2 and 9, 1938, "at the Borough of Lodi," "under the promise of marriage," Sinatra "did then and there have sexual intercourse with the said complainant, who was then and there a single female of good repute." An act "in violation of the revised statute of 1937."

After paying a $1,500 fine, the singer was released. About a month later on December 22, it was discovered that the plaintiff was married. The charge was changed to adultery and the fine was reduced to $500. Frank was only twenty-three.

In his singing, he imitated Billie Holiday's phrasing and trombonist Tommy Dorsey's breathing technique. He was never subject to arrest for his controversial mafia associations. Asked about his religious beliefs in a 1963 *Playboy* interview, he said, "I'm for anything that gets you through the night, be it prayer, tranquilizers or a bottle of Jack Daniel's."

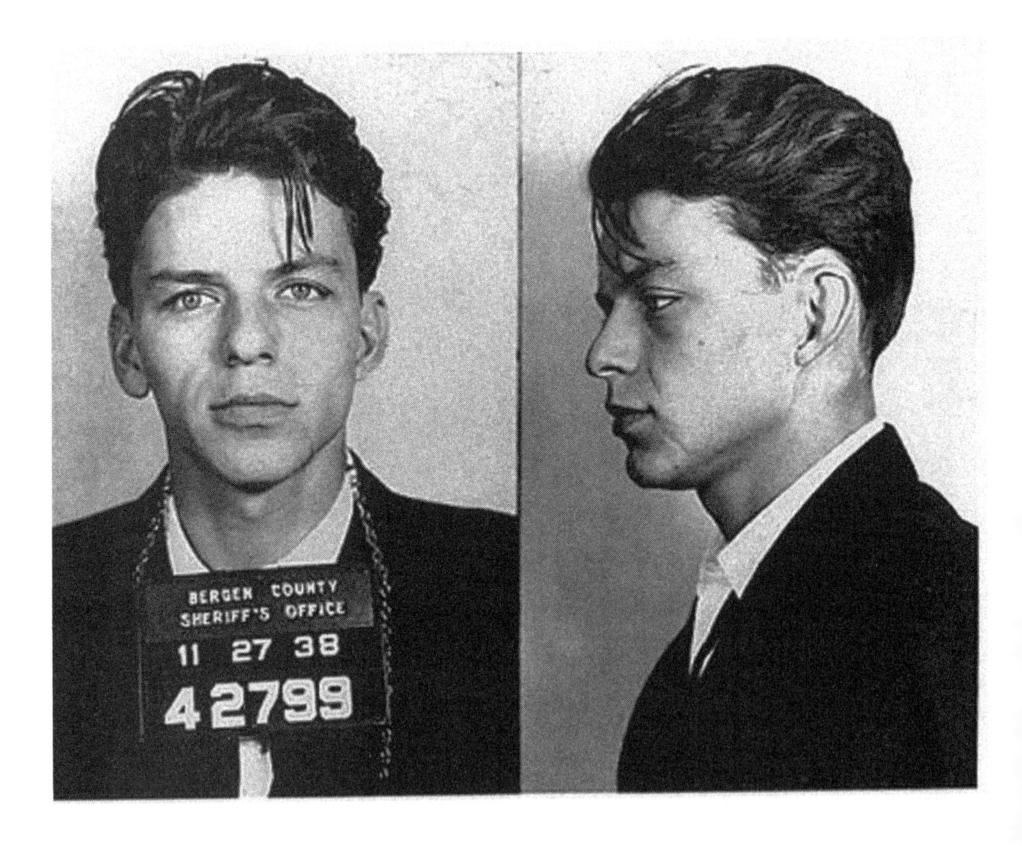

JOHNNY CASH

EL PASO, TEXAS, 10/04/1965

His father, a sharecropper from Kingsland, Arkansas, baptized him J. R. Cash later chose the name John because the Air Force didn't allow initials as names. His first hit was "Folsom Prison Blues" in 1956. In 1965 he was arrested at the El Paso airport for some amphetamines found in his guitar case. The following year he went into the slammer for trespassing; he had wandered into a field to pick flowers. In 1968 he gave a big free concert at Folsom Prison. During his career, he recorded over 1,500 songs, working with the greats. He died in Nashville on September 12, 2003.

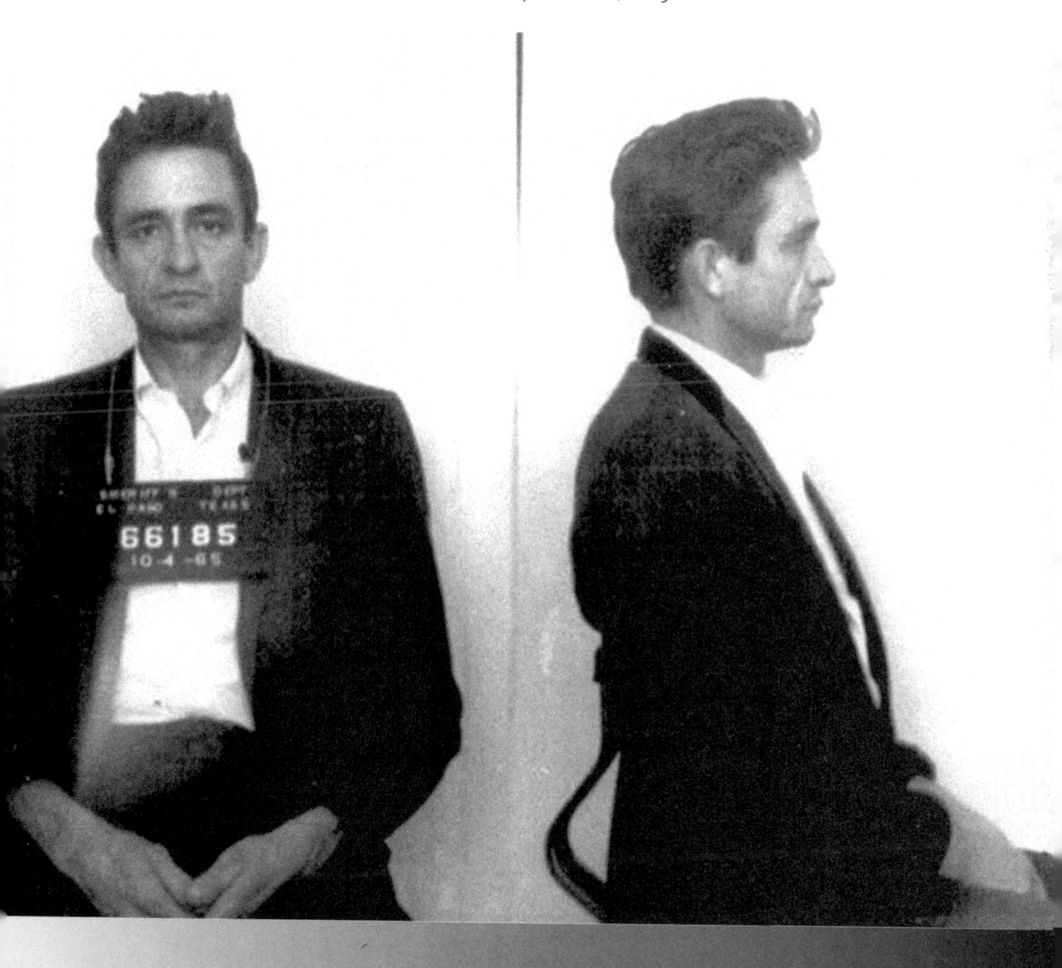

GLEN CAMPBELL

PHOENIX, ARIZONA, 11/24/2003

Another country giant (though less impressive than Johnny Cash). Another country boy, from Billstown, Arkansas, born to a poor, large family (twelve children). Over his forty-year career, he made seventy albums and sold over forty-five million records. He also appeared in a few movies; for example, he's the young man at John Wayne's side in *True Grit*. He was arrested in November 2003 in Phoenix, Arizona, where he was living with his wife and three children, for driving while intoxicated, leaving the scene of an accident, and aggravated assault on a police officer. He spent ten days behind bars—long enough to hold a concert for his jailmates.

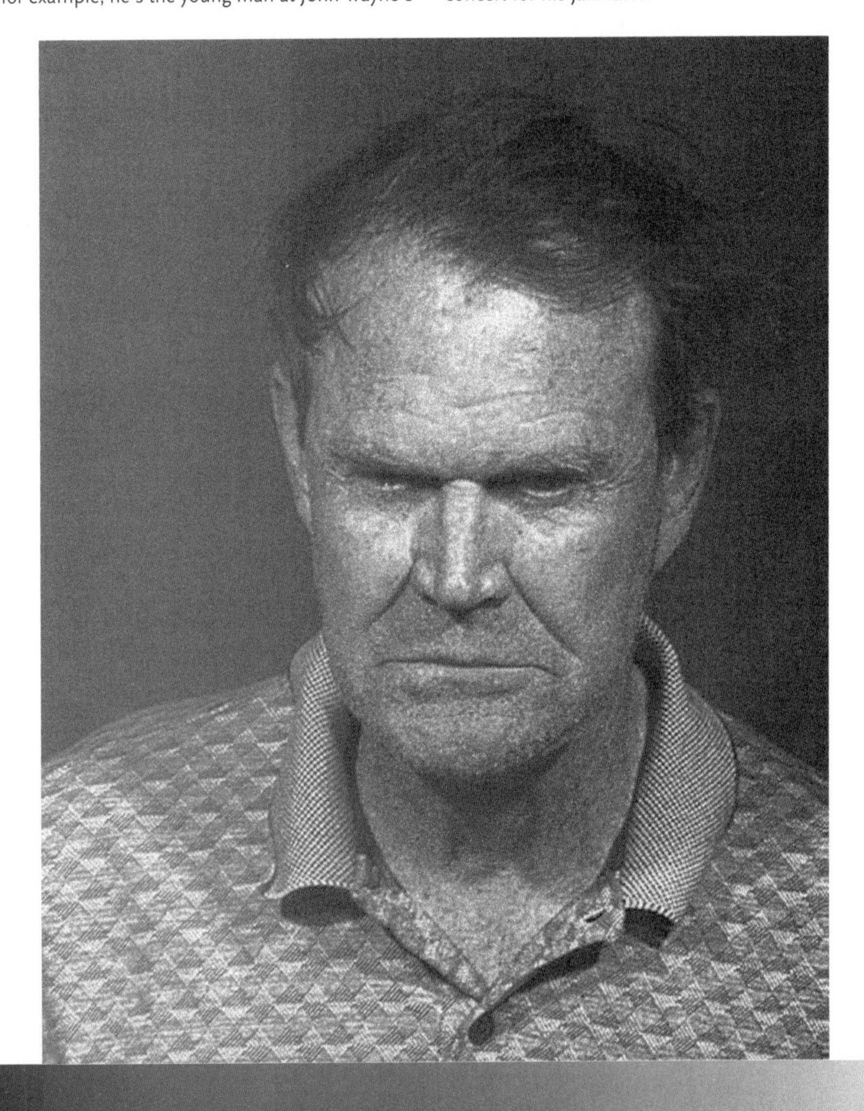

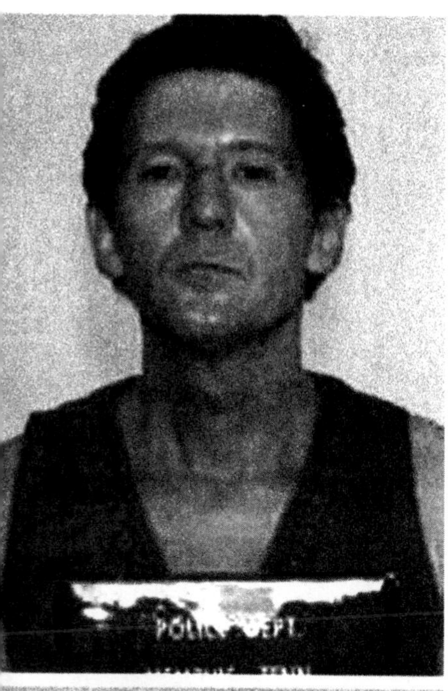

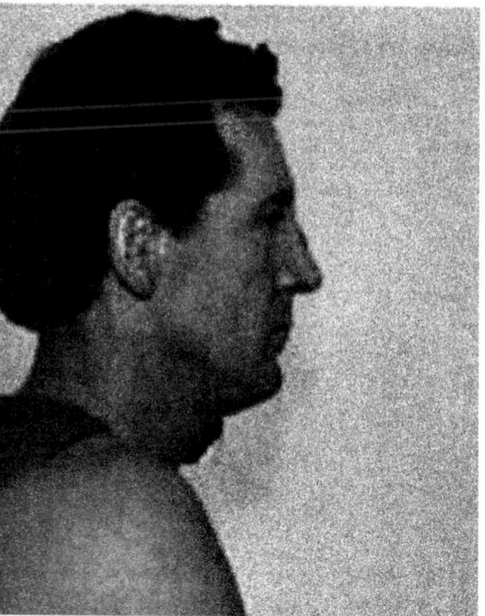

JERRY LEE LEWIS

MEMPHIS, TENNESSEE, 11/23/1976

He treated the piano like no one had ever dared to. On the bench he shook, waved his arms, sweated like a fountain, plunked on those keys like they were his enemies. With "Great Balls of Fire" he revolutionized rock n' roll and tried to contend with Elvis for the title of King. He was married six times, but, except for his controversial union with his thirteen-year-old second cousin, most of his marriages didn't last more than a year. During the course of his career, he was arrested several times. In November 1976, a guard at Graceland stopped him at the gate; no one had informed him about a guest. So he asked Lewis what he was doing there. Lewis pulled out a gun and jokingly responded that he had come to kill Elvis.

SCOTT WEILAND

LAS VEGAS, NEVADA, 11/19/2001

"I don't live in that building and I didn't go to see anyone, I just bought some drugs," lead singer of the Stone Temple Pilots Scott Weiland candidly told the officer who stopped him on June 1, 1998. In addition to getting arrested for entering private property, he was also caught with ten hits of heroin.

He was sentenced to a fine and a trip to rehab. Then when a judge found out that he didn't follow the plan, he got jail time, too. This was the second in a series of charges, every time for drugs, that would go on for years.

Like other musicians, he accepted the support of the Musician's Assistance Program, a foundation that helps stars in the music world get clean. Other program members include Guns N' Roses's Slash, Duff McKagan, and Matt Sorum, with whom Weiland recorded a couple of songs. When he wasn't confined to the clinic, he also managed to cut four albums with his band. Tours were often canceled due to his constant relapses.

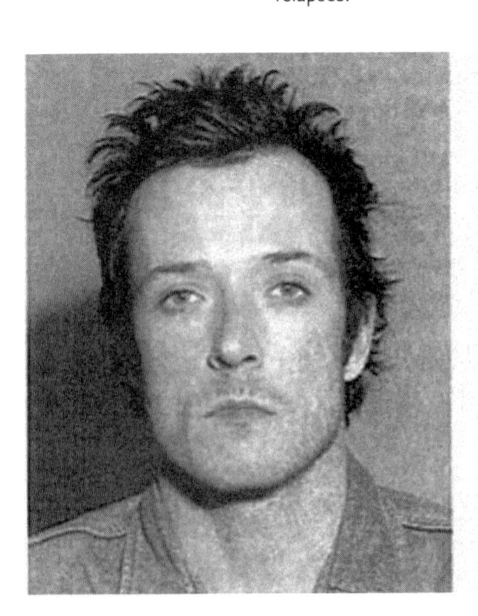

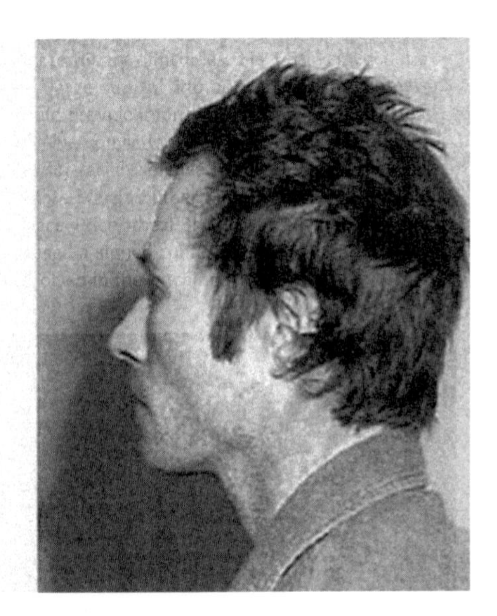

JACK WHITE
DETROIT, MICHIGAN, 12/2003

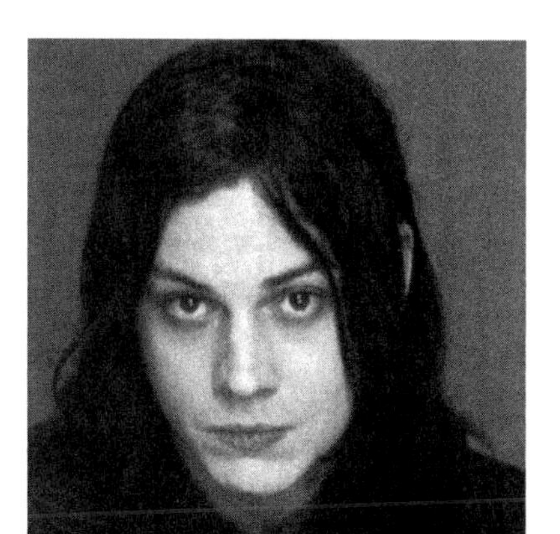

BILLIE JOE ARMSTRONG
BERKELEY, CALIFORNIA, 01/2003

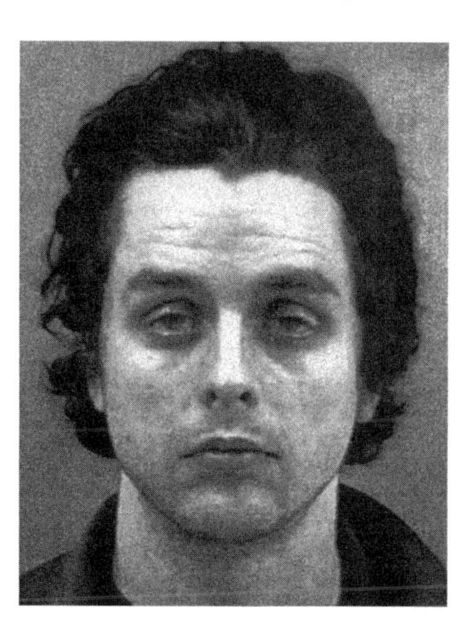

The latest arrivals in a long list. Billie Joe Armstrong and Jack White confirm that for the rock star, now and forever, the mug shot is practically a calling card. Armstrong, Green Day's lead singer, was caught in Berkeley in January 2003 while driving under the influence (the breathalyzer showed .18 while the legal limit is .08). White, the voice of the White Stripes, was arrested for a brawl in Detroit, on December 13, 2003, with Jason Stollsteimer, singer for the Von Bondies. The police don't know who started it. White, who is much bigger, probably won.

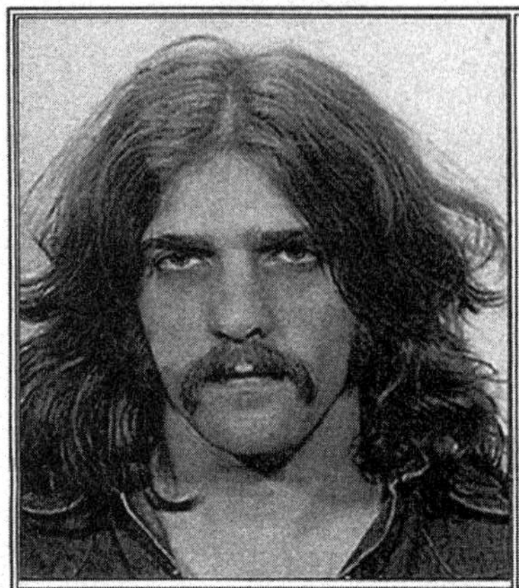

GLENN LEWIS FREY

AKA........... ,
AKA........... ,
SEX........... MALE
RACE.......... WHITE
DOB........... 11/16/1948
HEIGHT........ 5-9
WEIGHT........ 141
BUILD......... SMALL
HAIR COLOR.... BROWN
HAIR LENGTH... LONG
EYE COLOR..... BLUE
FACIAL HAIR... MUSTACHE
SPEECH........ NORMAL
S/M/T.........

GLENN FREY

COLUMBUS, OHIO, 05/1973

Inmate#: 287506
Booking#:391595
Last: WARNER
First: BRIAN
Middle: HUGH
Arr Date:09/21/01
DOB: 01/05/69
Sex: MALE
Race: WHITE
Height: 601
Weight: 140

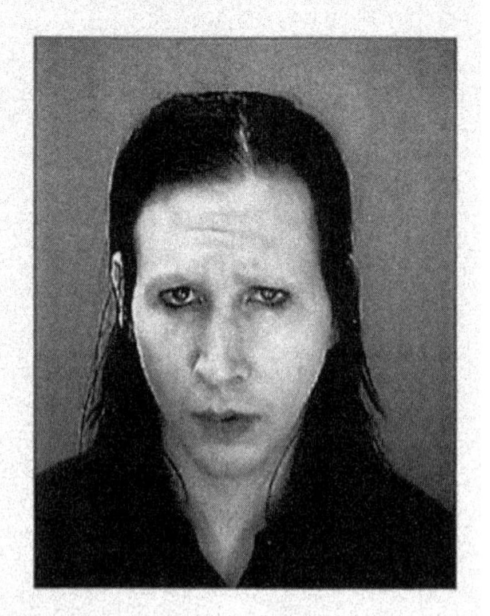

MARILYN MANSON

DETROIT, MICHIGAN, 09/21/2001

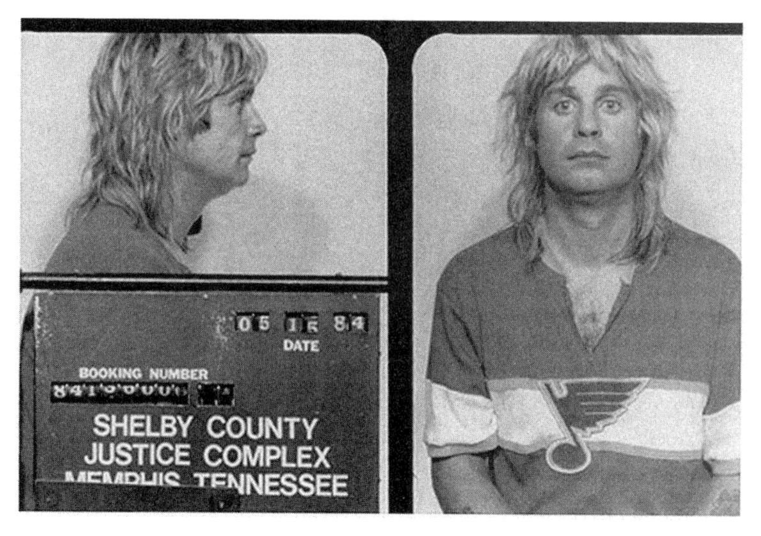

OZZY OSBOURNE
MEMPHIS, TENNESSEE, 05/15/1984

Police photography loves all music equally and doesn't make distinctions between musical genres, with the exception of classical music. It adores crooners like Frankie Valli, a singer who had not so much a voice as a seductive whisper, who was an admirer of Frank Sinatra, and who got himself arrested in 1965 in Columbus, Ohio, for an unpaid hotel bill his manager had skipped out on.

It loves the carefree guitar stylings of Glenn Frey of the Eagles, best known for *Hotel California*, who was also arrested in Columbus, in May 1973, for narcotics possession.

It's also fond of the tight little voice and onstage bats of metal king John Osbourne, a.k.a. Ozzy, locked up in Memphis, Tennessee, in May 1984 for public intoxication on Beale Street. It even appreciates the androgynous, pale, goth-esque Marilyn Manson (or, on the record, Brian Hugh Warner) who was incarcerated in September 2001 after a concert near Detroit, Michigan, for criminal sexual misconduct on a security guard and was let off with a $4,000 fine.

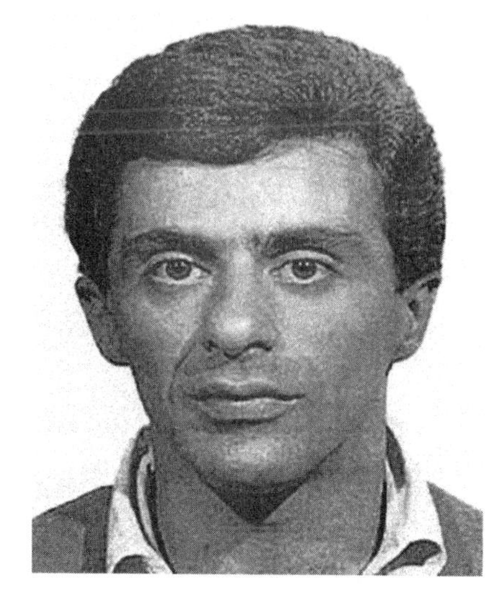

FRANK VALLI
COLUMBUS, OHIO, 09/1965

TUPAC SHAKUR

NEW YORK CITY, 03/08/1995

He knew prison even before he was born; his mother Afeni Shakur, a member of the Black Panthers, the revolutionary group of black Americans, got out of jail only a month before she brought him into the world.

Tupac Shakur's fame grew as quickly as his criminal record. Five albums during his life time, eleven posthumously; six arrests in five years, from 1991 to 1995. The charges range from resisting an officer to brawling to sexual assault. For the various offenses he was sentenced to serve four and a half years in prison.

But perhaps his most significant record is being the only artist to have a number one album on the charts while serving a prison sentence. He died on September 13, 1996, seven days after being shot outside the Tyson vs. Seldon boxing match.

This photo is from a 1995 arrest, when he was accused, and later convicted, of rape. According to the accusation, he offered a fan he had gone to bed with to his friends, encouraging them and using violence to force her. The rapper denied all wrongdoing.

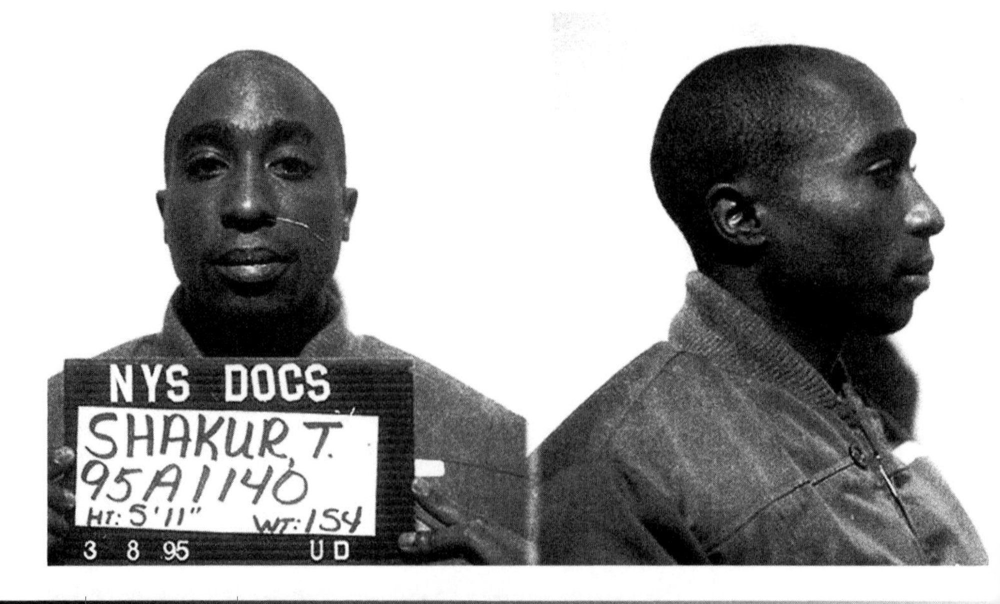

ROYAL OAK
POLICE DEPARTMENT

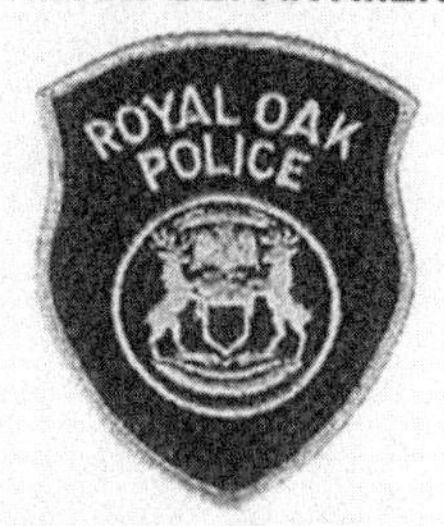

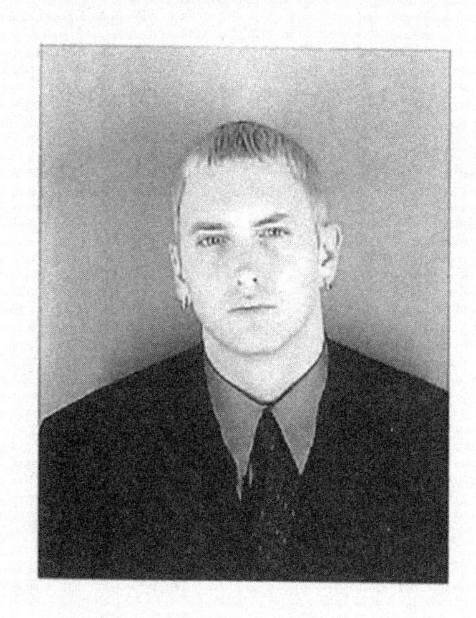

LAST: MATHERS
FIRST: MARSHALL
DOB: 10 / 17 / 72
SEX: MALE
RACE: WHITE
HEIGHT: 508
WEIGHT: 155
EYES: HAZEL
HAIR: BLOND OR STR
EVENT#: 24011906

IMAGE CAPTURED: / /

EMINEM

RED OAK AND WARREN, MICHIGAN, 06/2000

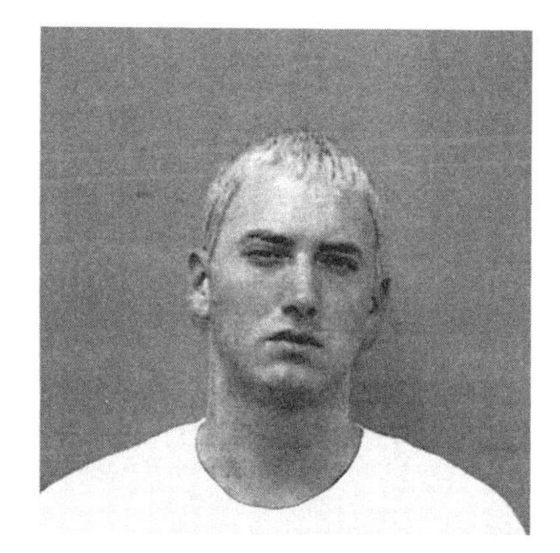

"I'm 'bout as normal as Norman Bates, with deformative traits." Or "You think I give a damn about a Grammy? Half of you critics can't even stomach me."

The story of Marshall Mathers III, or Eminem, represents the latest incarnation of the American dream, one where the optimist Frank Capra gets torn apart by nihilist James Ellroy.

Young, pale Marshall didn't know his father, and what's worse, he spent most of his childhood in an all-black Detroit neighborhood. At fifteen he was in a coma for ten days from a cerebral hemorrhage sustained during a fight. The following year, someone tried to shoot him. He escaped all this through music.

In 1999, thanks to the album *Slim Shady LP*, he became the greatest white rapper of all time. He has great musical talent and lyrics often so violent, sexist, and racist that they have triggered dozens of complaints and have been accused of corrupting youth. He was also denounced for beating someone who had harassed his mother with a baseball bat, and aiming a gun at someone he found with his wife Kim. The mug shots arise from his two arrests in 2000, both for carrying a concealed weapon.

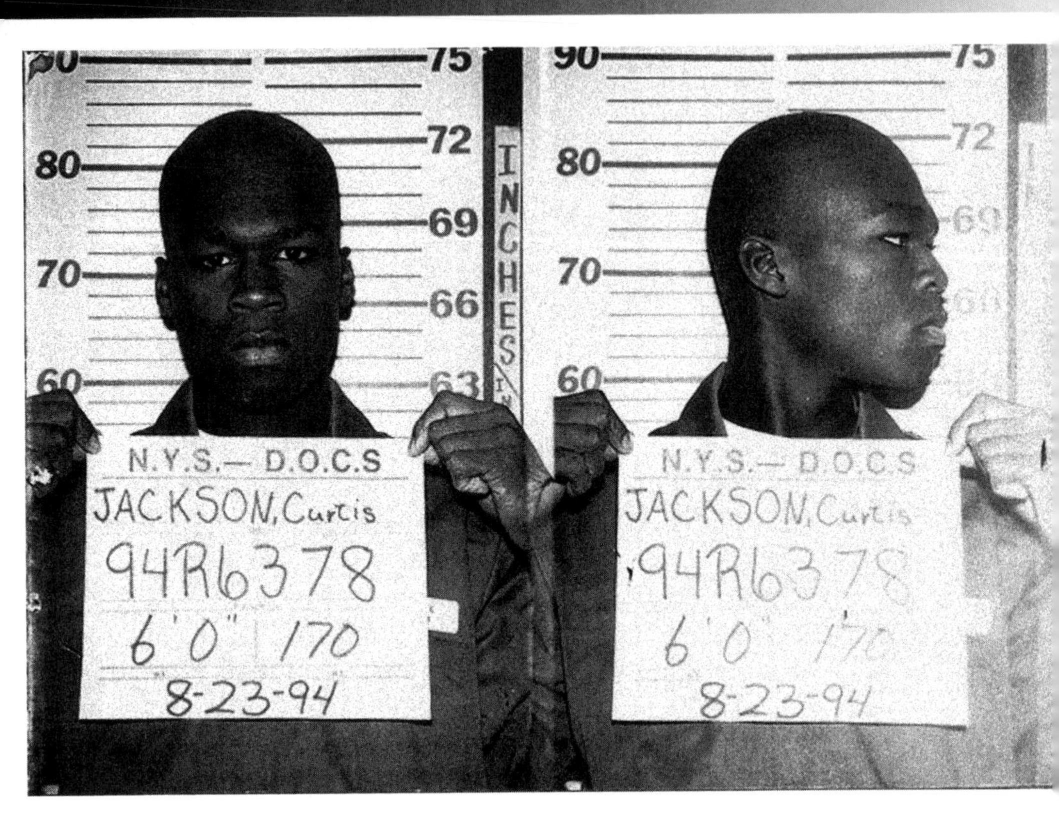

50 CENT

ALBANY, NEW YORK, 08/23/1994

In 1994 he went in for dealing heroin and crack. Curtis Jackson was nineteen, and he wasn't 50 Cent yet. He was born in Queens, New York City, to an absent father (like Eminem, the artist who was instrumental in his breakthrough). When Curtis was eight, he also lost his mother, who was murdered. He started out with Jam Master Jay of Run DMC. In 2000 he was shot nine times and was hit by three of the bullets. One nine-caliber bullet (which happens to cost fifty cents) is lodged in his cheek. Columbia Records tore up his contract. Thanks to Eminem, he made a comeback. In "21 Questions" he asks, "Would you leave me if your father found out that I was thuggin?"

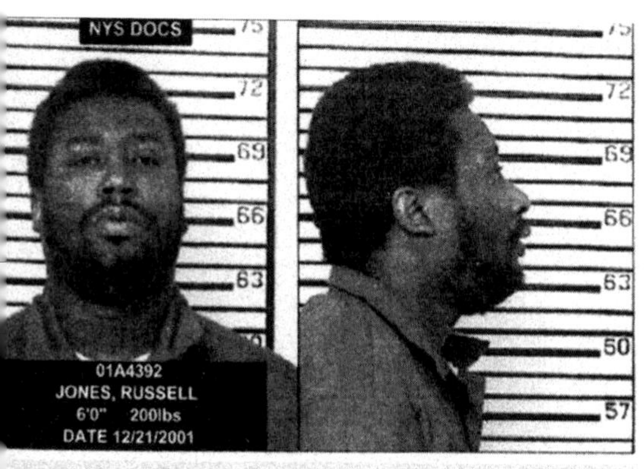

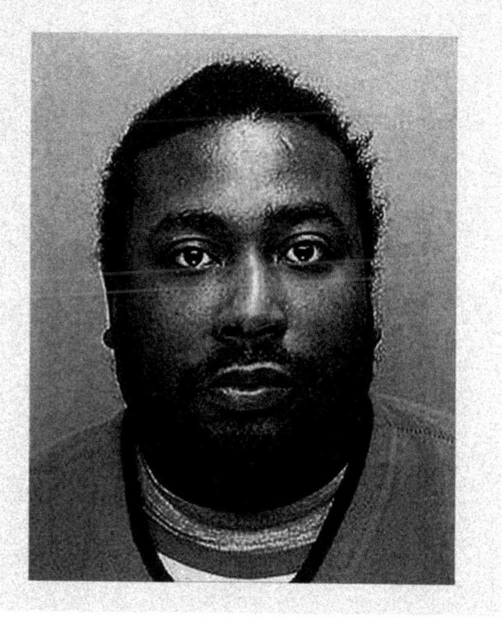

OL' DIRTY BASTARD

NEW YORK CITY, 12/21/2001

It's hard to tell which is thicker: his criminal record or his list of pseudonyms. Russell Tyrone Jones, previously of the Wu-Tang Clan, a.k.a. Big Baby Jesus, Osiris, Dirt McGirt, and especially Ol' Dirty Bastard, has spent more time in jail than out. Born in Brooklyn in 1968, he ended up in the pen many times, like many in his circle. He was released in May 2003 and jumped back into music. In a *Rolling Stone* interview, he described the sense of isolation he felt in prison: "Scared me a little. Sitting in the cell, watching my niggaz doing their thing. The music, they got it going on. I just want to jump in there like a swimming pool." On November 13, 2004, he collapsed while at the Wu-Tang's recording studio in New York City, and died shortly after. His death was ruled as the result of an accidental overdose.

GEORGE CLINTON

TALLAHASSEE, FLORIDA, 12/08/2003

"We took the middle ground between rock and blues and played mid-tempo funk." It's simple how funk was invented. The king of the bands Parliament and Funkadelic, Clinton created music, hairstyles, trends, brilliant slogans (applicable to everyone—"free your mind and your ass will follow"), and worked with everyone in the business worth anything (for example, Tupac Shakur, Pearl Jam, Soundgarden, Primal Scream, Rage Against the Machine, Prince) yet always remained on the fringes of success. His "Atomic Dog" is played more often than "Happy Birthday."

Surrounded by dreadlocks and conspiracy theories ("The defense department created the Internet. I know something's got to be wrong with it. You don't get anything that good for free"), he doesn't shy away from expressing himself on war, politics, conspiracies, and the psychology of aliens.

In December 2003, he was arrested at 2:00 a.m. in a parking lot in Tallahassee, Florida. Unable to make the crack pipe disappear, he tossed it into the backseat. He spent an hour at the police station, paid the $2,650 bail, and was able to leave after agreeing to enter a rehab program. He was born on July 22, 1940, in Kannapolis, North Carolina.

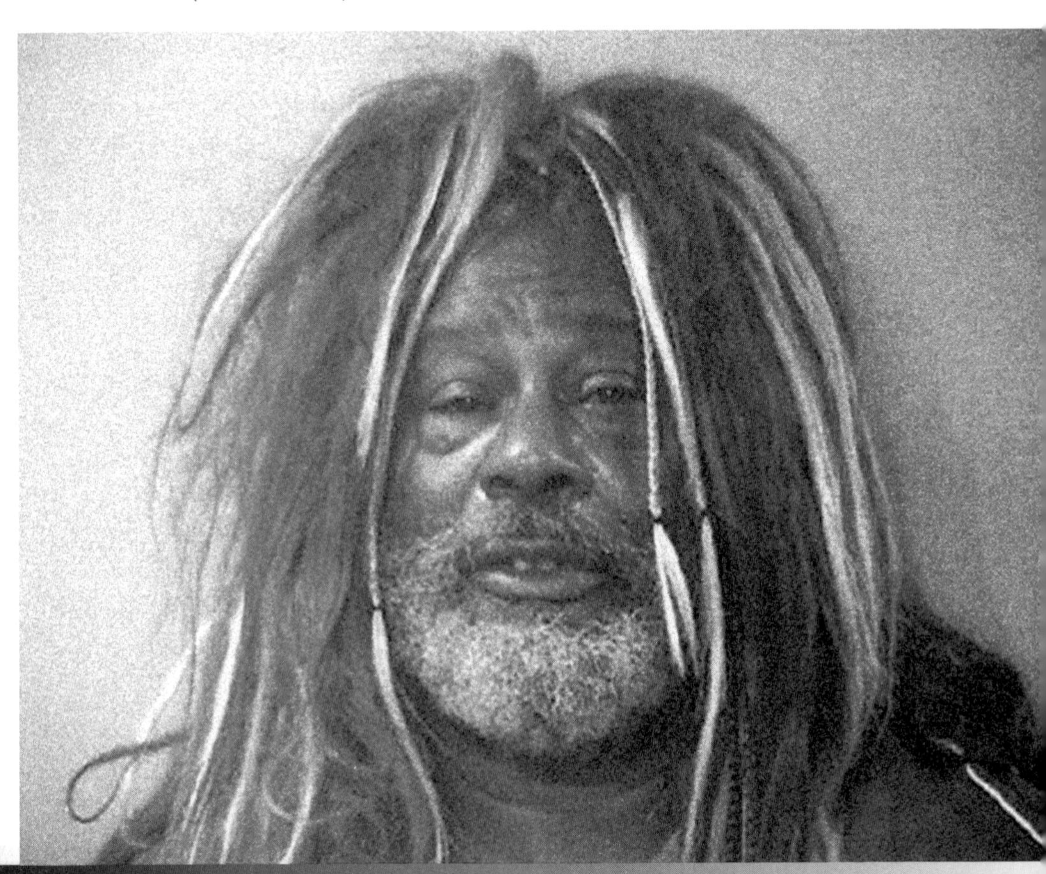

JAMES BROWN

AIKEN COUNTY, SOUTH CAROLINA, 01/28/2004

Six months before the foul deed documented in this photo, the "godfather of soul" (age seventy) and his wife (thirty-three) published a full page ad in *Variety*. It read: "Due to Mr. James Brown and Mrs. Tomi Rea Brown's heavy demanding tour schedule, they have decided to go their separate ways. There are no hard feelings, just a mutual show business decision made by both parties for the benefit of their carriers [sic]. Mr. Brown says, we both love each other but it has become difficult to function together. With love and affection we both reached this decision. We were a great team and we both have a great future. May God be with you, all our friends and fans. Mr. & Mrs. James Brown." The picture shows the Brown couple and their son with Goofy, smiling and happy at Disney World.

His latest arrest (for the time being) took place on January 28, 2004. James Brown was accused of having pushed his wife to the floor, causing "scratches and bruises to her right arm and hip." But this is only the most recent of the singer's transgressions. On July 3, 2000, he allegedly assaulted an employee of the South Carolina Electric and Gas Company with a knife, shouting, "you son-of-a-bitch white trash!"

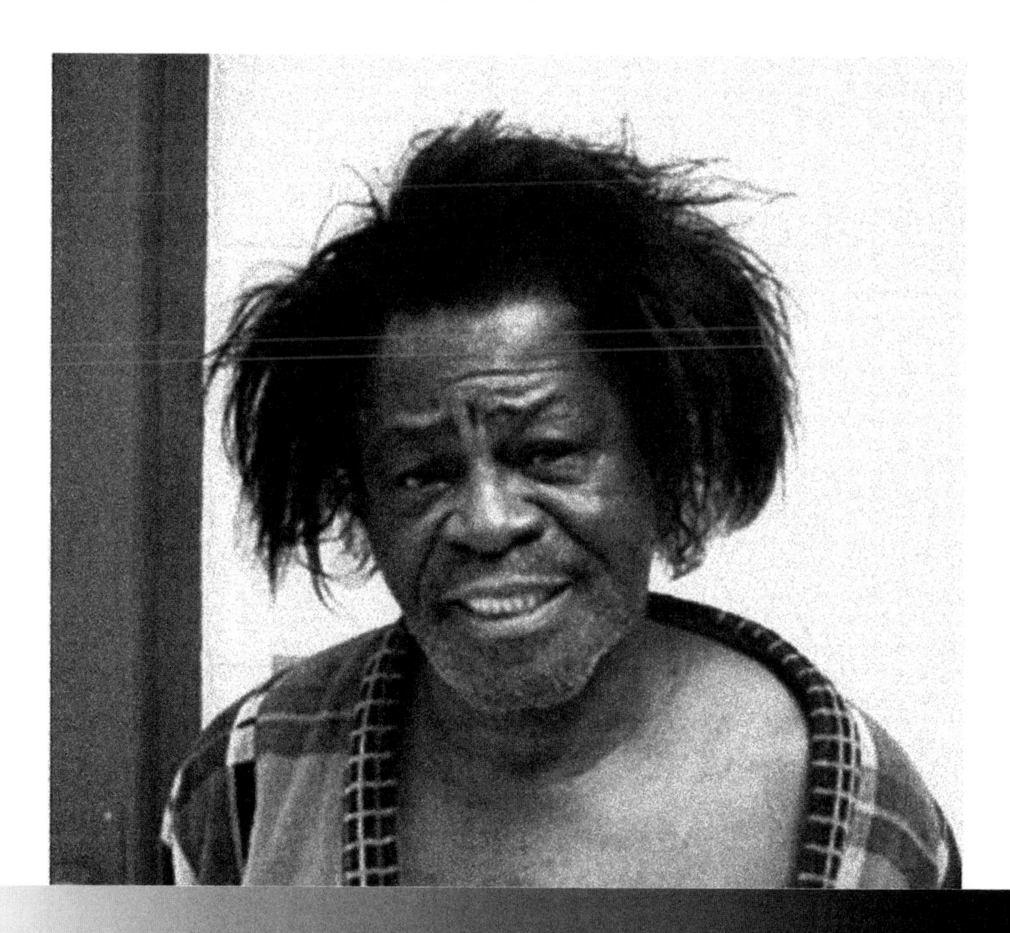

CHARLES BARKLEY

MILWAUKEE, WISCONSIN, 12/22/1991

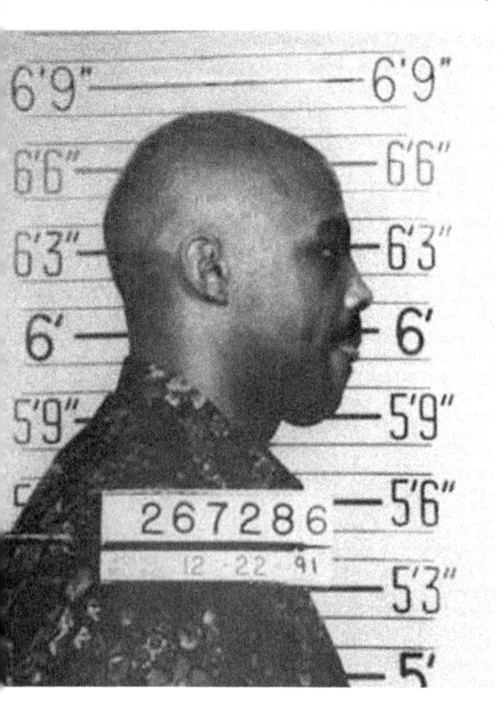

Only four players in NBA history have totaled over 20,000 points, gotten 10,000 rebounds, and had 4,000 assists. One of them is named Charles Barkley.

He was stopped by the Milwaukee police in December 1991 for disorderly conduct, after punching and breaking the nose of one Joseph McCarthy. A guy stupid enough to approach him in a bar and say, "Hey, Barkley, show me how tough you are." At the trial, which ended in 1992, Barkley was found not guilty. To the jury, it had been the defendant who had provoked the player.

DENNIS RODMAN

MIAMI BEACH, FLORIDA, 11/1999

"Before I let anyone inflict pain on me, I have to test it and make sure that I can handle it myself. Once I know that I can handle it, then when someone else tries to do it, I'm pretty much guarded." These are words from a 1997 interview of Dennis Rodman, former player for the Chicago Bulls. Their fight must have been a phase of this pain therapy that brought him and his wife, model Carmen Electra, to a Miami police station. In November 1999, they were arrested for domestic violence. The police found them in their hotel room shouting and covered with scratches.

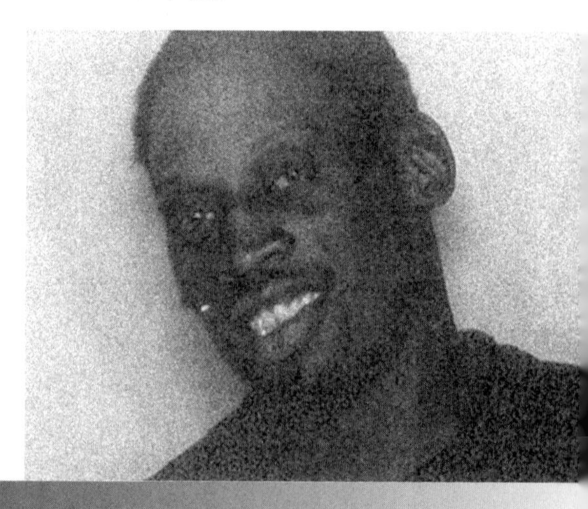

KOBE BRYANT

COLORADO, 07/04/2003

He was arrested on July 4, 2003, Independence Day, charged with the rape of a nineteen-year-old girl, an employee of a Colorado hotel, where the Los Angeles Laker had stopped after a basketball game. At first he denied having had sexual relations with the victim, then he claimed that it had been consensual. He said he had met her in the pool and she went up with him to his room. According to the interrogation, it seemed to have started with a tattoo on her lower back. Kobe Bryant risked, in addition to the end of his career and the loss of his sponsors, four years to life in prison. After months of media-crazed pre-trial proceedings, the accuser refused to testify and prosecutors dropped the case.

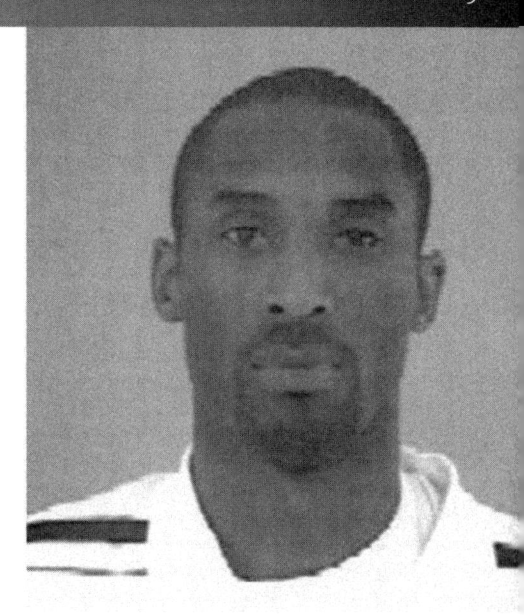

SCOTTIE PIPPEN

HOUSTON, TEXAS, 04/22/1999

Forward for the Chicago Bulls in the nineties alongside Dennis Rodman, and, most importantly, Michael Jordan. He got arrested on April 22, 1999, for passing a stopped car at a red light and going onto the wrong side of the road. They suspected that the crime was caused by intoxication, but Scottie Pippen refused to take the test.

The accusation was dropped before the trial started, because without the test there was no proof that the player had actually been drunk. Furthermore, various police officers testified in his favor, stating that on the night of the arrest he didn't seem tipsy at all.

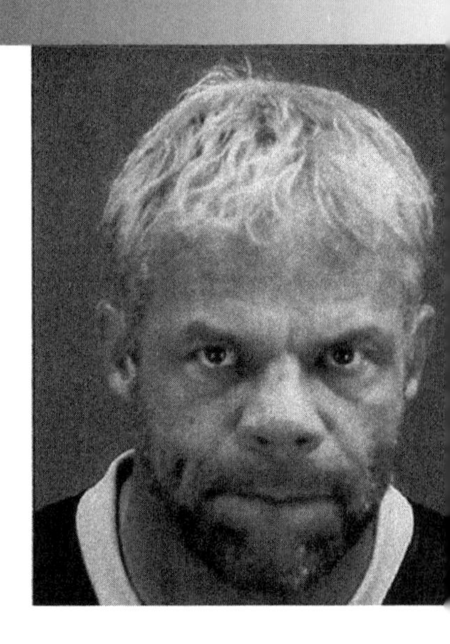

LEX LUGER

COBB COUNTY, GEORGIA, 05/01/2003

Police Case no. 03CS060:

> After a search of the house agents located a white bottle containing 26 hycrocodone bitartrate pills, 1 white bottle containing 500 hydrocodone bitartrate pills, 1 white bottle containing 361 Carisoprodol tablets, 1 white bottle containing 210 Dianabol tablets, 495 Oxyflux tablets (Clenbuterol), 98 Xanax pills, 6 boxes of Saizen 5 mg, 1 bottle of testosterone cyp 200 mg, 1 bottle of Laurabolin 50 ml, 2 bottles of Testosterona 200, 7 bottles of Nandrolona 300 L.A., 16 bottles of Boldenon 200, 19 bottles of Anabolic st. 20 ml, 18 bottles of Sustanon 250 mg, 19 bottles of Primobolan Depot 100 mg, 15 bottles of Primobolan Depot Lote K-004 19 Carisoprodol 350 mg and 5 hydrocodone bitartrate pills.

At the home of wrestler Lawrence Pfohl (a.k.a. Lex Luger), world heavyweight champion in the steroid category, the police arrived on May 1, 2003, to investigate the death of his girlfriend Elizabeth Hulette (stage name Miss Elizabeth), forty-two, also a wrestler. On April 19, a couple of weeks earlier, Luger had been arrested for beating Miss Elizabeth during a domestic argument.

ALEXEI YAGUDIN

AVON, CONNECTICUT, 08/2003

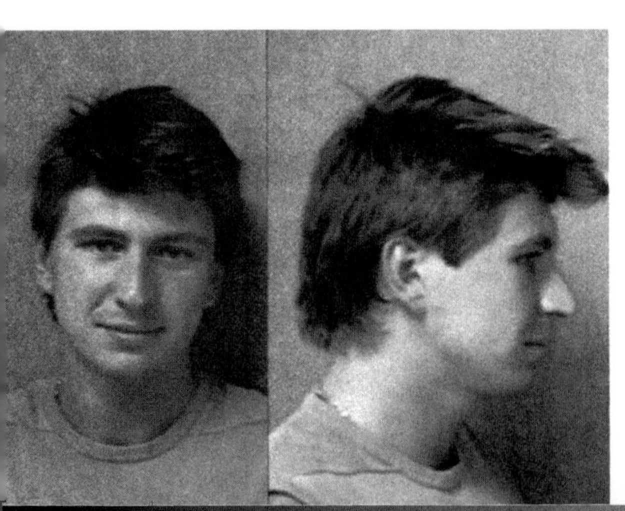

He is the only athlete in Olympic history to have received more than one perfect score. This occurred in Salt Lake City, February 14, 2002, for figure skating. In August 2003 he was arrested for driving while intoxicated in Avon, Connecticut. From St. Petersburg, Russia, born in 1980, he started skating at the age of four. He won his first world championship at eighteen. With the earnings he was finally able to buy a house and a jeep. Before that point, Alexei, his mother, and his grandmother were sharing an apartment—in typical Soviet style—with another family.

KIRBY PUCKETT

MINNEAPOLIS, MINNESOTA, 10/25/2002

Almost from the time he first joined the Minnesota Twins in 1984, Kirby Puckett was one baseball's best all-around players, and one of its most popular as well. During his 12-year career, he was named to the All Star team ten times, and helped the Twins to two World Series championships. He retired in 1996 at thirty-five due to glaucoma in his right eye, and was elected to the Baseball Hall of Fame in 2001, his first year of eligibility. He was arrested in October 2002 for assaulting a woman in the bathroom of a Minneapolis restaurant, but was acquitted in April 2003.

HENNEPIN COUNTY SHERIFF'S OFFICE

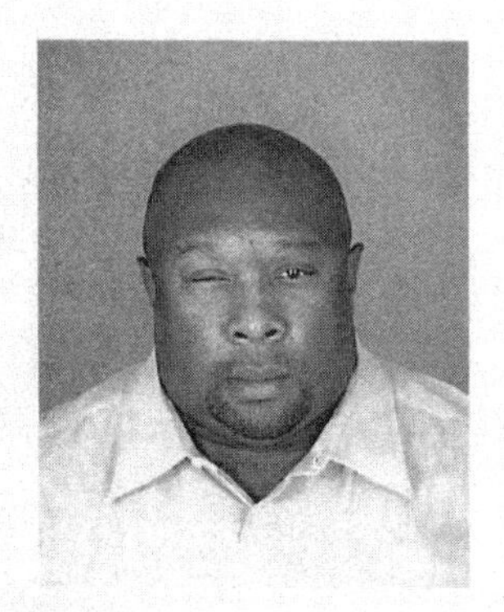

PUCKETT, KIRBY

Submitting Agency: Hennepin County SO 10/25/2002

Hennepin County Sheriff's Office

THE BIG SHOW

MEMPHIS, TENNESSEE, 12/03/1998

Height: 7', weight: 500 lbs. In the world of wrestling, Paul Wight was known to all as The Giant. In 1996 he won his first title in World Championship Wrestling (WCW). When he joined World Wrestling Entertainment (WWE), he changed his name to The Big Show.

He was arrested in Memphis, Tennessee, in December 1998. The accusation, later dropped, was exposing his genitals to a female employee of the hotel he was staying in for a WCW event.

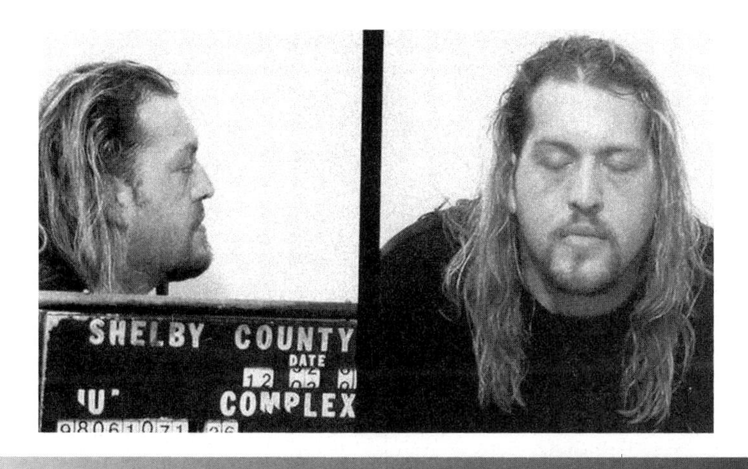

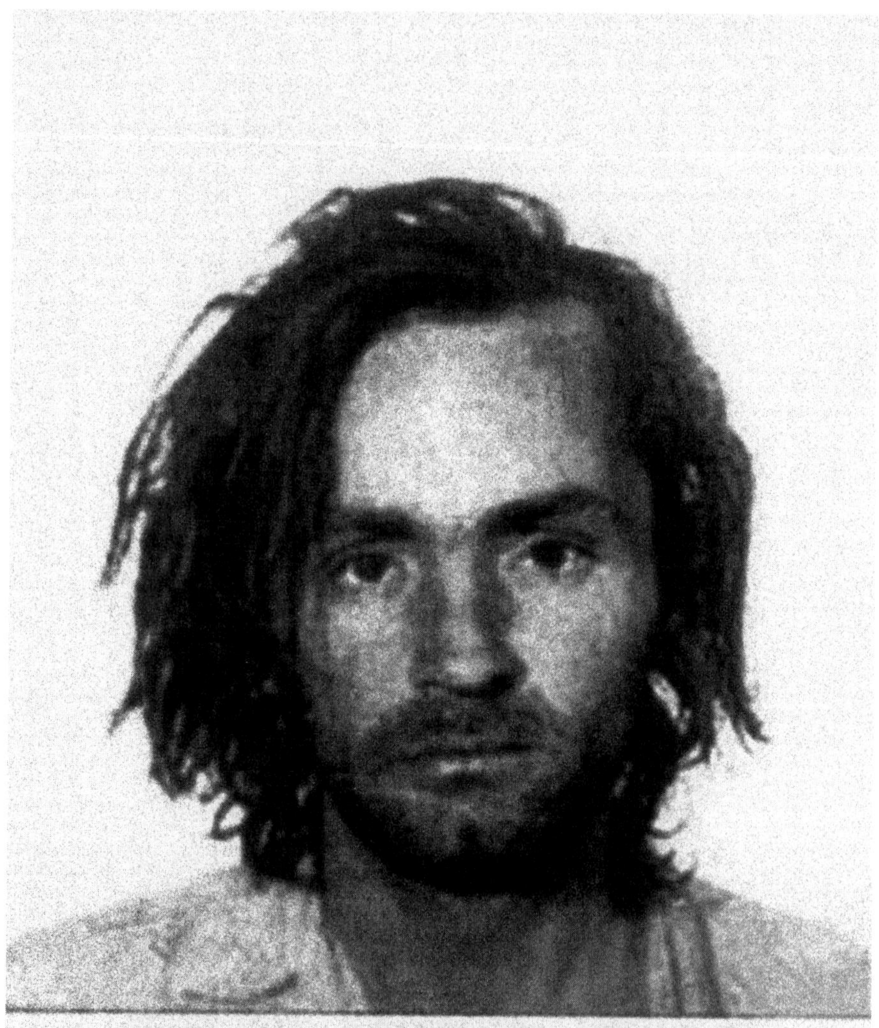
MANSON, Charles Milles
CII 966 856

CHARLES MILLES MANSON

DEATH VALLEY, CALIFORNIA, 10/12/1969

"My father is the jailhouse. My father is your system . . . I am only what you made me. I am only a reflection of you.

"I have ate out of your garbage cans to stay out of jail. I have wore your second-hand clothes . . . I have done my best to get along in your world and now you want to kill me, and I look at you, and then I say to myself, You want to kill me? Ha! I'm already dead, have been all my life. I've spent twenty-three years in tombs that you built. . . . The music speaks to you every day, but you are too deaf, dumb, and blind to even listen to the music . . . It is not my conspiracy. It is not my music. I hear what it relates. It says 'Rise,' it says 'Kill.' Why blame it on me? I didn't write the music."

The night of August 9, 1969, in a Los Angeles mansion, Charles "Satan" Manson and some of his followers killed five people, including Sharon Tate, the lady of the house, who was a twenty-six-year-old actress and the wife of director Roman Polanski, and eight months pregnant. The following night, in a nearby mansion, it was the LaBianca couple's turn.

Sentenced to death but serving life imprisonment because a California Supreme Court ruling invalidated all death sentences in California prior to 1972, in 1970 he released the album *Lie*.

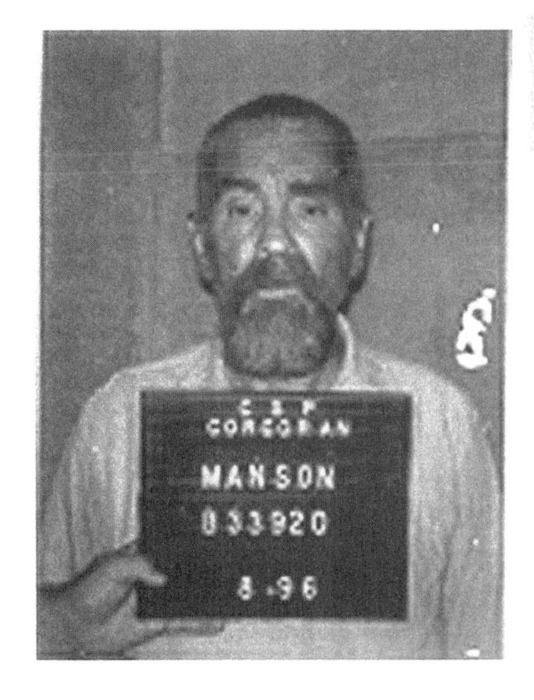

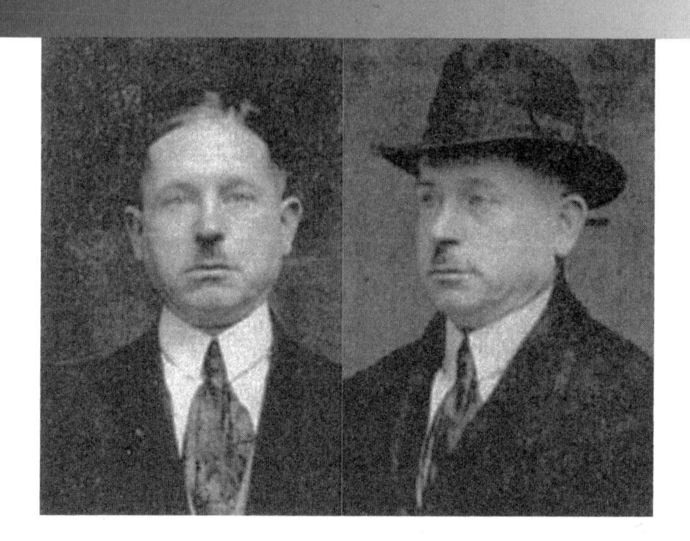

PETER KÜRTEN

DÜSSELDORF, GERMANY, 05/24/1930

From the diary of Peter Kürten, the vampire of Düsseldorf: "Today, the 23rd, in the morning, I told my wife that I was also responsible for the Schulte affair, adding my usual remark that it would mean ten years' or more separation for us—probably forever. At that, my wife was inconsolable. She spoke of unemployment, lack of means and starvation in old age. She raved that I should take my life, then she would do the same, since her future was completely without hope. Then, in the late afternoon, I told my wife that I could help her." Indeed, there was a large price on the vampire of Düsseldorf's head.

"Naturally, it was not easy to convince her that reporting me would not mean betraying me, but on the contrary, it was doing something good for humanity and for justice." The following morning the woman went to the police and reported her serial-killer husband.

Born into poverty in 1883, the third of thirteen children, Peter Kürten's background is one of petty theft and violence. He claimed to have killed for the first time at the age of nine, drowning two friends in a river, but his first verified homicide took place in 1913 during a robbery. "I entered a home on Wolfstrasse and went up to the second floor. I opened several doors without finding anything worth the effort to steal, when I saw a little girl about ten years of age asleep in bed." The day after the murder, which the girl's uncle took the rap for, Kürten returned to the scene of the crime and sat at a café across the street. Everyone was buzzing about the murder. "All that horror and indignation made me feel good." Other unpunished murders were to follow.

They brought him in for minor offenses. Convicted, he stayed in jail until 1921. When he got out, he married and found work in a factory where he was an active union member. The desire to kill came back with a vengeance in Düsseldorf. "Upon my return, the sunset was blood red," he notes in his diary, as if the city had been expecting him. The majority of his crimes took place between February and November 1929, as Hitler was gaining momentum. His notoriety grew, in his homeland and in Europe. He was the first serial killer to become a mass phenomenon. The newspapers called him "the vampire." Peter Lorre's frightened expression immortalized him in Fritz Lang's 1931 film *M*. Convicted of nine counts of murder and seven of attempted murder, mostly of little girls, he died on the guillotine on July 2, 1932.

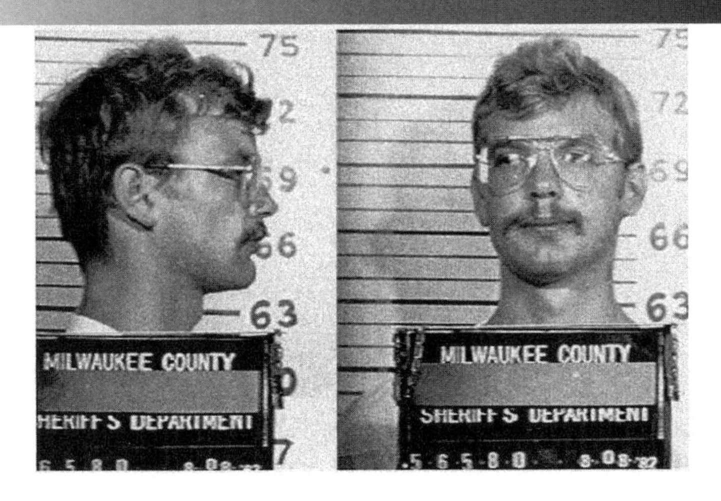

JEFFREY DAHMER

MILWAUKEE, WISCONSIN, 08/08/1982

"There's a fucking head in the refrigerator!" As he related this discovery, the first police officer signaled to the other to handcuff the blond, mild-mannered young man. It was July 22, 1991. Until that day, Milwaukee's renown was only due to the show *Happy Days*, with Fonzie and the Cunningham family spending their Saturdays doing the conga around the Leopard Lodge. An unlikely setting for a cannibal serial killer like Jeffrey Dahmer.

A nice, polite guy, at that moment in control of himself, Dahmer had, a couple of months before the arrest, convinced two police officers that the Laotian boy neighbors saw running down the street naked and terrified was not a drugged fourteen year old about to be hacked into pieces and cooked but his nineteen-year-old boyfriend just a little tipsy from drinking. This despite the fact that he was out on parole precisely for molesting a young boy.

Sentenced to fifteen consecutive life sentences for his many murders, Dahmer was still an atypical serial killer. All the fun, in his case, was post mortem. He didn't kill for the pleasure of it, but to arrange, even sexually, the corpses. After the verdict, he read this statement: "Your Honor: It is now over. This has never been a case of trying to get free. I didn't ever want freedom. Frankly, I wanted death for myself. This was a case to tell the world that I did what I did, but not for reasons of hate. I hated no one. I knew I was sick or evil or both. Now I believe I was sick. The doctors have told me about my sickness, and now I have some peace."

Jeffrey was born on May 21, 1960, in Milwaukee. He started developing sexual fantasies about corpses when he was around fourteen. He tested them out for the first time on a hitchhiker in June 1978.

At the end of that same year he joined the army and left for an American military base in Germany. A couple of years later he was discharged for alcoholism. Upon his return he was arrested once for drunken and disorderly conduct, and then again for sexual assault and exploitation of a child in 1998.

His father, Lionel, has written a heartwrenching book called *A Father's Story*. A model prisoner at the Columbia Correctional Institution in Portage, Wisconsin, he was killed the morning of November 28, 1994, by Christopher Scarver, a schizophrenic inmate who thought he was the son of God.

MARC DUTROUX

MARCINELLE, BELGIUM, 08/13/1996

In October 1996 in Brussels, the largest demonstration in the postwar period took place. A crowd of 300,000 people clad in white marched to protest the role of the police and the authorities in the case of Marc Dutroux, pedophile and assassin of Marcinelle, a small town near Charleroi and emigration destination for Italian miners. Already sentenced to thirteen years in 1989 for kidnapping five children, Dutroux got out in 1992 for good conduct. Between 1995 and 1996, with his wife and two accomplices, he kidnapped another six children. Only two were found alive.

He was arrested again on August 15 when the police discovered two girls, twelve and fourteen years old, in his house. They had been starved and raped in an underground cell in Dutroux's cottage. In another of his seven houses, they found the remains of two children and an accomplice, Bernard Weinstein, who had been drugged and buried alive.

Officially, the monster of Marcinelle was an electrician who collected unemployment benefits. In reality, he earned a living by selling stolen cars in Poland and Slovakia, and making and distributing amateur porn videos and selling girls like meat, to be groomed for prostitution.

Dutroux was born in Brussels on November 6, 1956. He was the first of five children of a calm couple who were teachers. When he was young, he was beaten by his parents. At fifteen, after their divorce, he left home and made money as a male prostitute. He had two children in his first marriage. In 1993 a man reported that he'd refused an offer from Dutroux of at least $3,000 to kidnap little girls. Even his mother, Janine, sent the police a letter: "I have known for a long time and with good cause my eldest's temperament. What I do not know, and what all the people who know him fear, it's what he has in mind for the future." They were both ignored.

A vast network of pedophiles was operating in a country renowned for Detective Hercule Poirot and the Brussels sprout. His accomplices included his second wife Michelle Martin, Michel Lelièvre, a young man, and Jean-Michel Nihoul, a businessman who recounted an orgy in a castle with politicians, police officials, and a former European Commissioner. In 1998 Dutroux managed to escape for three hours. This escape caused resignations, and a prosecutor killed himself. On June 22, 2004, a jury composed of eight women and four men gave him a life sentence. His ex-wife got thirty years, Lelièvre twenty-five, Nihoul five. At the trial, with dignity and despair, the two lone survivors testified.

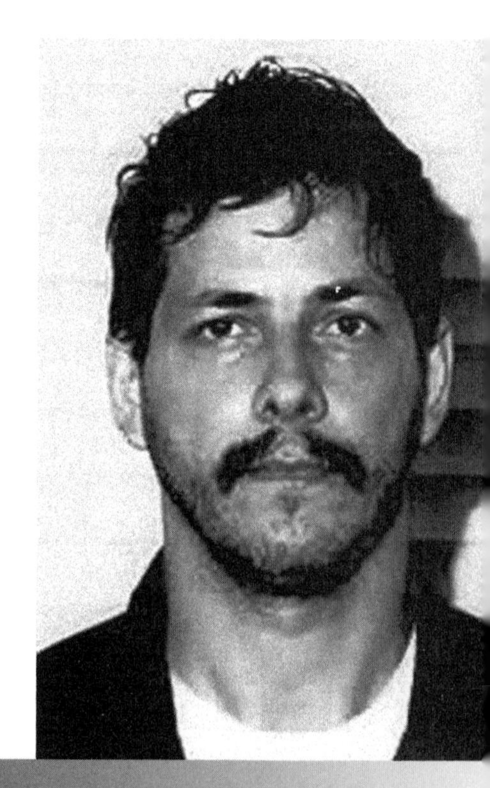

PIETRO PACCIANI

FLORENCE, ITALY, 05/1987

In Mercatale Val di Pesa, near Florence, he was known in his native Italy as "the Flame" because of his ruddy complexion and his quick temper. In 1951 he murdered his girlfriend's lover by stabbing him nineteen times and then forced her to have sex next to the corpse. In 1987 he was arrested for abusing his two daughters, calling them into bed, even together, after chasing away his wife.

Given a life sentence for first degree murder, he cried out in the courtroom that he was "as innocent as Christ on the cross." He was later acquitted during the appeal in February 1996. That same day Giancarlo Lotti and Mario Vanni (the "Snackmates") were arrested. The former admitted to the crimes, the latter talked about a doctor who paid for the killings.

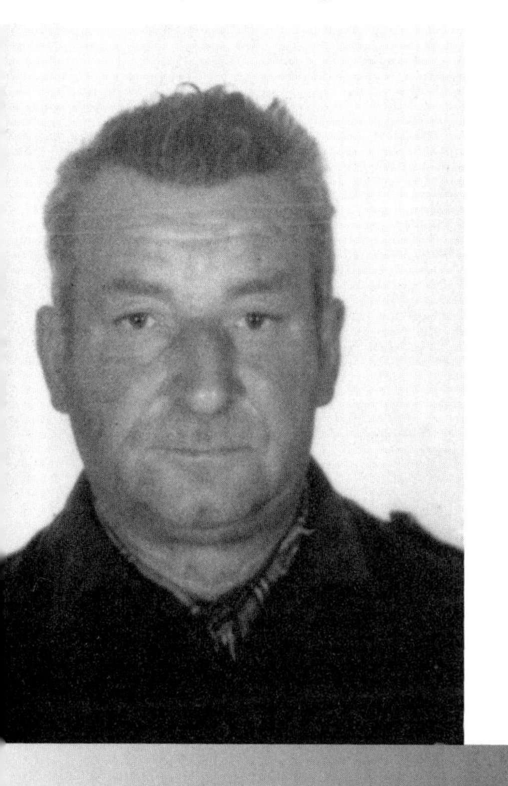

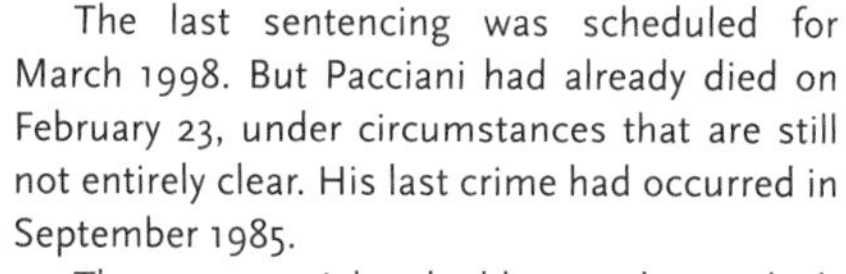

The last sentencing was scheduled for March 1998. But Pacciani had already died on February 23, under circumstances that are still not entirely clear. His last crime had occurred in September 1985.

There were eight double murders, which took place between 1968 and 1985, attributed to the Monster of Florence and his accomplices. Many elements linked the killings: the outskirts of Florence, the victims (couples having sex in their cars), the methods (the man killed immediately, the woman's pubic area often removed, in three slices), and the type of bullet (Winchester, H series). Finding that type of bullet in Pacciani's garden would be the strongest proof of his guilt.

But there were still many elements to clear up. Florence, that delightful candy store for foreign tourists, was in the eighties colored with either flowing or congealed blood. During the investigation, satanic masses were discovered, orgies in rest homes, an organization of hundreds of peeping toms. Writer Thomas Harris—who created Hannibal Lecter and *The Silence of the Lambs*—took notes at the trial.

Several leads, all plausible, were followed step by step and one by one rejected. In the beginning, even a random boy popped up. On August 21, 1968, the six-year-old son of the murdered woman was sleeping in the back seat of the car. He was awakened by the gunshots. Two hours later, in the middle of the night, he showed up at a nearby house to ask for help. He was sleepy and asked to be put to bed. He said he'd been carried on someone's shoulders, and the man, to calm him down, was singing Antoine's "La Tramontana": "Since the day is no longer day, since the sun is no longer sun, since the dawn has grown distant, I have lost the guiding wind."

Today Pietro Pacciani's house is inhabited by a young Ethiopian couple and their children.

RICHARD RAMIREZ

LOS ANGELES, CALIFORNIA, 12/12/1984

At the preliminary hearing, he shouted to photographers "Hail Satan!" with his arm outstretched to reveal the pentagram tattooed on his palm. On November 7, 1989, he was sentenced to death for thirteen counts of murder, and thirty other felonies, including rape, burglary, and sodomy. He declared to reporters: "I am beyond good and evil . . . I will be avenged. Lucifer dwells within us all." Outside the court, he promised: "I'll see you in Disneyland."

The "Night Stalker" had a method: at night he came in through the window, killed the man, then raped the woman, cut her with a knife, and carved her eyes out. Later, in most cases, he killed them. Seventy-nine-year-old ladies and six-year-old little girls alike. He terrorized California during the summer of 1985. The survivors spoke of a good looking, curly haired, Hispanic male, driving an orange Toyota station wagon.

The police finally identified him: Texan, twenty-five, with several previous offenses. The media broadcast his mug shot. While attempting to steal a car in a Hispanic neighborhood in East LA, he was recognized and arrested and nearly mobbed to death. In prison he received love letters. In 1996, at San Quentin, he married one of his many admirers. He loved the song "Night Prowler" by AC/DC. Los Angeles is the world capital of cinema and of serial killers.

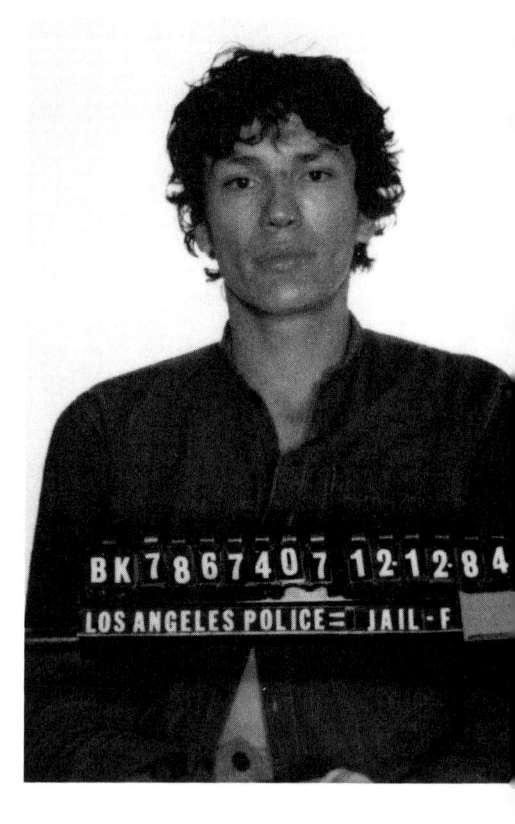

NIKOLAY SOLTYS

SACRAMENTO, CALIFORNIA, 08/31/2001

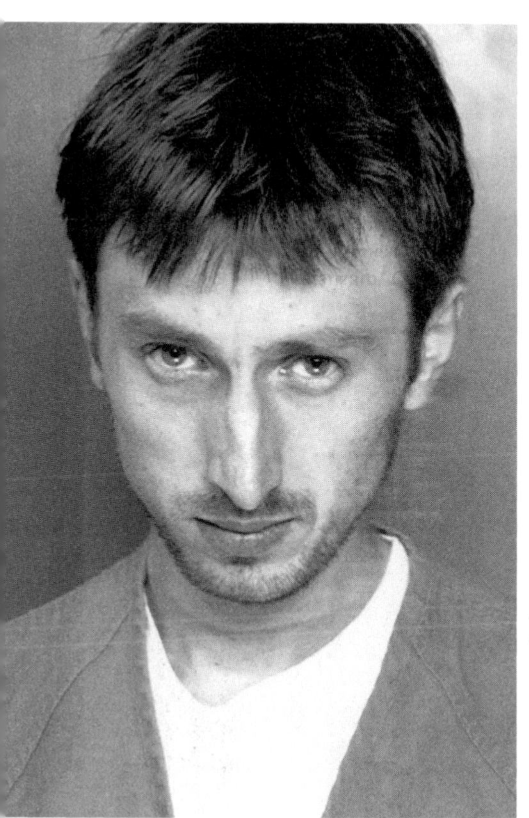

When the Sacramento police rushed to the scene of the mass murder, they found themselves in Russia. The assassin's neighbors and victims were all immigrants. "We've had some difficulty communicating," one police officer said. In the city, the Russian community numbered seventy thousand. It was August 20, 2001. A twenty-seven-year-old unemployed Ukrainian immigrant exterminated much of his family: two cousins, both nine years old, an uncle, an aunt, and his wife who was three months pregnant. Then he picked up his three-year-old son, Sergei, and stabbed him, too. The FBI offered $50,000 for his capture. He was arrested after ten days, found behind his mother's house on a tip from his brother. Soltys was convinced that his family members were trying to poison him.

The pre-trial proceedings revolved around a seemingly marginal problem. Were there six or seven murders? Seven. The district attorney stated: "The murder of a fetus can be prosecuted as long as the prosecutor can prove it is 7–8 weeks old." Born in Onishkovtsy, a village near Ternopol, to a family of evangelical Christians, Soltys joined his relatives in the U.S. in 1998. He hanged himself in his cell on February 14, 2002.

ARTHUR AND NIZAMODEEN HOSEIN

STOCKING PELHAM, GREAT BRITAIN, 06/12/1970

The body was never found. It was probably eaten by pigs, after being thrown, in tiny pieces, into a pigpen. The body belonged to Muriel McKay, fifty-five, wife of the deputy to Rupert Murdoch, Australian media magnate, who was kidnapped the evening of December 29, 1969, in their elegant Wimbledon home. During the five-week abduction, the kidnappers phoned eighteen times, asking for one million pounds. It ended on February 7 with the arrest of brothers Arthur and Nizamodeen, thirty-four and twenty-two respectively, two West Indians, born in Trinidad, who owned a farm in Stocking Pelham. The investigators were clued in by an anonymous phone call: a frightened woman said she was in the same room as a kidnapped woman. Then a shot was heard and the line went dead.

In 1979 the brothers were given life sentences. They meant to kidnap Murdoch's young wife who at that time was staying in Australia with her husband. Muriel McKay had borrowed their Rolls Royce.

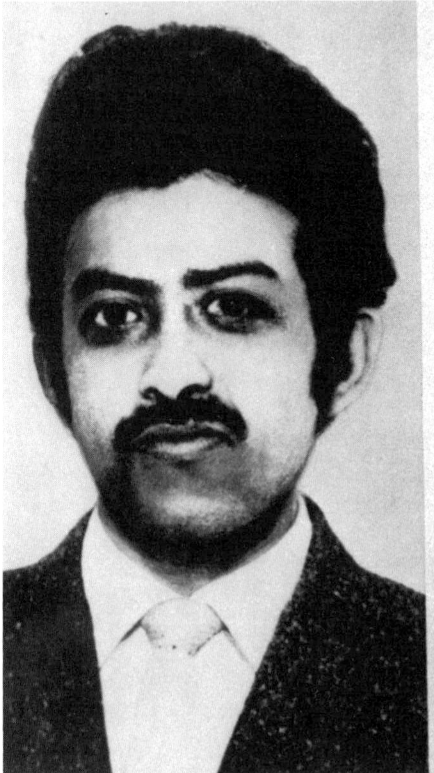

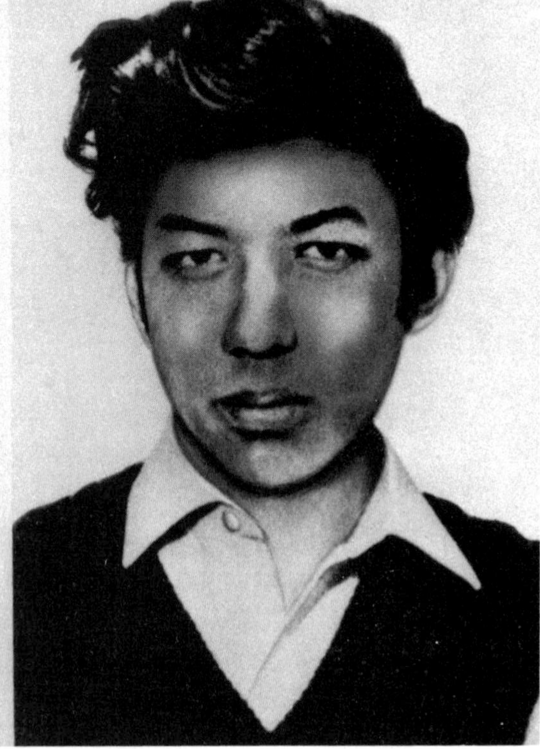

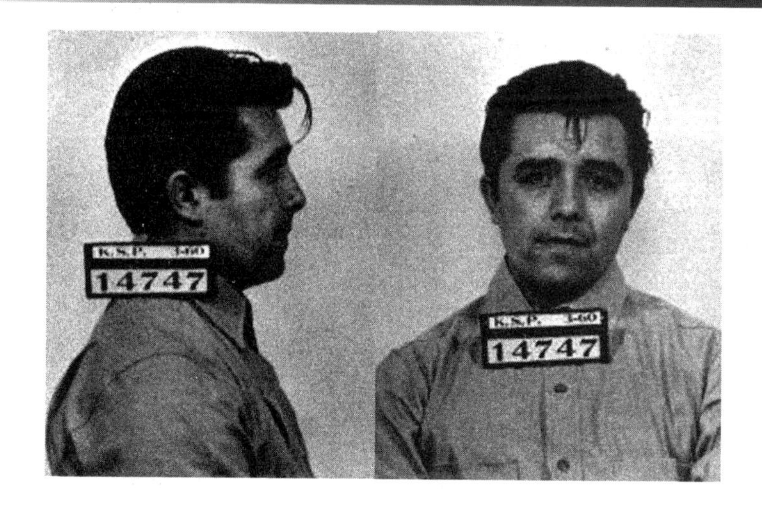

PERRY SMITH
LAS VEGAS, NEVADA,
01/02/1960

In 1959 a short *New York Times* article caught Truman Capote's eye:

> Holcomb, Kan., Nov. 15—A wealthy wheat farmer, his wife, and their two young children were found shot to death today in their home. They had been killed by shotgun blasts at close range after being bound and gagged. . . . There were no signs of struggle, and nothing had been stolen. The telephone lines had been cut.

Six years later *In Cold Blood* came out, the novel that catapulted Capote to fame and established the non-fiction novel as a new literary genre. On one side there was the ideal family, on the other the killers, a couple of bad eggs. Hickock, who came up with the idea, grew up in a poor but stable family. In Smith, a scoundrel with Cherokee and Irish blood in his veins, the writer recognized his own double. It was an epic of rural America at that time, in which evil never ceased to be human. Like when Smith, before the shooting, on impulse, gently adjusted the pillow behind the head of one of the victims.

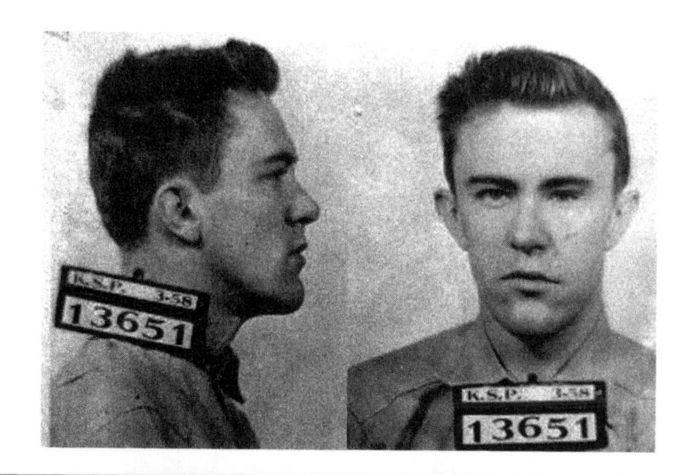

DICK HICKOCK
LAS VEGAS, NEVADA,
01/02/1960

JACK KEVORKIAN

SPRINGFIELD, MICHIGAN, 04/1999

Life is so strange that even a serial killer can be driven by good intentions and ultimately raise crucial questions about life and death.

Kevorkian: This is a video tape recording on Tuesday, October 23, 1991, at around 8:00 p.m. at the home of Mr. and Mrs. Miller in Roseville. And we're here to discuss actually what's called physician-assisted suicide. And we're here to discuss the wishes of Sherry Miller, Mr. and Mrs. Miller's daughter. And Mrs. Marjorie Wantz, whose husband, Bill, is here. Sherry's parents are here, Mr. and Mrs. Miller, her son Ray, her son Gary, her daughter Susan, brothers and sisters. And Sherry's very good friend, Sharon Welch.

Sherry Miller, then forty-three, suffered from multiple sclerosis. She died shortly thereafter, near Lake Orion, Michigan, by inhaling carbon monoxide. In the nineties, Jack Kevorkian, a.k.a. Doctor Death, assisted in the deaths of over 130 people. In 1999 a Michigan court gave him a ten to twenty-five year prison sentence. When the verdict was announced, Judge Jessica Cooper said, "You had the audacity to go on national television, show the world what you did, and dare the legal system to stop you. Well, sir, consider yourself stopped." Supported by his patients and by public opinion, though criticized by the American Medical Association, he was tried five times before he was convicted.

The video resumes:

Kevorkian: You realize, of course, the implications of your decision.
Miller: Yup, I do.
Kevorkian: What is the implication of your decision?
Sherry: There's no turning back.
Kevorkian: What will happen?
Sherry: All I have to say is no.
Kevorkian: What is it you want? Put it in plain English.
Sherry: I want to die.

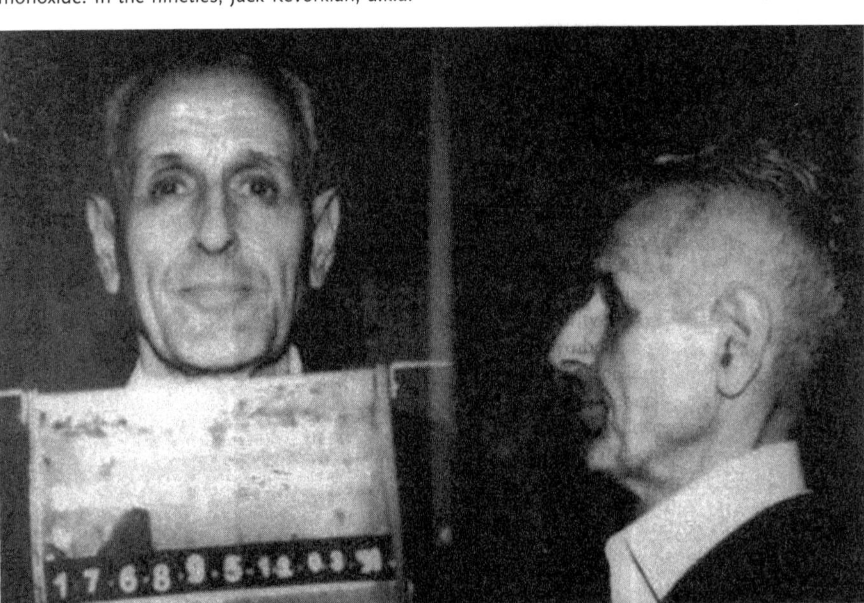

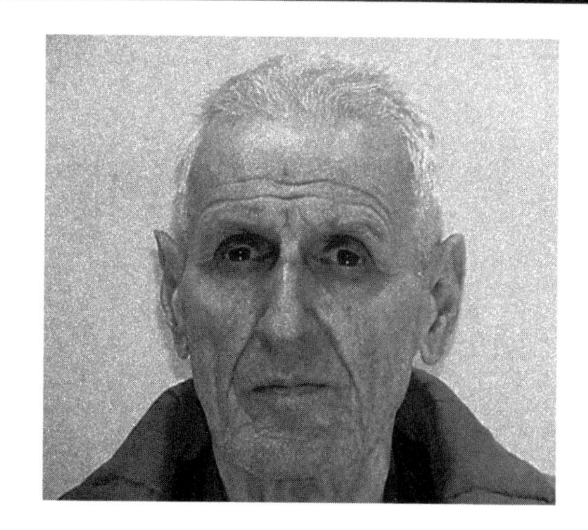

Kevorkian: That's as plain as you can put it.
Sherry: Yeah. And I know there's no turning, I know that. And this is not an overnight decision . . . [inaudible] waited too long. I cannot do anything myself. I waited too long.
Kevorkian: Have you ever wavered in this decision? Have there been days when you said well, maybe I better think about it?
Sherry: No. I would not be here—I would not be in my situation, no. Never, no.
Kevorkian: Are you afraid at all? Do you have any fears?
Sherry: No, no, none. . . . [inaudible] No fears.

Jack Kevorkian was born in Pontiac, Michigan, on May 26, 1928. He received his medical degree in 1952.

Four years later he published the article "The Fundus Oculi and the Determination of Death," in which he discusses the practice of photographing a dying person's eyes at the moment of their passing. His colleagues began calling him Dr. Death.

In 1961 he recounted his experiments on blood transfusion from the dead to the living. He thought it could be useful in the Vietnam War. In 1970 he invested his savings in the production of a film based on George Handel's *Messiah*.

His first article on euthanasia came out in the eighties. In 1989, on his kitchen table, he created the Thanatron, his suicide machine. It cost him thirty dollars. On June 4, 1990, in Kevorkian's Volkswagen van, Janet Adkins was killed, a fifty-four year old from Portland suffering from Alzheimer's disease. In 1995 he opened a suicide clinic in Springfield, Michigan. March 14, 1998, marked the hundredth suicide. Later that year CBS aired a video showing Kevorkian giving a lethal injection to a patient with Lou Gehrig's disease. He said, "Had Christ died in my van with people around Him who loved Him, the way it was, it would be far more dignified. In my rusty van."

ALBERT H. FISH

NEW YORK CITY, 1903

A letter from the cruelest man in history arrived on November 12, 1934. For six years, the Budd family hadn't heard any news of their daughter, Grace, who was taken away at age ten by a kindly old man.

It reads:

My dear Mrs. Budd,

In 1894 a friend of mine shipped as a deck hand on the Steamer Tacoma, Capt. John Davis. They sailed from San Francisco for Hong Kong, China. On arriving there he and two others went ashore and got drunk. When they returned the boat was gone.

At that time there was famine in China. Meat of any kind was from $1 to $3 a pound. So great was the suffering among the very poor that all children under 12 were sold for food in order to keep others from starving. A boy or girl under 14 was not safe in the street. You could go in any shop and ask for steak—chops—or stew meat. Part of the naked body of a boy or girl would be brought out and just what you wanted cut from it. A boy or girl's behind which is the sweetest part of the body and sold as veal cutlet brought the highest price.

John stayed there so long he acquired a taste for human flesh. On his return to N.Y. he stole two boys one 7 one 11. Took them to his home stripped them naked tied them in a closet. Then burned everything they had on. Several times every day and night he spanked them—tortured them—to make their meat good and tender.

First he killed the 11 year old boy, because he had the fattest ass and of course the most meat on it. Every part of his body was cooked and eaten except the head—bones and guts. He was Roasted in the oven (all of his ass), boiled, broiled, fried and stewed. The little boy was next, went the same way. At that time, I was living at 409 E 100 st., near-right side. He told me so often how good Human flesh was I made up my mind to taste it.

On Sunday June the 3, 1928, I called on you at 406 W 15 St. Brought you pot cheese—strawberries. We had lunch. Grace sat in my lap and kissed me. I made up my mind to eat her.

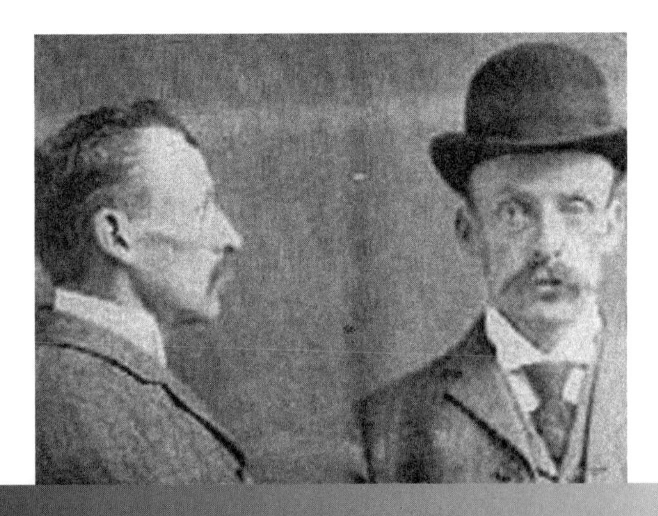

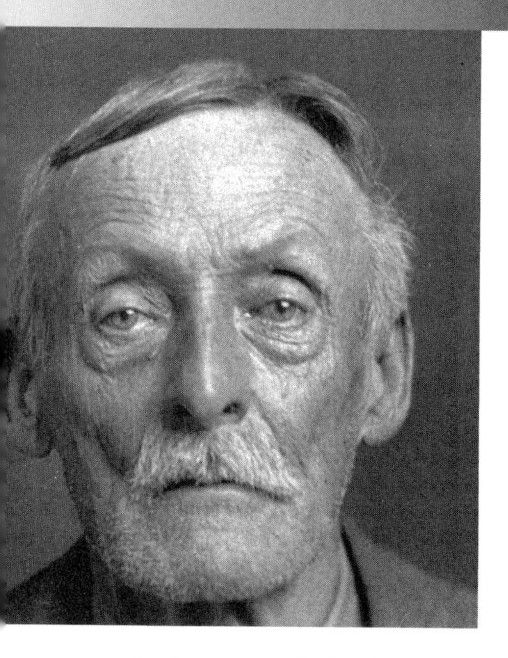

On the pretense of taking her to a party. You said Yes she could go. I took her to an empty house in Westchester I had already picked out. When we got there, I told her to remain outside. She picked wildflowers. I went upstairs and stripped all my clothes off. I knew if I did not I would get her blood on them.

When all was ready I went to the window and called her. Then I hid in a closet until she was in the room. When she saw me all naked she began to cry and tried to run down the stairs. I grabbed her and she said she would tell her mamma.

First I stripped her naked. How she did kick—bite and scratch. I choked her to death, then cut her in small pieces so I could take my meat to my rooms. Cook and eat it. How sweet and tender her little ass was roasted in the oven. It took me 9 days to eat her entire body. I did not fuck her tho I could of had I wished. She died a virgin.

The police found Fish from a logo printed on the envelope. They asked him why he had written to Grace's family. He responded, "I just had a mania for writing."

He was born Hamilton Fish, in Washington, D.C., in 1870. His first sadomasochistic impulses developed in the orphanage where he grew up. "I always had a desire to inflict pain on others and to have others inflict pain on me. I always seemed to enjoy everything that hurt," he confessed to the court psychiatric examiner. He got married in his late-twenties. Left by his wife, he devotedly raised their six children alone. His work as a painter brought him to live in at least twenty-three different states. He confessed to having killed at least one child in every state. He chose mostly boys, because he preferred them to girls. He primarily chose blacks, because he believed, correctly, that the police wouldn't work as hard to find them.

His criminal record lists many arrests (at left, a mug shot from 1903) and charges for petty theft and obscene letters. He alternately believed that he was Christ or that he was obeying the angels who appeared to him. He liked to insert needles into his pelvic area. The X-ray from prison showed at least twenty-nine. Deemed mentally sound, he was found guilty on at least fifteen counts of homicide and another hundred or so of child abuse. The "Gray Man," as the press called him, was a gentle and calm man with an air of extreme indifference. The idea of being put to death didn't faze him. He explained to the psychiatrist, "I have no particular desire to live. I have no particular desire to be killed. It is a matter of indifference to me." He died on the chair at Sing Sing on January 16, 1936. A reporter for the *Daily News* wrote, "his watery eyes gleamed at the thought of being burned by a heat more intense than the flames with which he often seared his flesh to gratify his lust."

GUSTAV VÖPEL

BERLIN, GERMANY, 11/1948

There may be a noble side to the story: Herr Gustav Vöpel may have been an anti-Nazi dissident who was sentenced to fifteen years in jail. It is certain, however, that from 1945 to 1948, appointed by the Allied forces, he killed forty-eight people as the Berlin executioner, then became an executioner of the State.

He preferred to work with an axe because "the guillotine can fail, the gears can stick, the blade can jam. The axe is more humane. Furthermore, according to custom, the risk is that if the condemned survives, he can go back home a free man."

Representing the long arm of the law made him believe he was beyond good and evil, and he began committed robberies and kidnappings. Someone reported him, but he seldom appeared at the trial, citing previous work obligations as an excuse.

In this paradoxical mug shot he wears a mask, perhaps to protect his safety, seeing that his occupation was not very popular.

The mechanism broke in 1950. For the umpteenth robbery he was sentenced to seven years in prison and five years of suspended civil liberties. His wife was also charged as an accessory.

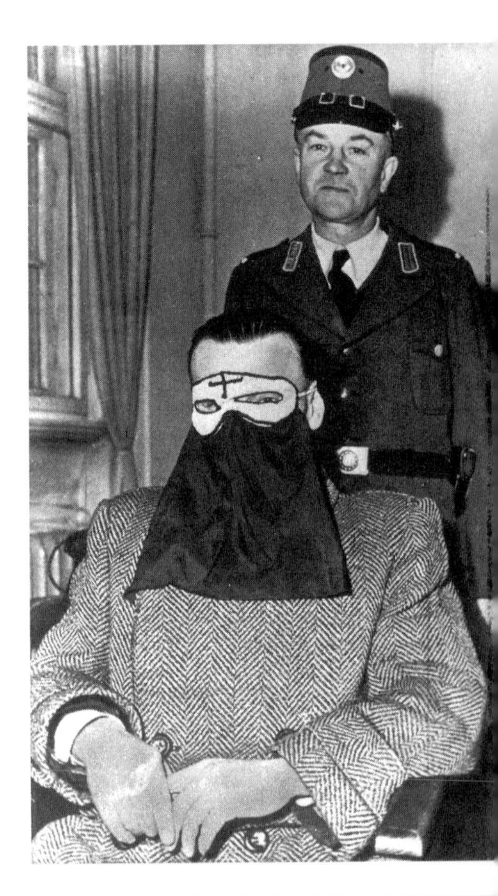

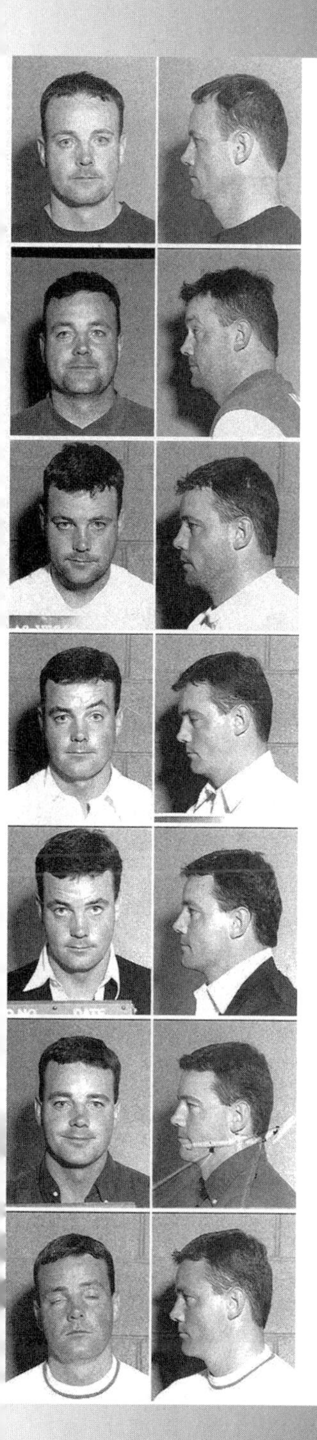

JOHN WAYNE BOBBIT

LAS VEGAS, NEVADA

Little John and his little penis came into the world on March 23, 1967. Nobody had heard of them until the night of June 23, 1993, when they were separated by Lorena, wife of the former, who cut off her husband's penis with a large knife and threw it out the window of a moving car. Found by the side of the road, the reproductive organ was reattached through an excruciating and complicated surgical procedure. To pay for the operation and to gratify his own ego, John Wayne Bobbit agreed to appear in a couple of pornographic movies called *Frankenpenis* and *John Wayne Bobbit . . . Uncut*. The tagline was inviting: "Ever since all this happened, all everyone wants to see is my penis . . . Now you can!"

At the trial, Lorena was acquitted because she had acted on impulse, not premeditation. In a separate trial, John was charged with domestic violence.

In 1997, the ex-Marine became a minister for a Las Vegas church. From February 3 to February 26, 2001 he was married to writer Dottie Brewer. He got married again to Joanna Ferrell, but filed for divorce in September 2005. A few days prior to filing, he was arrested by the Las Vegas police for domestic violence. Neither of his two subsequent wives has considered taking action.

CAMILLO CASATI STAMPA

The marquis loved to watch. The marquise loved to be watched. The marquis was rich, elegant, knew everybody. The marquise was a young, beautiful brunette. And she really liked men.

This was the game between Camillo Casati Stampa, or "Camilluccio," and the lovely Anna Fallarino. An exciting game. A dangerous game. Even if nobody lived to tell the tale of how everything really happened, judicial truth tells us that among the dozens of men they picked up on the beach or the street to satisfy their appetites and who then disappeared, the lady liked one—Massimo Minorenti—a little too much.

On the night of August 30, 1970, the marquis entered his apartment on Via Puccini in Rome, with a .12 caliber Browning shotgun. He killed Massimo Minorenti, twenty-four, college student, a lover loved a little too much, killed his second wife, then committed suicide by shooting himself through the mouth with a large caliber shotgun. A few months prior he had written in his diary, a big green leather notebook, that "Anna has completely slipped away from me, but I am bound by the sickness I have for her."

As in all murder-suicide cases, there is no mug shot. The culprit has already paid the price. In its place an identification photo is used. ID cards and passports are, for everyone, in case of necessity, preemptive mug shots.

The tragedy has an epilogue. Some time after the tragedy, Anna Maria Casati Stampa, the marquis's then young daughter, sold her father's villa, San Martino di Arcore, outside Milan, to a promising Milanese entrepreneur by the name of Silvio Berlusconi. The intermediary, acting as conservator on the young marquise's behalf, was a sincere Roman lawyer, Cesare Previti, who on that very occasion struck up a friendship with the future prime minister. The villa changed hands for the unheard of sum of 500 million lire (roughly the cost of a common apartment in Milan), and was probably supplemented by another payment "on the side."

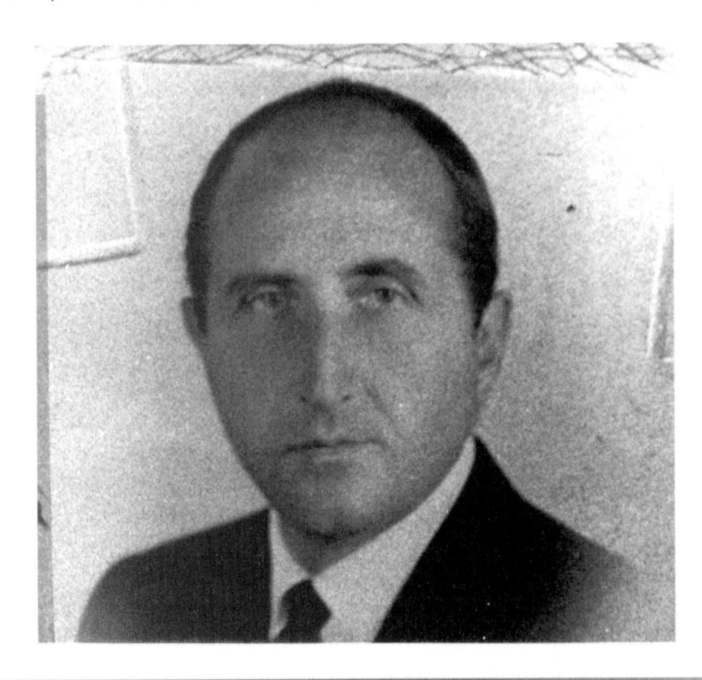

O. J. SIMPSON

O stands for Orenthal, J for James. A great football player and, after his retirement, a mediocre actor and convict. Accused of uxoricide, Simpson was the star of a live car chase watched by 95 million Americans. During the eight-month-long trial, the verdict was contaminated by racial and political considerations, starting with the dispute between the prosecution and the defense over the criteria that they should use to select the jury. Ten women (eight of whom were black) and two men found Simpson not guilty on October 3, 1995.

The facts: On June 12, 1994, Nicole Brown, who had separated from O. J. two years prior, and Ronald Goldman, her companion, were killed in Los Angeles while her children were upstairs sleeping. Simpson's lawyers promised that he would turn himself in. But at 6:45 p.m. his white Ford Bronco was spotted on Interstate 405. TVs broadcast the chase filmed by dozens of helicopters. When he surrendered, they confiscated a fake moustache and goatee, family photos, a passport, $8,000 in cash, and a loaded .357 Magnum.

In 1997, a civil court found him liable for the wrongful death of Goldman, battery against Goldman, and battery against Brown. He was ordered to pay $33 million in damages, so in 2000 he moved to Miami, Florida, where a law protects the pensions, assets, and income of convicted criminals against claims made in other states.

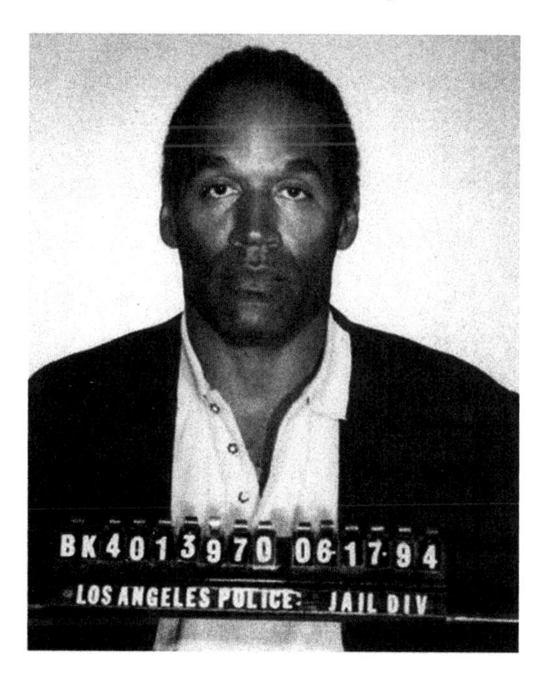

EARL AKIN JIMMY SNOWDEN CECIL PRICE LAWRENCE RAINEY

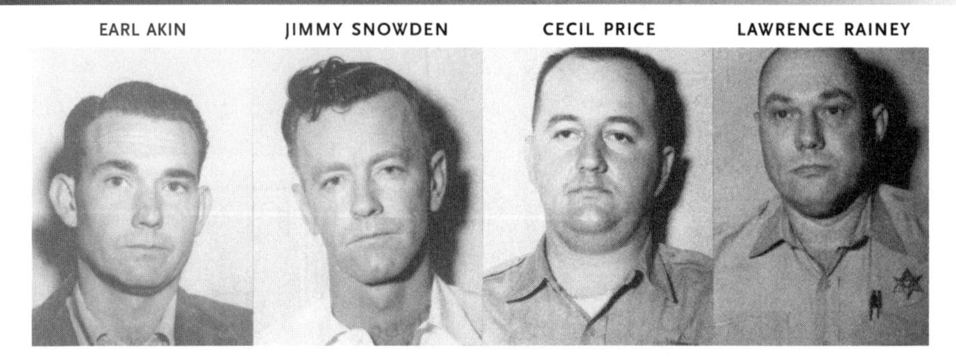

THE MISSISSIPPI BURNING CASE

JACKSON, MISSISSIPPI, 12/04/1968

When the verdict was read at the trial for the murder of James Chaney, Michael Schwerner, and Andrew Goodman, Judge Cox said: "They killed one nigger, one Jew, and a white man—I gave them all what I thought they deserved."

On December 29, 1967, Wayne Roberts and Sam Bowers were sentenced to ten years in prison, Billey Wayne Posey and Sheriff Cecil Price to six, and Jimmy Snowden and Horace Barnette to four. Another eleven men were acquitted for not having committed the act or for insufficient evidence.

On the night of June 21, 1964, after attending a political meeting, three civil rights activists were stopped by the police in Neshoba, Mississippi, for speeding. At the police station one of them, Michael Schwerner, asked to make a phone call because he wanted to warn other activists that the area they were in was dominated by the Klu Klux Klan, and because no one had known where they were on the previous day. Unexpectedly, they were released. But death awaited them outside of jail. Three cars blocked their station wagon and they had to stop. What forced them to get out was Sheriff Price's squad car. From that moment on all traces of them were lost. The assailants took them to a field, beat them senseless, and then killed them. Then they buried their bodies in a pit.

FBI agent John Proctor (Gene Hackman in *Mississippi Burning*, a movie inspired by the crime, which Alan Parker made in 1988) worked for six months to reconstruct the events, encountering extraordinary difficulties. He was helped not by the large sum of $30,000 offered to whomever could provide information, but by the local kids.

The conviction marked the end of the impunity of racial violence in the U.S. Several weeks before Martin Luther King Jr. received the Nobel Peace Price, the FBI announced that they possessed a signed confession from a Klan member involved in the lynching.

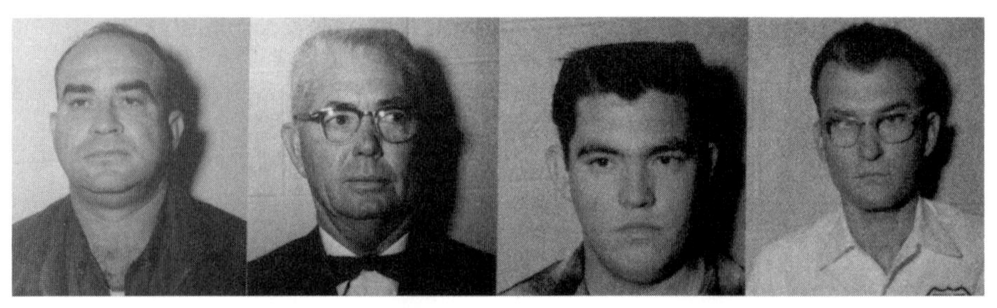

OLEN BURRAGE B. L. AKIN JIMMY LEE TOWNSEND BILLEY WAYNE POSEY

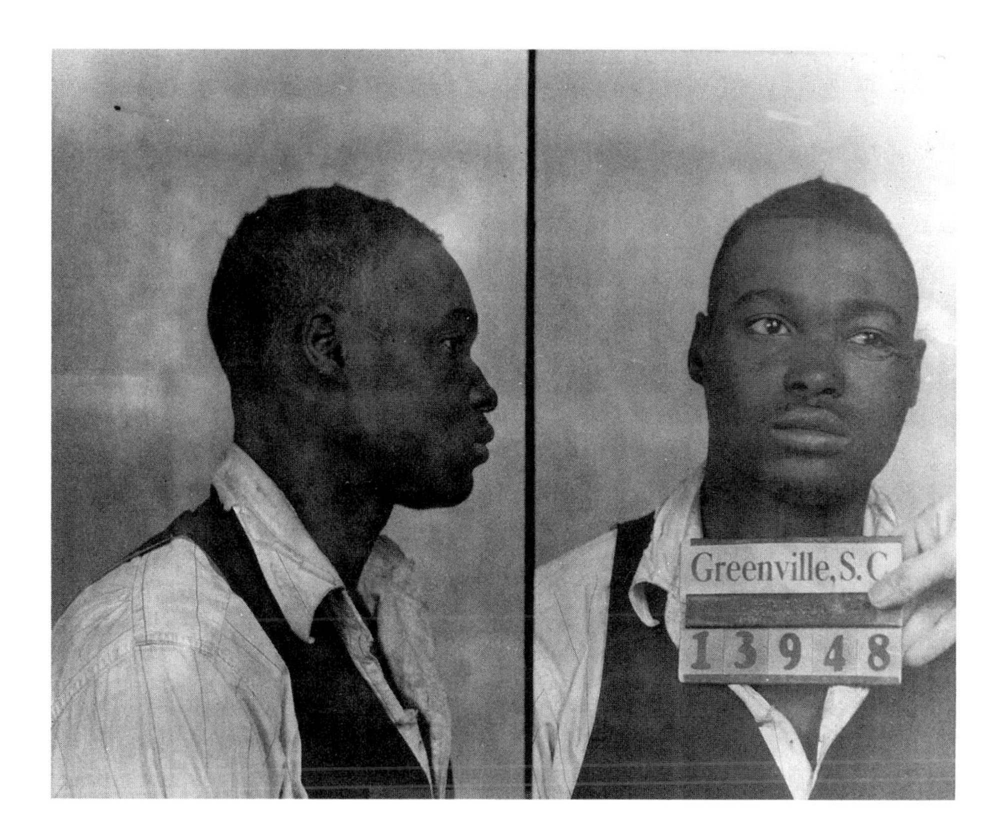

WILLIE EARLE

GREENVILLE, SOUTH CAROLINA, 02/16/1947

Between 1998 and 2002, 446 people were accused of lynching in Greenville County, South Carolina. According to an Associated Press analysis of crime statistics in 2003, blacks accounted for forty-seven percent of these lynching charges, though they made up just eighteen percent of the state's population. Civil rights activists expressed their concern: defining "lynching" as any sort of attack by two or more people meant skewing the history of African-Americans in the U.S.

The first law against lynching in South Carolina was instituted in 1951 in response to strong public opinion that culminated in large-scale protests. What triggered the anger of South Carolina blacks was the slaying of Willie Earle, twenty-four, pictured in the photo. The young man was arrested on February 16, 1947, for the attempted murder of Thomas Watson Brown, a white taxi driver, wounded and robbed the night before. Two days later, some white men wearing taxi driver caps removed him from jail, took him outside county lines, beat him, stabbed him, and then finished him off by pistol whipping his face.

In his mug shot, his expression betrays a condemnation. How is one to read this photo, the judge's bias, and Earle's own brutal murder?

THE DUQUESNE CASE

01/02/1942

From the FBI report on the Duquesne case: "On January 2, 1942, 33 members of a Nazi spy ring headed by Frederick Joubert Duquesne were sentenced to serve a total of over 300 years in prison. They were brought to justice after a lengthy espionage investigation by the FBI. William Sebold, who had been recruited as a spy for Germany, was a major factor in the FBI's successful resolution of this case through his work as a double agent for the United States."

The mug shot fixes the faces of nine members of the organization led by Duquesne. From the top left: Lily Stein, a Viennese waiting for American citizenship who earned a living posing as a model for various painters; Else Weustenfeld, a German-born American citizen and secretary; Evelyn Lewis, an American sculptor and playwright; Frederick Duquesne, a writer born in South Africa; Rene Mezenen, French, a steward for the transatlantic clipper service; Axel Wheeler-Hill, a Russian emigrant, truck driver; Richard Eichenlaub, German restauranteur, naturalized American; Felix Jahnke, by trade a soda vendor, held American citizenship; Paul Scholz, a German who worked in German book stores in New York City from which he distributed Nazi propaganda.

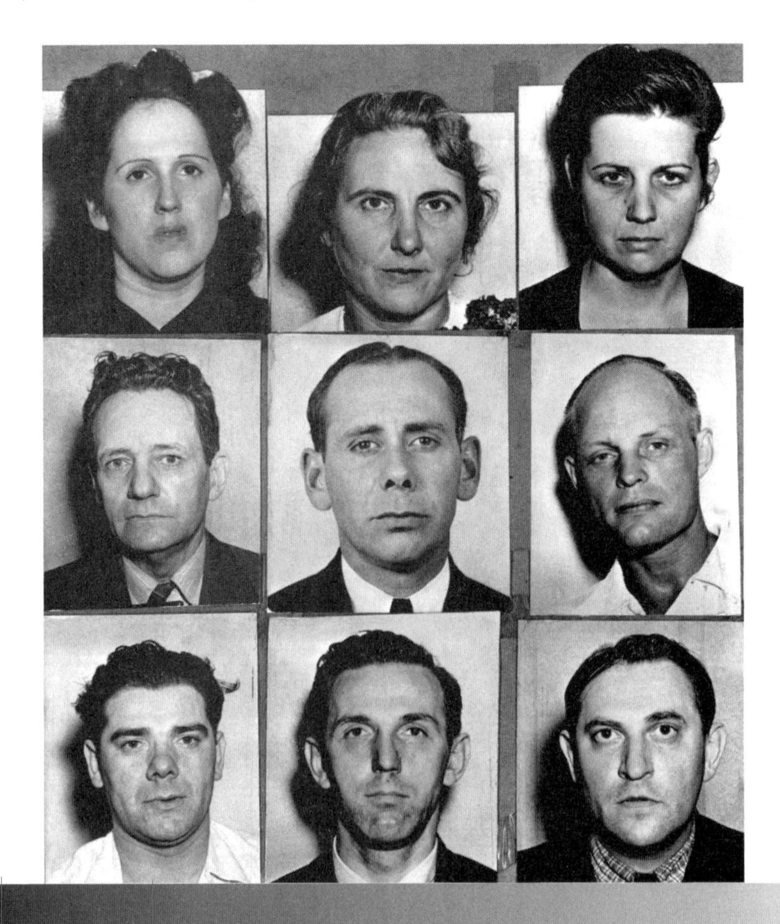

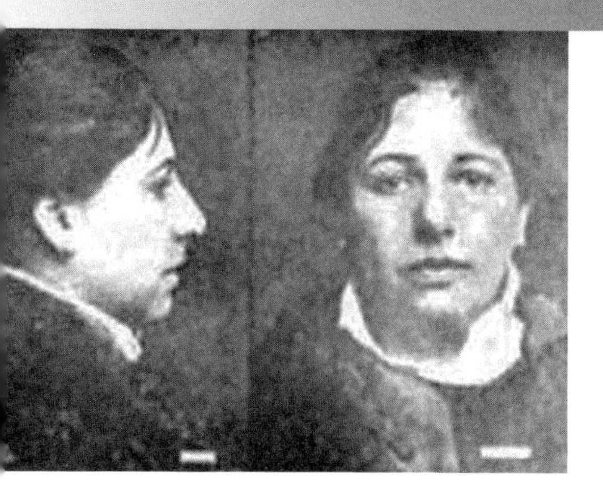

MATA HARI

PARIS, 02/13/1917

In 1905 Paris, the Orient was in style. Margaretha Geertruida Zelle was twenty-nine, with a failed marriage behind her and a few fantasies in her head, such as elevating striptease to an art form. She wasn't particularly beautiful, she was flat chested and straight hipped, but when she appeared onstage practically nude riding a white horse, men went crazy.

A newspaper of the time described her as "slender and tall with the flexible grace of a wild animal, and with blue black hair." Another described her as "so feline, extremely feminine, majestically tragic, the thousand curves and movements of her body trembling in a thousand rhythms."

People said she was a Hindu artist. In reality, she was born in Leeuwarden, Holland, the daughter of a bankrupt merchant. At eighteen she married a much older retired lieutenant, who had a moustache but was bald, and was insanely jealous. He took her with him to Java in the Dutch Indies. In eleven years of marriage, the couple had two children, one of whom died poisoned, possibly by a servant for reasons that were never made clear. Abandoned by her husband, Margaretha moved to Paris where she became the lover of a French diplomat who helped her achieve her dream of becoming a dancer. Dancing and stripping under the name Mata Hari, which means "sun" (literally, "eye of the dawn") in Malay, for years she packed the most famous nightspots in Europe.

Trends pass, the body withers, demand diminishes. At the outbreak of World War I in 1914, she learned another trade. At some point, sexual pleasure turned into something else, and slowly but surely, she got deeper into it. In 1916, at forty, she fell in love with Vladimir de Masloff, a twenty-one-year-old Russian minor official, who had lost an eye on the warfront. For her sweetheart she agreed to pass German information to France. The Germans suspected her, and in the hopes of framing her as a double-agent, they indicated that she was a German spy in a code they knew the French could intercept and decipher. At the trial, she declared, "Harlot, yes. But traitoress? Never!" The prosecutor, Captain Bouchardon, stated: "Without scruples, accustomed to make use of men, she is the type of woman who is born to be a spy." The *New York Times* described her as "a woman of great attractiveness and with a romantic history." She was executed by firing squad in Paris at the fog-filled dawn of October 15, 1917. During those same days, in Moscow, the world was changing. Today there is an active association in Holland fighting to clear her name.

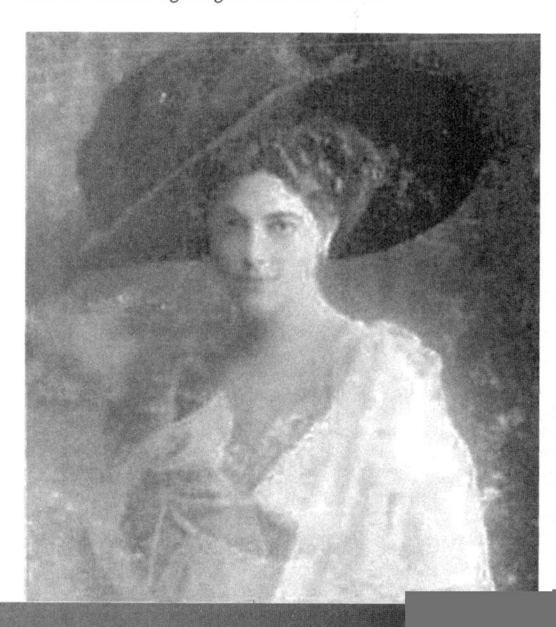

TOKYO ROSE

IKEBUKURO, TOKYO, 03/07/1946

In a Chicago Japanese imports store, perhaps still today, survives one of the victims of the second world war. Iva Ikuko Toguri, married name D'Aquino, is perhaps the only woman constrained to live and suffer for a nickname.

American soldiers battled in the Pacific against Japan, ally of Nazi Germany and Fascist Italy. Radio Tokyo transmitted English-language programs, one reason being to wear down the morale of those at the front.

The legend of Tokyo Rose was born, the sadistic and irreverent voice that delivered ominous news. When the war ended in 1945, Iva tried to go back to America.

She was a first-generation Japanese-American who went to Tokyo in 1941 to help an ailing relative and later stayed in Japan because the war broke out, earning money by working for the radio under the name Orphan Ann. She read the bulletins written for her by American and Australian prisoners of war who had been forced to work for the enemy. One day she announced that several American ships had sunk. That sealed her fate. In 1949 she was charged with high treason (in what the press defined as the most expensive trial in history) and she was sentenced to ten years behind bars. She got out in 1956 for good behavior.

In 1980 she divorced her husband, Felipe D'Aquino, whom she had married during the radio years, because the United States had never allowed him to enter the country. Her entire life was intertwined with the media: in 1977, to be able to start a family, she accepted an offer from an American journalist to be interviewed as the infamous Tokyo Rose. She was pardoned that year, after an episode of the TV show *60 Minutes*, in the last official act of President Gerald Ford.

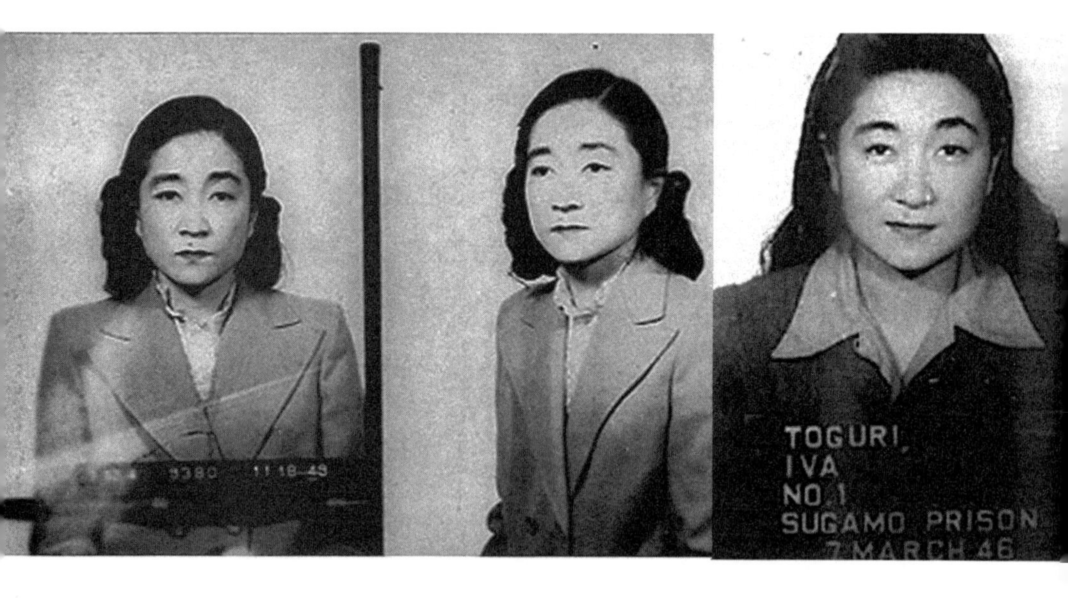

AXIS SALLY

FRANKFURT, GERMANY, 1948

Mildred Elizabeth Sisk was born in Portland, Maine, on November 29, 1900, the year that Frederich Nietzsche and Oscar Wilde died. In 1907 her parents divorced, and her mother got remarried to a dentist, Robert Bruce Gillars. Out of respect for her stepfather, her name became Mildred Gillars. She was still a long way from Axis Sally, Tokyo Rose's blond, Nazi younger sister.

Since childhood she had dreamed of being an actress. She gave it a shot in New York, performing in second rate vaudeville shows. In 1935 she emigrated to Germany where she taught English, which paid less, for example, than teaching Russian. To make more money, she agreed to be an announcer for Radio Berlin, where she remained until Germany's defeat in 1945. From December 11, 1941, to May 6, 1945, her sexy American voice swept over Europe all the way to North Africa.

She liked to taunt the allied soldiers by telling them their wives were cheating on them at home, and she also transmitted messages in code. On May 11, 1944, while awaiting the D-Day landing in Normandy, she played a tearful American mother, heartbroken because she had dreamed of her son's death in battle.

Arrested in Frankfurt in 1946, she was repatriated to Washington, D.C. The trial began on January 25, 1949. To compound her culpability was the fact that she had masqueraded as a Red Cross worker to persuade soldiers to record messages for their families. Then she'd edit the messages and make them part of the pro-German propaganda. One of the extenuating circumstances, at least in the sentimental news media of that time, was her relationship with the Nazi Max Otto Koischwitz, once a New York professor who became her lover in Berlin and pushed her toward treason.

On March 26, 1949, she was sentenced to spend between ten and thirty years in prison. In 1959, when she was up for parole, Mildred waived the right, but two years later she changed her mind and was released.

In her final years she taught music in a Catholic girls' school in Columbus, Ohio. She died on June 25, 1988, at age eighty-seven.

A Battle of the Bulge veteran recalls: "They played a few American records first. I don't remember everything she said. She said, 'Your wives and girlfriends are probably home in a nice warm building, dancing with some other men. You're over here in the cold.' It was cold and it was snowing. She said, 'There was a big push on up North; you might as well give up. The war's over, the German army captured fifty thousand Americans. They are going all the way to Paris.' We didn't believe her."

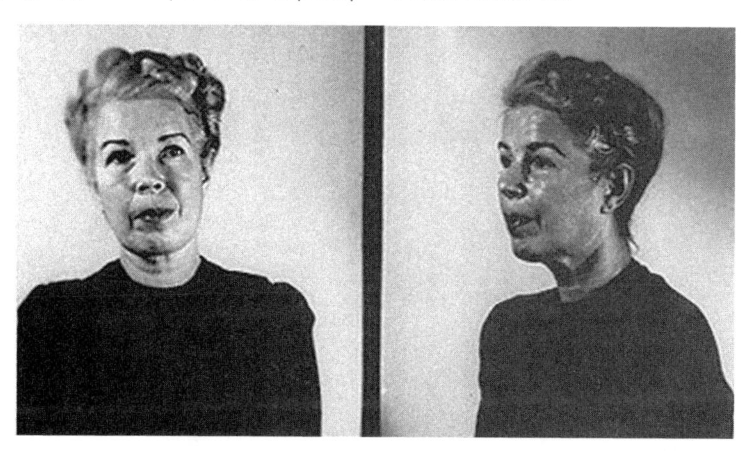

GEORG-HANS REINHARDT

NUREMBERG, GERMANY, 02/22/1948

Is a soldier a soldier, no matter which regime he kills for?

General Georg-Hans Reinhardt had a military curriculum that commanded nothing less than complete respect. From 1938 to 1941 he led the IV Panzer Division in Poland, and the XXXXI Panzer Corps in Yugoslavia, France, and finally, on the Eastern front.

From October 1946 to April 1949 he was tried, along with another 199 manufacturers, financiers, ministers, and soldiers in the Nuremberg Trials. Over the course of the trials, four of the defendants committed suicide.

Hans Reinhardt was the supporting actor in the biggest tragedy of the twentieth century. In this procession, his importance is due primarily to the expression on his face. Desperate incredulity at their defeat is overruled by defiance and indignation. As a soldier he probably thought that every loser was guilty, that there would never be absolution for the defeated. He has no number. He holds a placard with his own name, a gesture demanded by the allies as a sign of guilt. Born in 1887, he survived until 1963.

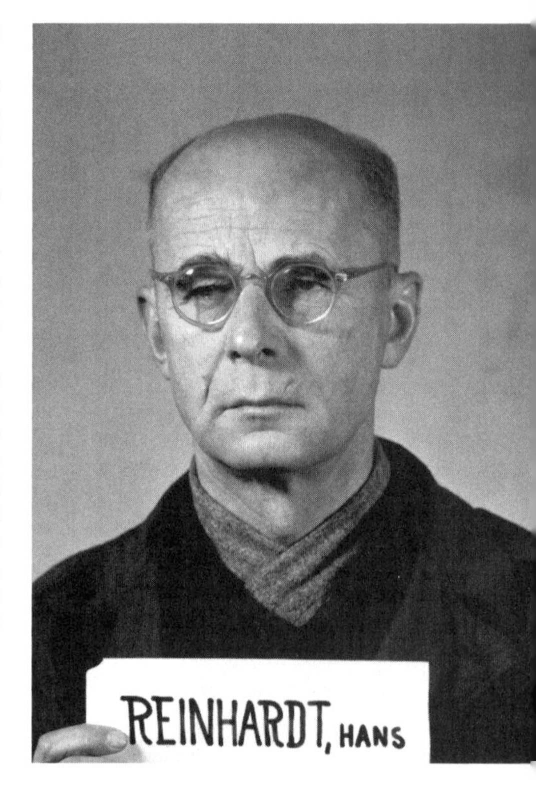

RUDOLF HOESS

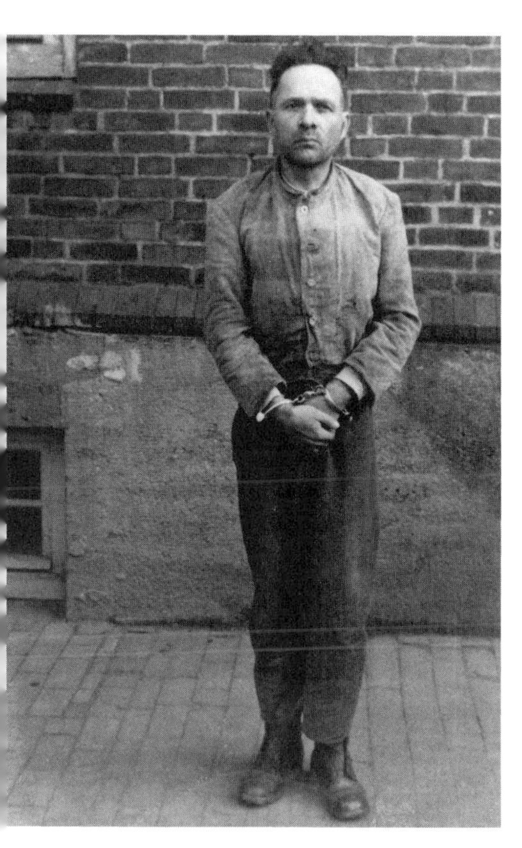

The director of the Auschwitz concentration camp was executed in 1947. He was born in 1900.

From Primo Levi's foreword and Alberto Moravia's afterword in the Italian edition of Rudolf Hoess's autobiography, *Commandant of Auschwitz*:

Levi: In the summer of 1941, Himmler "personally" notified Rudolf Hoess that Auschwitz would be something different from a place of affliction; it had to be "the largest extermination centre of all time," and Hoess and his colleagues would have to come up with the best technology . . . Hoess and his assistant got the brilliant idea of resorting to Cyclon B, a poison used on rats and cockroaches, and it was all for the best. After testing it on nine hundred Russian prisoners, Hoess felt "greatly at ease": the mass killing had gone well both quantitatively and qualitatively—no blood, and no trauma.

Moravia: He was an average man, of mediocre intelligence, of mediocre emotional capacity, of average social importance; in short, in every way a perfect petit bourgeois and therefore the ideal citizen for mass society. Hoess was neither a sadist nor an impassioned ideologue; in other circumstances he would have made a good bureaucrat. Instead he was the greatest executioner the world has ever seen.

ÉMILE-ANDRÉ POUPLEAU

AUSCHWITZ, POLAND, 1942

The testimony of Wilhelm Brasse, a prisoner, assigned to the identification service at the Auschwitz camp:

> The seat was attached to a rotating platform which was about ten centimeters thick. At the center of the platform was a hole that enabled it to be attached to a fixed metal pivot, in its turn, on the ground. Thanks to this system, the platform with the seat could rotate on its axis. I should specify that inside the seat and platform there was a mechanical system that allowed the photographer to move the platform with the individual being photographed; in such a way to position him in front of the lens, facing front and in profile. Thanks to this system, the photographer could make changes without getting up.
>
> Naturally, posing for photographs was not a habitual occupation for the prisoners, who were photographed only once during their stay at the camp. The prisoner, upon entering the room where the camera was located, climbed onto the platform and sat down. Two photos of the face were taken, one with the head turned slightly to the side, and the third was in profile.
>
> To change the position of the photographed subject with respect to the lens, it was necessary to turn on the mechanism that made the platform rotate. When the photographer finished the three poses, he shouted "Weg" (out): at that time, the prisoner had to rise from the chair, slide down the platform, and place his feet on the ground. For a brief moment the prisoner's body was slightly bent forward, before standing up. In that exact moment, the Kapo Malzt, when he was the photographer, decided to make the platform rotate, very brusquely, and right after shouting "Weg." The prisoner, taken by surprise, lost his balance and fell to the ground, to Malzt's great delight.

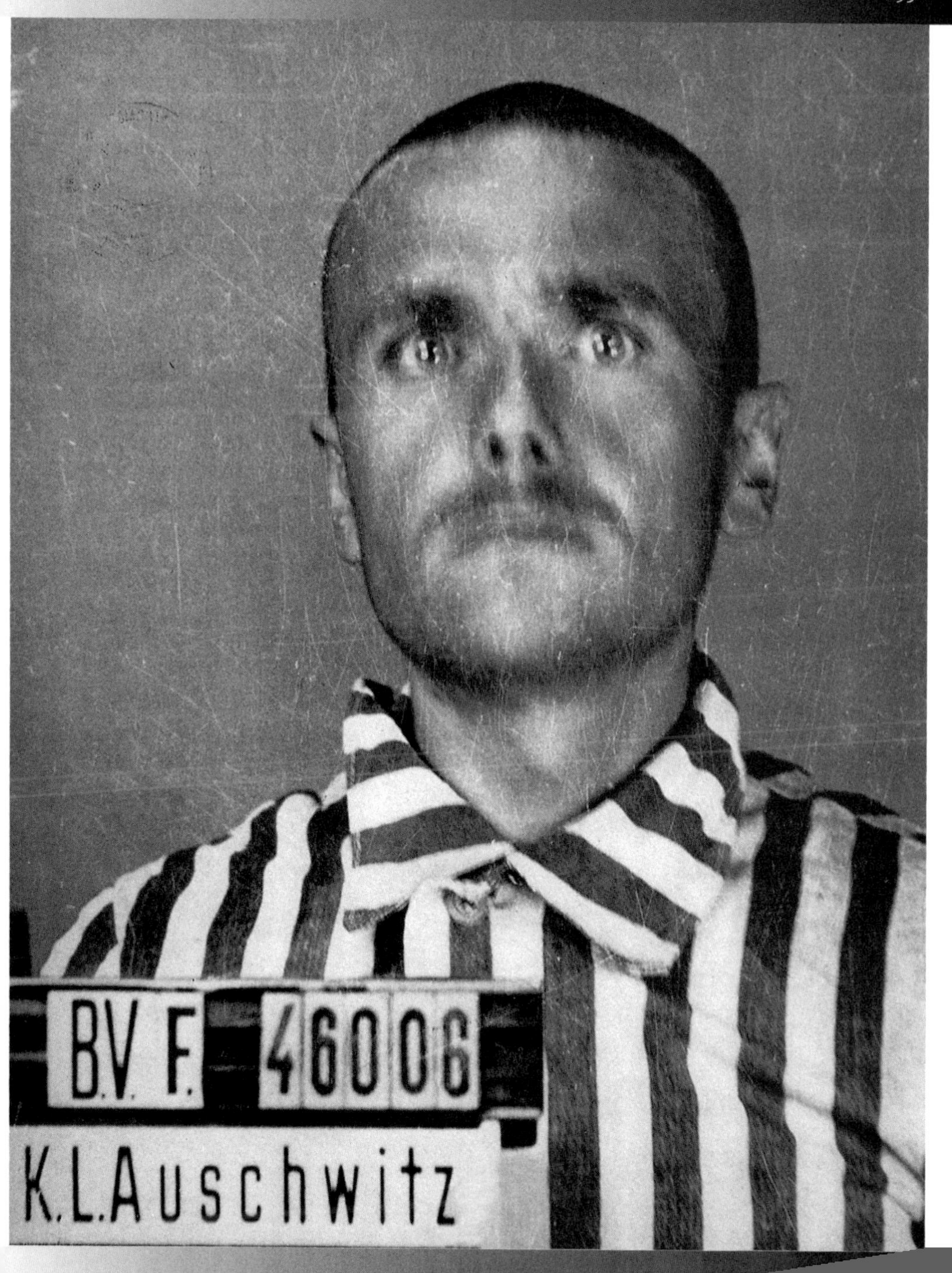
B.V. F. 46006
K.L.Auschwitz

CONCENTRATION CAMP INTERNEES

AUSCHWITZ, POLAND, 1940–1945

Sometime after the opening of the Sachsenhausen camp in 1936, in addition to the procedures to complete upon entry—registration, sanitization, uniform distribution—for the most fortunate, there was the photographic ritual. Only those not immediately put to death received the honor of being photographed. The Nazis needed to find the most efficient way to connect identification numbers to the faces and bodies of the prisoners.

For all the others, for all the millions sent to the chamber upon arrival, the identification photo would have been a waste of time. In other words, undergoing this rite marked the passage from certain death to probable, but postponed, death.

The camps were equipped for photography and development of film. In relation to the number of internees, a varying number of them—a dozen at Auschwitz, ten at Buchenwald, about four at Sachsenhausen and at Mauthausen—were sent to the photographic services department. Bernhard Walter, the SS officer responsible for the Auschwitz photo laboratory, said that "the work consisted of taking three shots for each internee. Then three copies of each shot were made. Two went to the political office, the third was kept at our office."

Most of the archives and identification photos were destroyed just before January 27, 1945, the day the Red Army liberated Auschwitz. About 39,000 remained. This is why, even now, the criteria for prisoner identification are not completely clear. Sometimes the name of the camp is listed, sometimes the date of entry into the camp, followed by first and last name and date of birth, or by some sort of abbreviation.

The Nazi extermination camps always had an ambiguous relationship with photography. Few images, even those not for identification, escaped destruction.

From this incident of millions of identification photographs being destroyed in order to prevent the victors from getting them, emerged an awareness rare for the twentieth century, of the political significance contained in each and every identification document.

On page 152, an internee describes a real identification machine, designed to reduce effort and error to the minimum. The Nazis knew that pictures of the victims were a weapon only if they remained in the tormentors' hands. Therefore, before the liberation, they destroyed millions of photos. In other hands, those images would become memory.

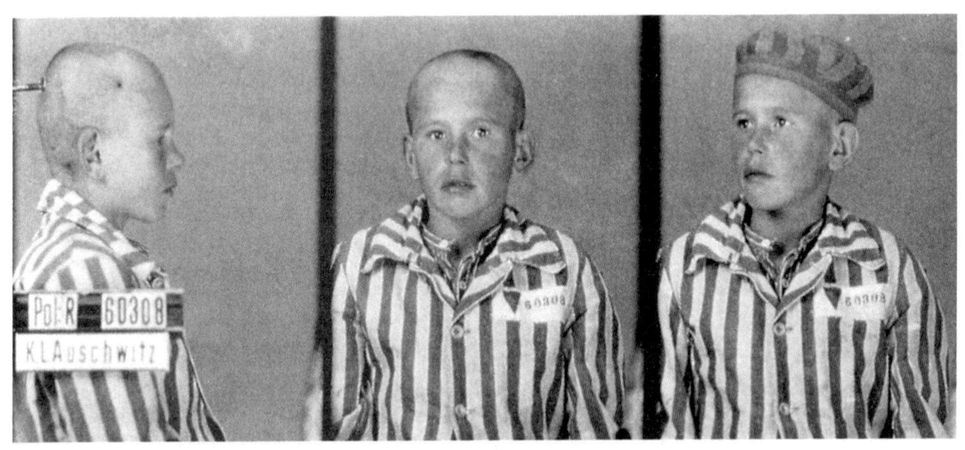

RUSSIAN PRISONER

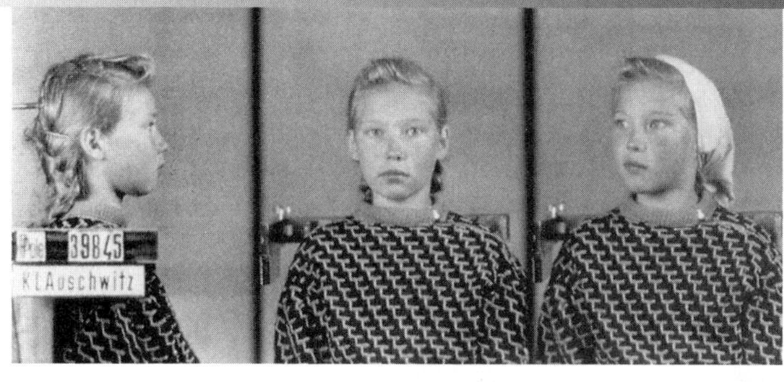

ROZALIA KOVALCZYK

NOACHIM LEIMAN

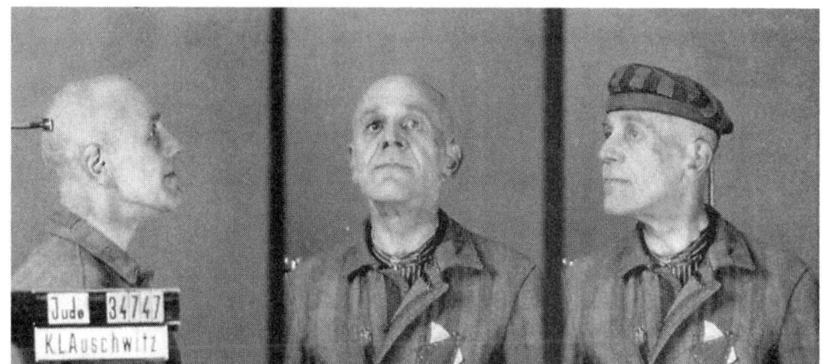

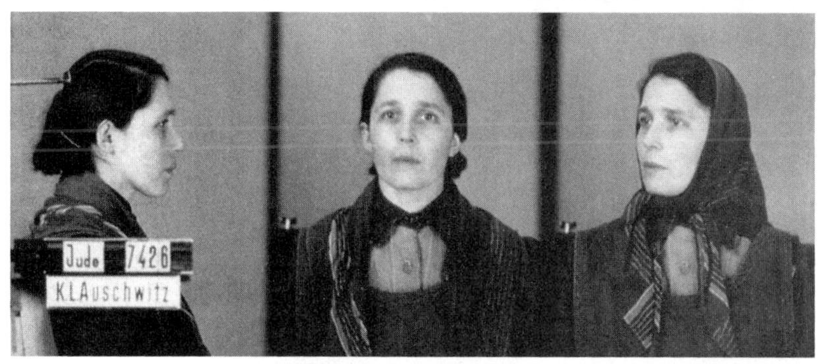

MARIA SMIALEK

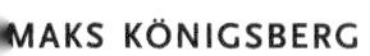

MAKS KÖNIGSBERG

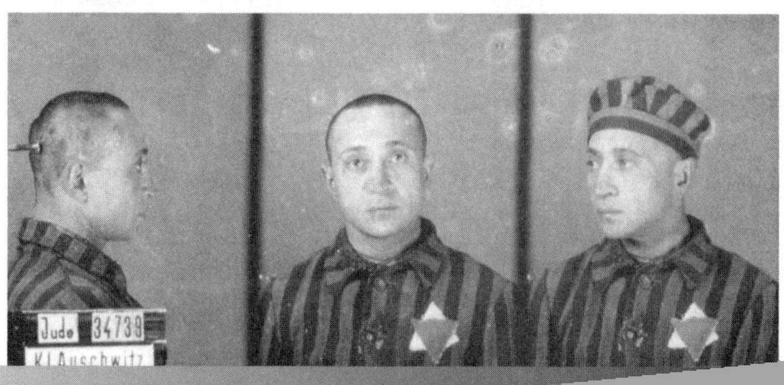

CHU CHIN KUAY

BANGKOK, THAILAND, 04/18/2001

Early police photography liked corpses, liked to establish predator and prey. Pictures of dead people, by definition those no longer able to do harm, clearly rendered the mug shot's function as a crime-fighting tool obsolete.

This Taiwanese man was photographed at the moment before his death. His photo was thus linked not only to the beginnings of identificatory art, but also to the ancient use of displaying criminals in a public square. He was executed by gunfire for drug trafficking, with five other people, in the first Thai public execution partially aired on television.

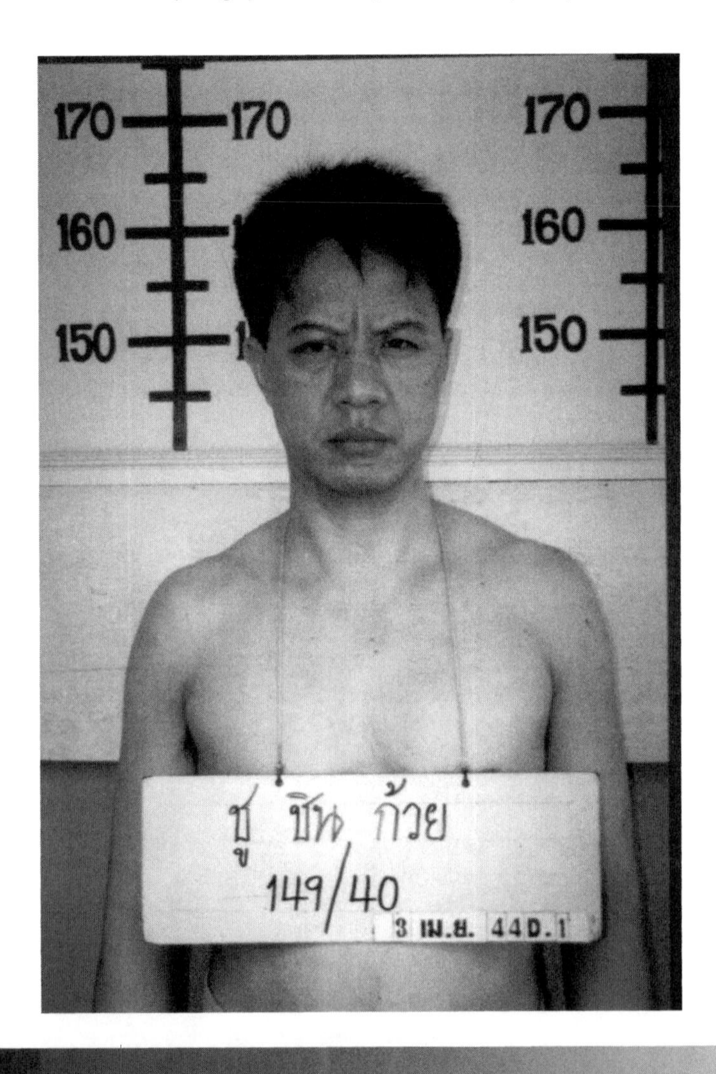

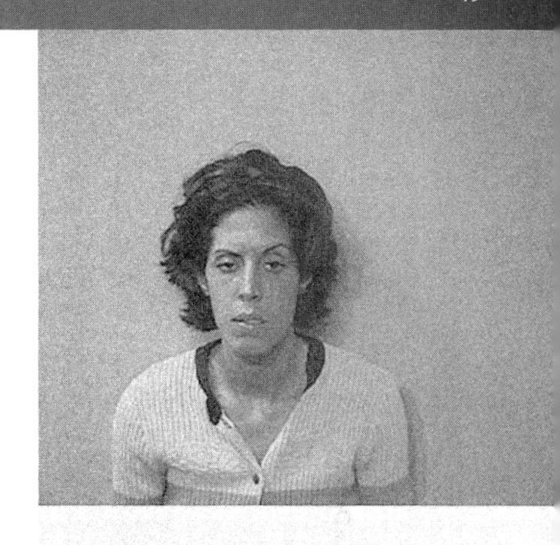

NOELLE BUSH

TALLAHASSEE, FLORIDA, 01/29/2002

In an anonymous phone call to the Orlando police from a drug rehabilitation center: "One of the women here was caught buying crack cocaine tonight. And a lot of the women are upset because she's been caught about five times. And we want something done because our children are here . . . She does this all the time and she gets out of it because she's the governor's daughter . . . She gets treated like some kind of princess."

The governor is Jeb Bush, the president's brother, elected in 2000 precisely because of the scandals that were going on in the state. The princess is his daughter Noelle, arrested on January 29, 2002, for trying to buy Xanax with a fake prescription.

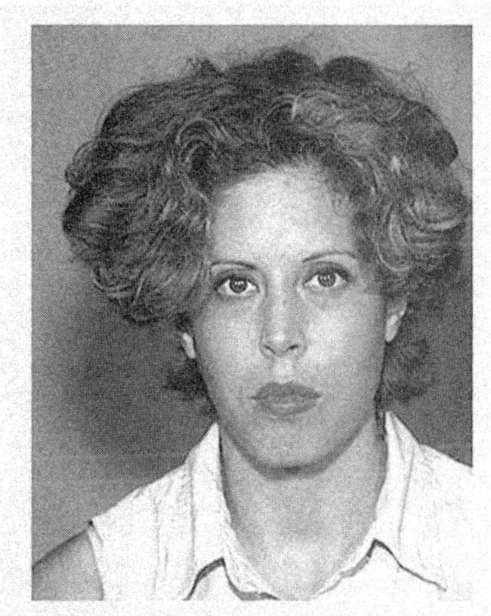

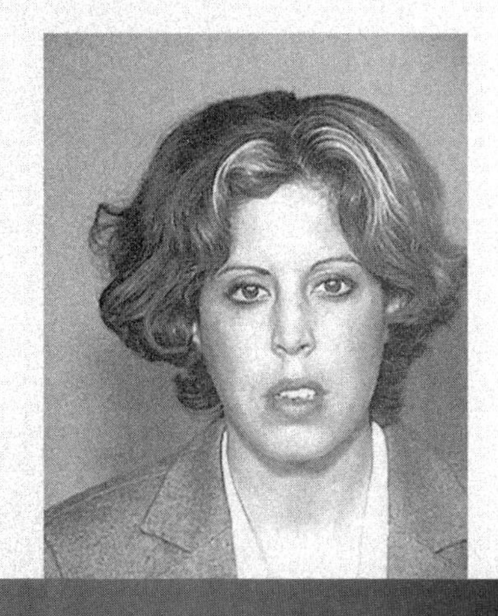

ROGER CLINTON

HERMOSA BEACH, CALIFORNIA, 02/24/2001

Luckily for him, before leaving the White House, his older half-brother Bill Clinton decided to make things right. In 2001, as the final act in his presidential term, Bill pardoned him along with another 140 (including Patty Hearst) of his 1985 conviction. Bill was then the governor of Arkansas. Roger was sentenced to fifteen months for selling cocaine. Soon after his pardon, he was fined $1,351 and two years probation for driving while intoxicated. Moreover, it had yet to be explained why in 1999, the daughter of Rosario Gambino, an American drug trafficker, wrote him a check for $50,000.

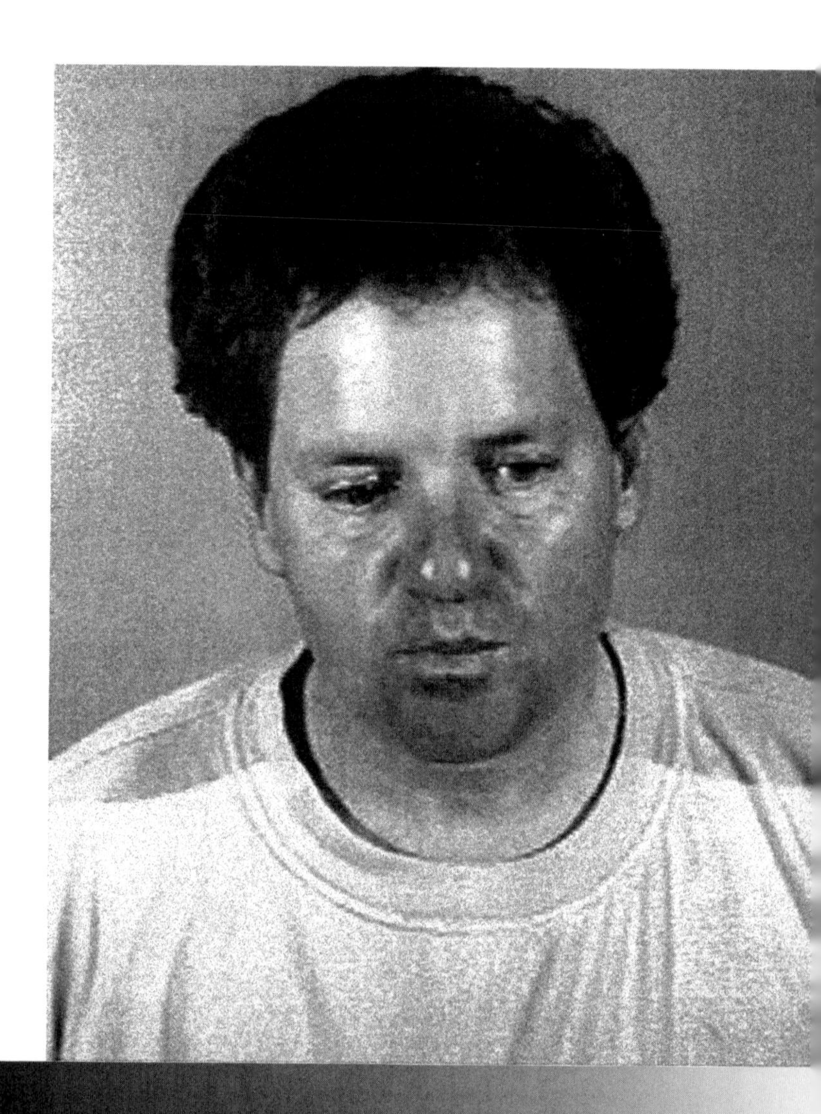

ALBERT A. GORE

BETHESDA, MARYLAND, 12/19/2003

The last black sheep in the family of Albert Gore III, son of Al, Clinton's vice president who in the presidential elections of 2000 was left a victim of the Bush brothers and the Supreme Court. The first incident occurred in 1996, when Albert III was thirteen and was caught with some friends smoking marijuana (or maybe oregano) at the end-of-the-year dance. In 2003 he was stopped for not having his headlights on, arrested for having a joint, a cigarette box containing what appeared to be marijuana, and a crushed soda can that reeked of marijuana. In addition to the unpleasant facts on young Albert, there's the arrest of his sister, Sarah, at age sixteen for drinking beer at a party. Everyone knows that in America, getting a mug shot taken is an event.

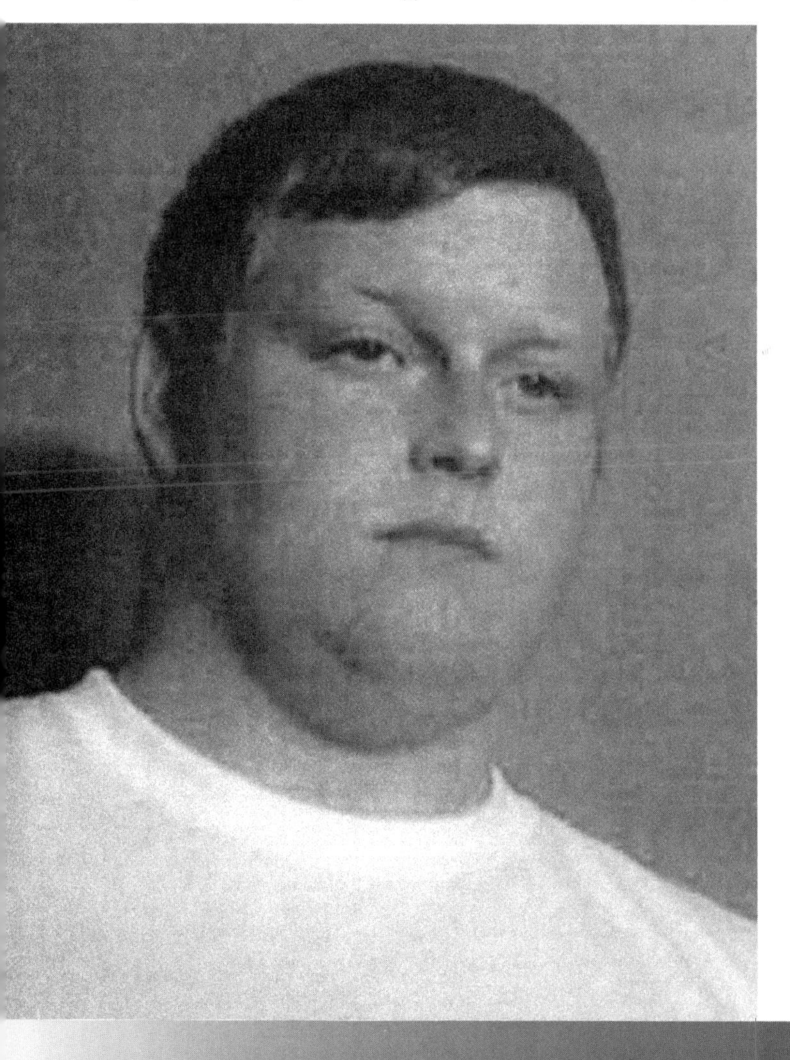

ALPHONSE BERTILLON

PARIS, 1912

The grammar of twentieth-century police photography is indebted to the conformist genius of the founder of anthropometry (here, photographing himself for fun in 1912), the great systematizer of photographic investigation, description, and measurement, identity as a combination of numbers.

Every human being can be described, essentialized (and captured) through the graduated measuring of the body by following a statistical premise formulated years earlier by Adolphe Quételet. Two men taken at random have a 1 in 4 chance of being the same height. The more measurements taken (length of the arm, foot, nose, chest, pinky, armspan, head, forehead, etc.), the lower the probability. Using fourteen measurements, the probability becomes 1:286,434,456. Virtually no margin of error.

Unfortunately for Bertillon, at the turn of century it was discovered there was a 1 in 67 billion chance that two different people would have the same fingerprints. Unfortunately for Bertillon, in America in 1903 two criminals called Will West came onto the scene. His misfortunes (which we will later discuss) don't erase the fact that for almost thirty years Alphonse Bertillon represented the triumph of positivist science over crime, of bourgeois reason over social evil.

Born in Paris in 1853, Alphonse rapidly understood the possibilities of studying crime using statistical methods, of which his father, Adolphe, was one of the leading proponents. One of his biographers, Jürgen Thorwald, writes: "He was a young man with a drawn, pale face, with a cold, melancholy expression, slow movements, and a monotone voice. He suffered from intestinal disturbances and horrible migraines, and had such an icy, reserved character that he seemed almost repulsive. This dryness was accompanied by a natural wariness, with a tendency toward sarcasm, rancor, and a fastidious pedantry, entirely devoid of any sort of aesthetic sensibility" (*Crime and Science: The New Frontier in Criminology*, Harcourt, Brace & World, 1967).

Alphonse joined the police force on May 15, 1879. By 1882 he had already begun to apply his method. His magnum opus, *La photographie judiciarie avec un appendice sur la classification et l'identification anthropométriques*, came out in 1890. For decades, police photography was called "bertillonage" everywhere in the world. Incredible stories were told about how his method enabled the arrests of eight hundred criminals in just three years.

February 1, 1892, marked the creation of the Criminal Identification Service for the Prefecture of Paris, which was extended by decree to the entire French territory on August 11, 1899. Until his death in 1914, Alphonse Bertillon ran it himself, amassing about 110,000 mug shots in only four years. In 1894, at the height of his career, he took on the task of doing handwriting analysis in the famous Dreyfus case, showing himself to be someone who holds the accused guilty to the point of obtuseness and who, in this case, was ultimately proven wrong by the acquittal.

His method was exported to the United States, England, and Italy, where in 1898 the European police, meeting in Rome for the anti-anarchy congress, adopted Bertillon's compendium as a practical and theoretical bible.

He believed that the essential nucleus of each person's identity lay in the shape of the ear, but over time, after criticizing it for years, he was fairly able to accept the fingerprint method, conceptualized in France by Francis Galton and in Great Britain by Scotland Yard's Richard Henry, and applied experimentally in British Bengal from 1886 to 1894.

When on October 16, 1902, a servant's corpse was found in a Paris dentist's apartment at 107 Faubourg Saint-Honoré, Bertillon's squad identified the assassin from the fingerprints he left in the apartment—"the only witnesses that don't fall through and never lie," as he wrote with his typical literary flair in the October 24 report. The culprit was Henri-Leon Scheffer, born in 1876 and photographed for a burglary a few months earlier. The triumph was complete, even if, ironically, it was thanks to someone else's invention.

The year 1903 signaled the downfall of his method based on a combination of photography, measurements, and description (the "portrait parlé"). At Leavenworth prison in the United States, a new inmate was photographed and measured. His name was Will West. The officer took the standard fourteen measurements and realized he had measured an identical person before. A search through the prison's records revealed that another William West had been at Leavenworth for two years, and that, astoundingly, his measurements were the same as the new arrival's. The director summoned them both and found that the measurements were indeed identical. This was all the more astonishing since the two men were not related. A fundamental discovery in twentieth-century physics announced itself: the act of measuring always carries a certain level of imprecision. The act of taking fourteen measurements exponentially increases the risk.

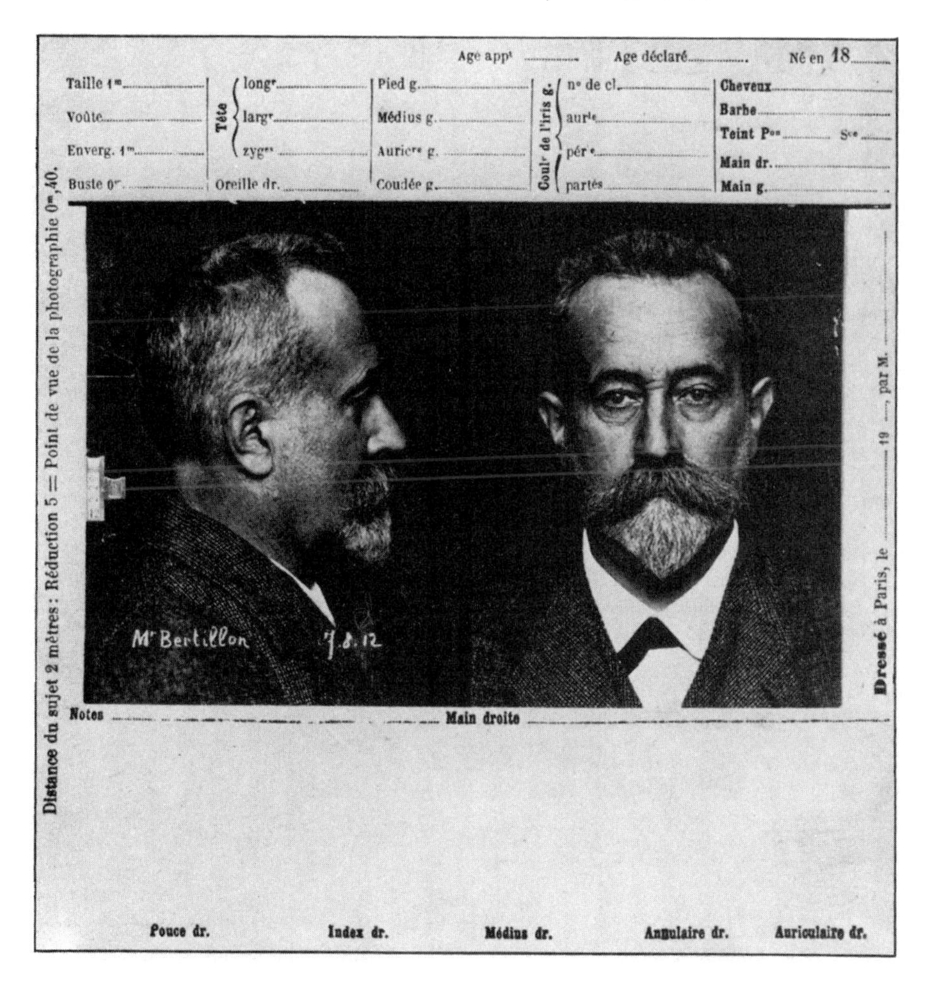

Age appt .... Age déclaré .... Né en 18 ....

Taille 1m .... Voûte .... Enverg. 1m .... Buste 0m ....

Tête { longr .... largr .... zyges .... } Oreille dr. ....

Pied g. .... Médius g. .... Auricre g. .... Coudée g. ....

Coulr de l'iris g. { no de cl. .... aurle .... pére .... partés .... }

Cheveux .... Barbe .... Teint Pon .... Sce .... Main dr. .... Main g. ....

Distance du sujet 2 mètres : Réduction 5 = Point de vue de la photographie 0m,40.

Dressé à Paris, le .... 19 ..., par M.

Notes .... Main droite ....

Pouce dr. Index dr. Médius dr. Annulaire dr. Auriculaire dr.

ZLEPPANA SVEKUTZKY

MOSCOW AREA, CA. 1880

Cesare Lombroso had a problem and asked his friends what to do. In his catalogue of criminal types there were far too few women.

Around 1880 in the vicinity of Moscow, his friend Pauline Tarnowsky tracked down some photographs and sent them to the great scientist. The caption of this photo reads: "Zleppana Svekutzky at 16—a village couple's daughter—poisoned five people, two of whom died. Strangely adamant in denying her accomplice." Alphonse Bertillon had recently joined the police force, and faraway Russia was drawn to, though wary of, French ways. As the syntax of police photography had not yet been embraced, real masterpieces were able to emerge in the absence of rules. The girl poses between two perfectly mustached, symmetrical guards standing in the background. She's wearing what looks like festive clothing. She's barefoot. So small that her feet don't touch the ground. The sun is low, casting long shadows—hers, and her toes', perfectly distinguishable on the ground, and the guard's. Walter Benjamin wrote that art is characterized by its ability to be strengthened by each successive gaze. You would never get tired of looking at this photo.

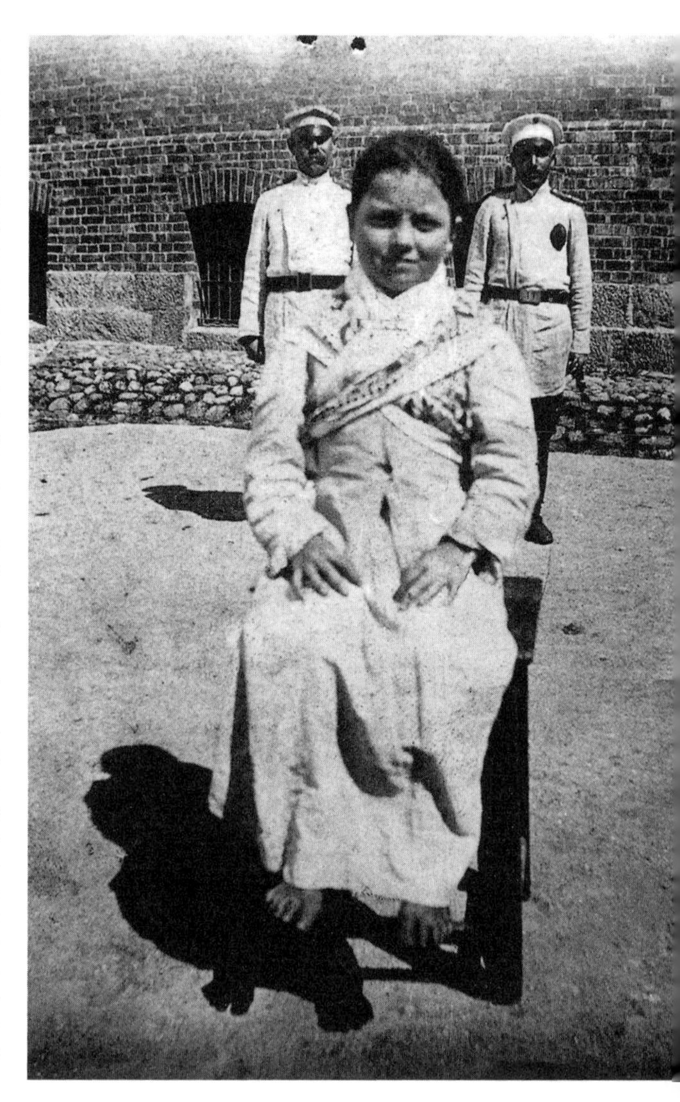

KATHARINA MILEK

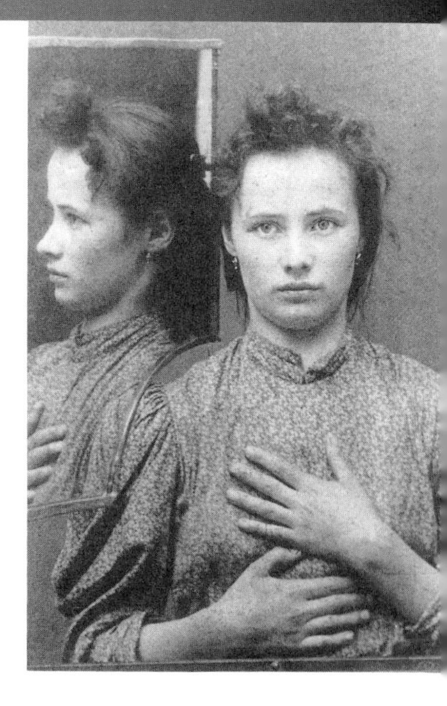

The scientist notes: "Accomplice in the Schmalleger uxoricide." Mr. Schmalleger "poisoned his second wife in order to marry Milek and probably killed his first wife also." The photograph of this marvelous young love is collected with many others (including the one below) in an album of foreign criminals, in which Cesare Lombroso wrote by hand the offense and the circumstances for each picture.

A side mirror placed above the culprit's right shoulder allowed the photographer to capture the front and the profile of the accused in a single frame (even if the profile in the reflection is backward, therefore incorrect). The so-called English system was criticized by Alphonse Bertillon because it hindered the photo's use for identification documents and the pose's usability for police purposes—for example, hands intensely and unconditionally photographed in the act of shielding the body.

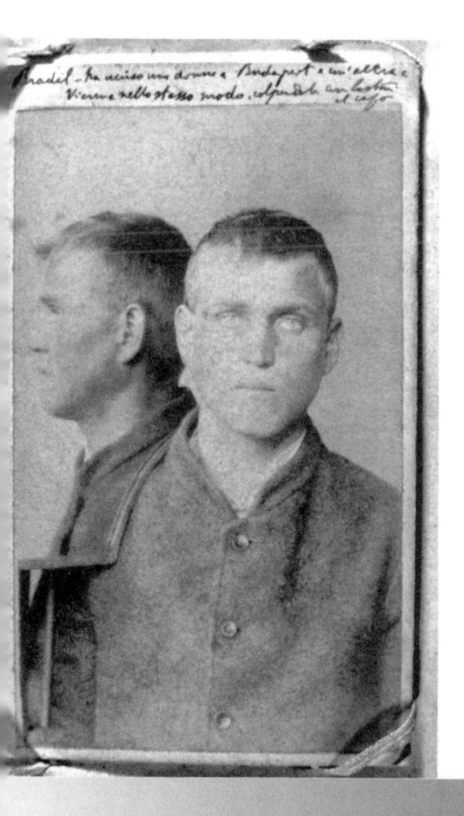

BRADEL

In the same album (this photo is opposite Katharina's) another Jekyll and Hyde from early in the century. In this case as well, Cesare Lombroso noted the criminal's history by hand. "Bradel. Killed one woman in Budapest and another in Vienna in the same way, by bludgeoning the head." It is perhaps the earliest existing mug shot of a serial killer.

It still uses the English system, which preceded the advent of the "Gemelle di Ellero," the camera patented by Umberto Ellero that captures front and profile views at the same time. "The Cameras are fixed focus," Ellero writes, "the Gemelle working by taking two images simultaneously. Observe the subject's expression and when you find it suitable, press the release. That's all there is to it." The Gemelle (twins) was used by the Italian state until 1959 (with royalties paid to the inventor), its use spreading to police departments, prisons, military bases, and insane asylums all over the world.

HELEN GILLIS

WASHINGTON, D.C., 07/30/1934

In 1928, at age sixteen, she married the bandit Lester Gillis, who became notorious under the nickname Baby Face Nelson. Six years later, in 1934, Baby Face was public enemy number one and FBI agents were authorized to "shoot to kill."

He, Gillis, started out with auto theft in 1922. This was followed by kidnappings, killings, partnership with John Paul Chase, admission into John Dillinger's gang, until he became one of the most famous bandits of the Great Depression. On November 27, 1934, Baby Face was killed in a shoot-out with police in Barrington, Illinois, the same state where most of their strikes hit the bull's-eye and also where, at that time, Al Capone had complete power.

Two days later Helen was also arrested. Her maiden name was Wawzynak. Theirs was a story that blended love and crime, one that the United States, especially during that period, loved to talk about and put in the spotlight.

Helen died of old age in 1987, fifty-three years after her husband, who was around long enough to father their two children. She was buried by his side in Chicago's St. Joseph's Cemetery.

July 30, 1934.

I U 01

WANTED

WASHINGTON, D. C.

MRS. HELEN GILLIS, with aliases, MRS. JOSEPH J. MARR, MARIAN VIRGINIA MARR, MARION VIRGINIA MARR, MRS. JIMMIE WILLIAMS, MRS. LESTER M. GILLIS, MRS. "BABY FACE" NELSON, MRS. LESTER GATES.

HARBORING FUGITIVE

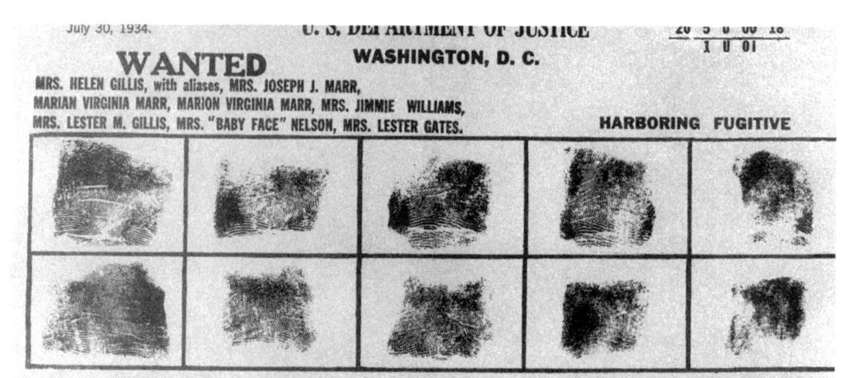

DESCRIPTION

Age, 21 years (1934); Height, 5 feet, 2 inches; Weight, 94 pounds; Build, small; Hair, brown, bobbed; Eyes, blue; Complexion, fair.
Scars and Marks - small brown mole 2 inches above left inner wrist; forehead has four horizontal lines from wrinkles.

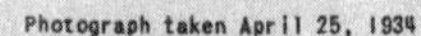

Photograph taken April 25, 1934

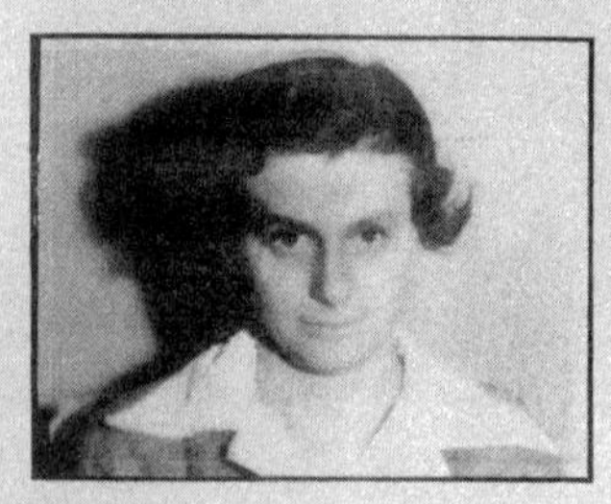

Marion Marr.

CRIMINAL RECORD

As Mrs. Marion Virginia Marr, arrested Sheriff's Office, Madison, Wisconsin, April 23, 1934; charge, harboring U. S. fugitive; released to U. S. Marshal.
As Marian Marr, #2984, arrested U. S. Marshal, Madison, Wiscons April 25, 1934; charge, harbori U. S. fugitive; sentence, 18 mo sentence suspended, placed on bation; probation revoked June 1934.

RELATIVES

Lester M. Gillis, husband, subject of Identification Order #1223.
Mrs. Robert C. Fitzsimmons, sister-in-law, 5516 South Marshfield Avenue, Chicago, Illinois.
Mrs. Mary Gillis, mother-in-law, 2119 6th Street, Bremerton, Washington.
Mrs. Edwin Gillis, sister-in-law, 3238 Osceola Avenue, Chicago, Illinois.
Mrs. William McMahcn, sister-in-law, 2119 6th Street, Bremerton, Washington.

Mrs. Helen Gillis is wanted by the United States Marshal, Madison, Wisconsin on charges of harboring John Herbert Dilling and Thomas Leonard Carroll (both deceased), Fugitives from Justice, and for violating her probationary sentence.

Law enforcement agencies kindly transmit any additional information or criminal record to the nearest office of the Divis of Investigation, U. S. Department of Justice.

If apprehended, please notify the Director, Division of Investigation, U. S. Department of Justice, Washington, D. C., or the Special Agent in Charge of the office of the Division of Investigation listed on the back hereof which is nearest your c

(over)

Issued by: J. EDGAR HOOVER, DIRECTO

TERESA CRUPI

CATANZARO, ITALY, 07/07/1936

In a faraway world, parallel to Helen Gillis's existence—to her casual encounter with love, fame, and disgrace—flows the life of this woman, of whom her descendants know only what is noted in her police file. Uniting these two existences is that both were subject to the complex descriptive parameters developed by Alphonse Bertillon in the 1890s. Teresa Crupi was born to "Salvatore and Covelli, Rosaria" in Limbadi, Calabria, on November 21, 1916. If she were still alive, and she may be, she would be eighty-eight. From her mug shot, held at the Rome Criminology Museum and taken in Catanzaro, Calabria, on July 7, 1936, one is struck by her watery eyes, the right still seeming on the verge of tears almost a hundred years later, and the position of her head in profile weighed down by her thoughts. One is struck by the simplicity with which everything is written by hand. Education: illiterate, profession: farmer, reason for arrest: homicide. It is in the absence of details that the human face begins to resemble a map. A silent work of art in which years, deeds, suffering, and guilt collapse into a momentary expression.

At the bottom, like tombstones, her fingerprints.

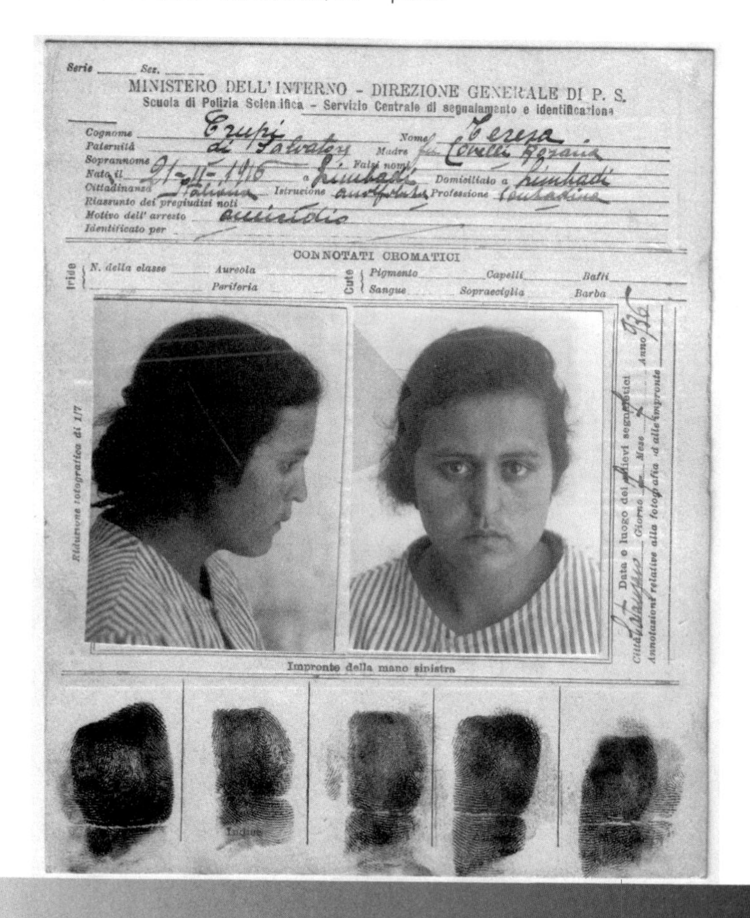

Serie ____ Sez. ____

MINISTERO DELL'INTERNO - DIREZIONE GENERALE DI P. S.

Scuola di Polizia Scientifica - Servizio Centrale di segnalamento e identificazione

Cognome Crupi Nome Teresa
Paternità di Salvatore Madre fu Covelli Rosaria
Soprannome Falsi nomi
Nato il 21-XI-1916 a Limbadi Domiciliato a Limbadi
Cittadinanza Italiana Istruzione analfabeta Professione contadina
Riassunto dei pregiudizi noti
Motivo dell'arresto omicidio
Identificato per

CONNOTATI CROMATICI

Iride { N. della classe ____ Aureola ____ Periferia ____
Cute { Pigmento ____ Sangue ____ Capelli ____ Sopracciglia ____ Baffi ____ Barba ____

Riduzione fotografica di 1/7

Data e luogo dei rilievi segnaletici Città ____ Giorno 7 Mese ____ Anno ____

Annotazioni relative alla fotografia ed alle impronte

Impronte della mano sinistra

P.G.

1926

Homosexuality reveals hidden strategies, fears, and pleasures that, like the motive, inhabit the history of police photography. A case in point, that of the homosexual requires further devices of neutralization.

If for thieves and prostitutes frontal and profile shots suffice, if the tattooed call for the entire figure and the naked body (sometimes also copying the design on paper, even the post mortem tanning and conservation of the ornamented skin), the homosexual is asked to show, like another face, his bare buttocks. The part that magically synthesizes (and neutralizes) the whole.

Below the photo, kept at the Lombroso Museum in Turin, it reads: "P.G. aged 17 who in 1926 used a pretext to persuade a carter to go with him to the hill: after reaching a secluded spot, he shot the revolver at him. He was carrying the weapons and the bullets displayed here. After the deed, he took a long ride on horseback as he occasionally liked to do. He was sentenced to Assise for 12 years of imprisonment." Poor carter. And poor P.G.

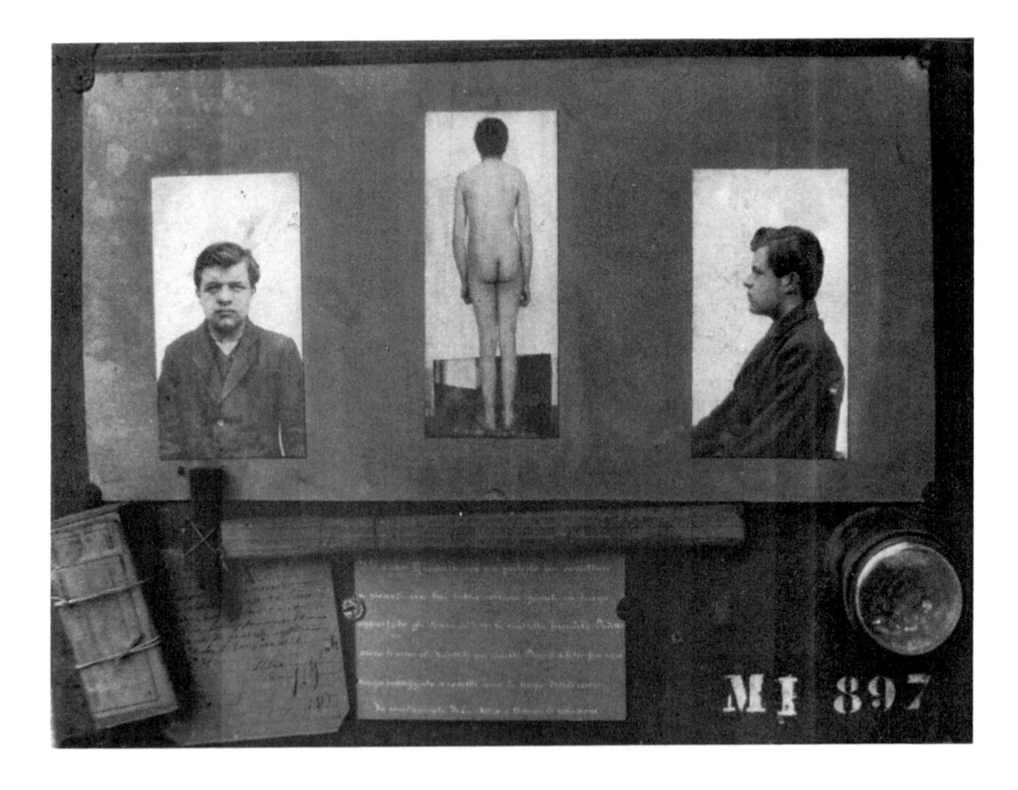

GIOACCHINO DI PASQUALE

Placing the head of robbers, in this case Gioacchino di Pasquale, on an overturned bucket was part of a common practice. In the late nineteenth century there were hundreds of Italian brigands and American outlaws photographed post mortem. Sometimes decapitated. In this case, the image's function is no longer useful for possible future investigations. Instead it serves as an example for others. The use of the postcard spread during this period with the advent of the railway and postal system, and such photographs of dead targets and their smiling hunters became postcards to send to friends and relatives.

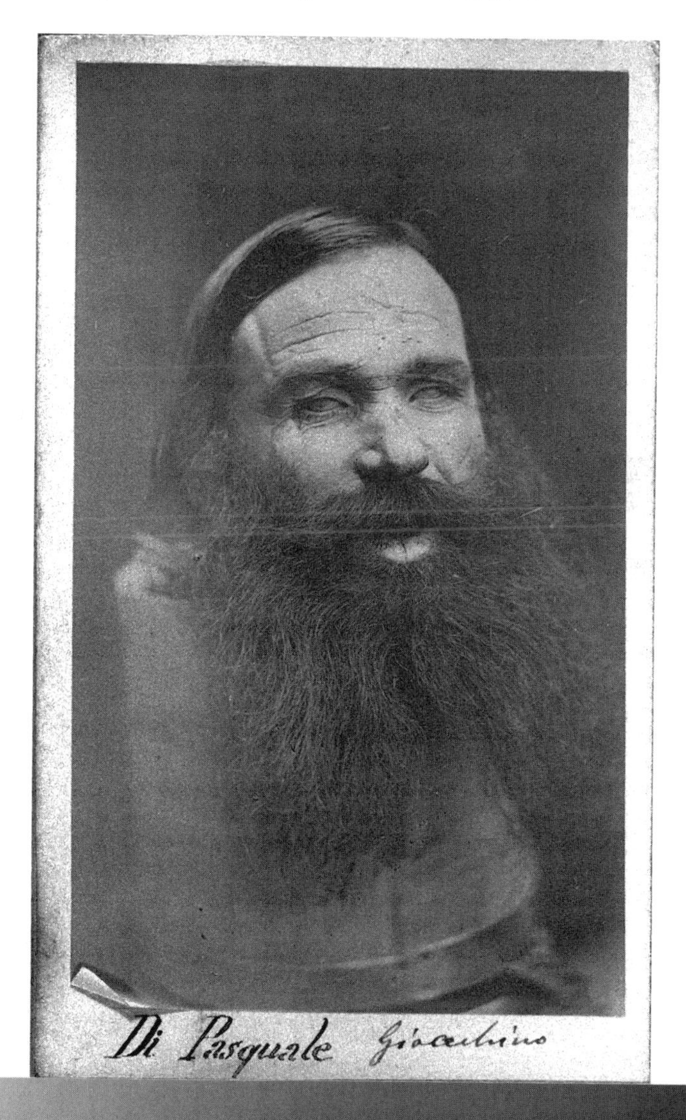

FRAGMENTS

Nothing like the collection of ears, noses, eyes, eyebrows, temples, foreheads, mouths, smiles that the classic identification photo splinters into, revealing its magical, almost animistic core underneath, which has dwelled in modernity since its origins.

The advent of commodities as concentrated quotidian desire, "abounding in metaphysical subtleties" as Karl Marx writes, led to seeing in every possible object—clothing, inventions, and even body parts—obscured meanings, hidden correlations between the whole and its parts, in an omnivorous and unconscious fetishistic orgy. The real is opened like a book, but an indecipherable book. It is both a land of conquest and source of danger. Everything is an object of attraction, everything a source of fear. The magical instrument with which to exorcise these overly intense emotions is scientific objectivity, faith in the possibility of neutralization and possession, measurement and appraising, everything that escapes the domain of the European bourgeoisie.

Before the discovery of fingerprints, a universal code and essence of identity was searched for in everything. In the shape of the ear, which to Bertillon varied from person to person, in the numerical relationship between the length of various parts of the body, in the inventory of the shapes of noses, of mouths, of eyes, of cheekbones, described in a manner much more literary than scientific by Cesare Lombroso.

The aim, almost Cartesian, is to locate in the body the opening to the soul, an incontrovertible sign of temperament. At the origin of this mammoth work of cataloguing the body of the criminal, the madman, or the genius, lies a need for control through possession.

The photograph is the primary weapon used to put this strategy into effect. Its presumed objectivity implies the idea of capture, the act of empowering and immortalizing the gaze creates the illusion of having the dangerous or disturbing individual under control, the offender's gaze and body trapped forever on plate or paper, available for each subsequent consultation, suggesting the idea of having not only the criminal's countenance under lock and key, but also their soul. The literature on the subject dispenses with descriptions of the fear and resistance that the lunatic and the criminal provoked in the police photographer. In "Little History of Photography," Walter Benjamin describes the anguish of observing one's own petrified face in the earliest daguerreotypes, the fear that those little copies would reciprocate the gaze of the original.

Objectivity is a facade, a slogan, the final descendent of the ancient superstition of the image's power to steal the soul of the individual depicted. In order for this illusion of control to be complete, the momentary gaze of the photograph had to unfold into a net of smaller acts of taking possession. Descriptions, measurements, rules, uniforms, among others. To be effective the gaze had to be as broad as possible. The work of photographic and documentary representation goes along with an obsessive taxonomic effort, meant to categorize the entire universe. Hence the appearance of the museum, the temple of that clandestine relationship between magic and science that started in the nineteenth century and extended, at varying levels of intensity, into the following century.

Museums for everything in existence were born. Bourgeois imperialism documented itself, its victories and its failures, its attractions and its fears, deluding itself in order to create a sense of security. In an extreme and desperate attempt at symbolic neutralization, the body of the criminal was divided into its parts, ordered in homogeneous series, and archived as if this were the way it could cease causing harm, as if by preserving and controlling the detail, the whole could be comprehended and disarmed.

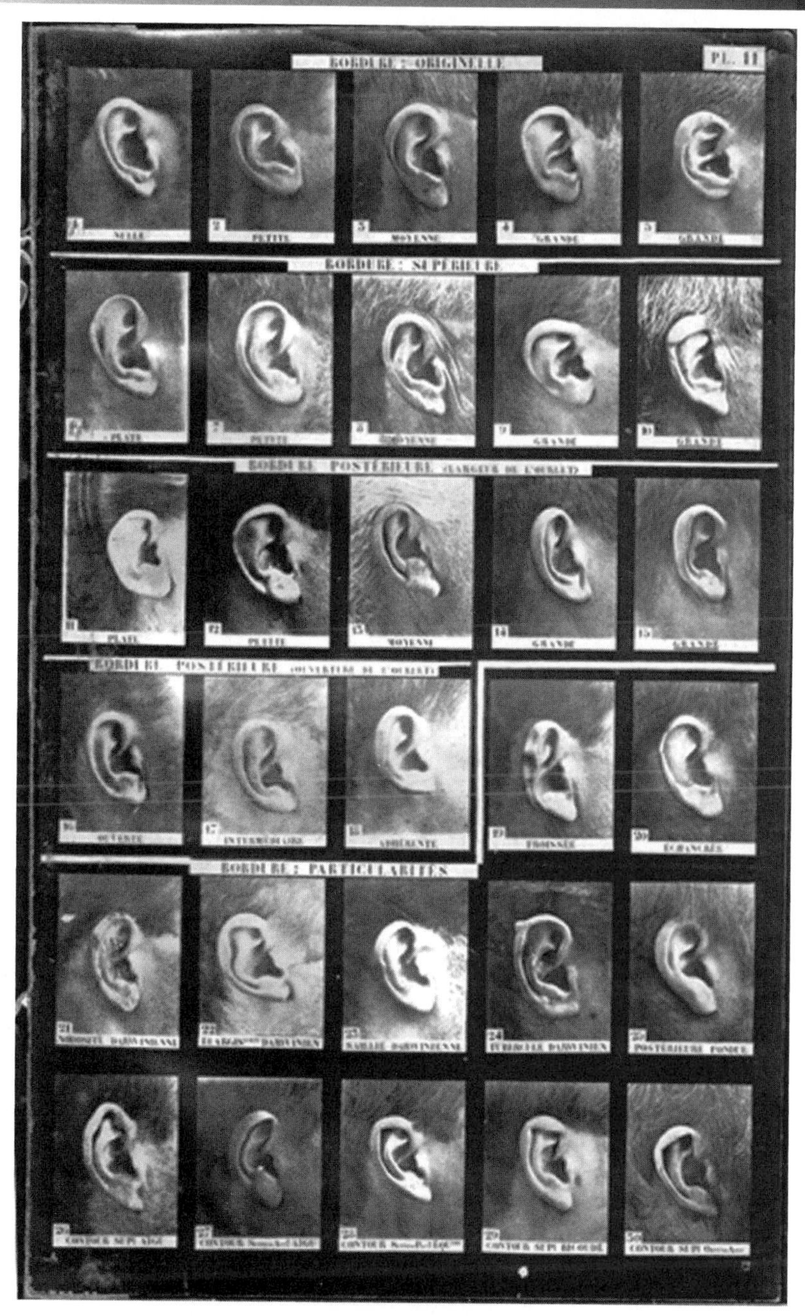

EARS

NOSES

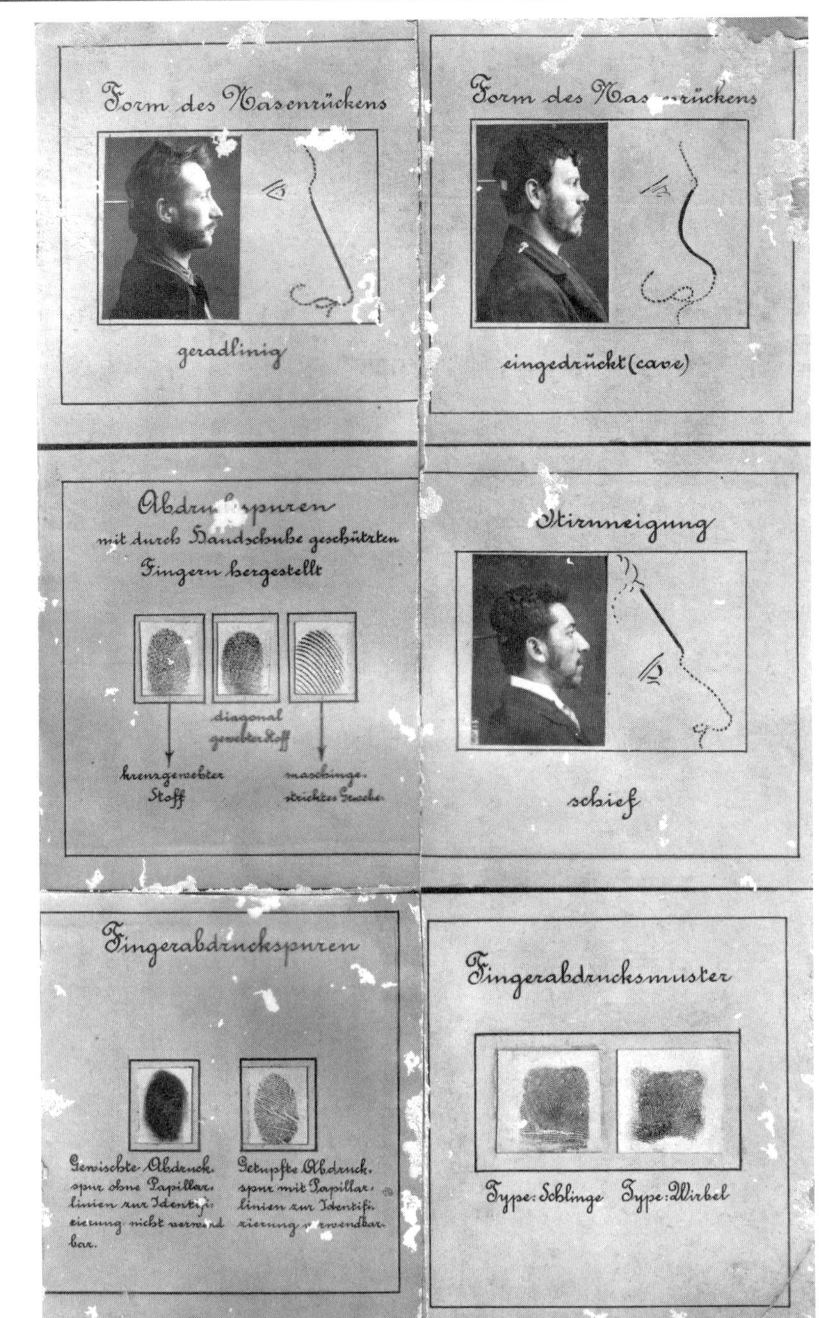
Form des Nasenrückens
geradlinig
eingedrückt (cave)
mit durch Handschuhe geschützten
Fingern hergestellt
diagonal
gewebter Stoff
kreuzgewebter
Stoff
Stirnneigung
schief
Fingerabdrucksspuren
Gewischte Abdruck-
spur ohne Papillar-
linien zur Identifi-
zierung nicht verwend-
bar.
Getupfte Abdruck-
spur mit Papillar-
linien zur Identifi-
zierung verwendbar.
Fingerabdrucksmuster
Type: Schlinge
Type: Wirbel

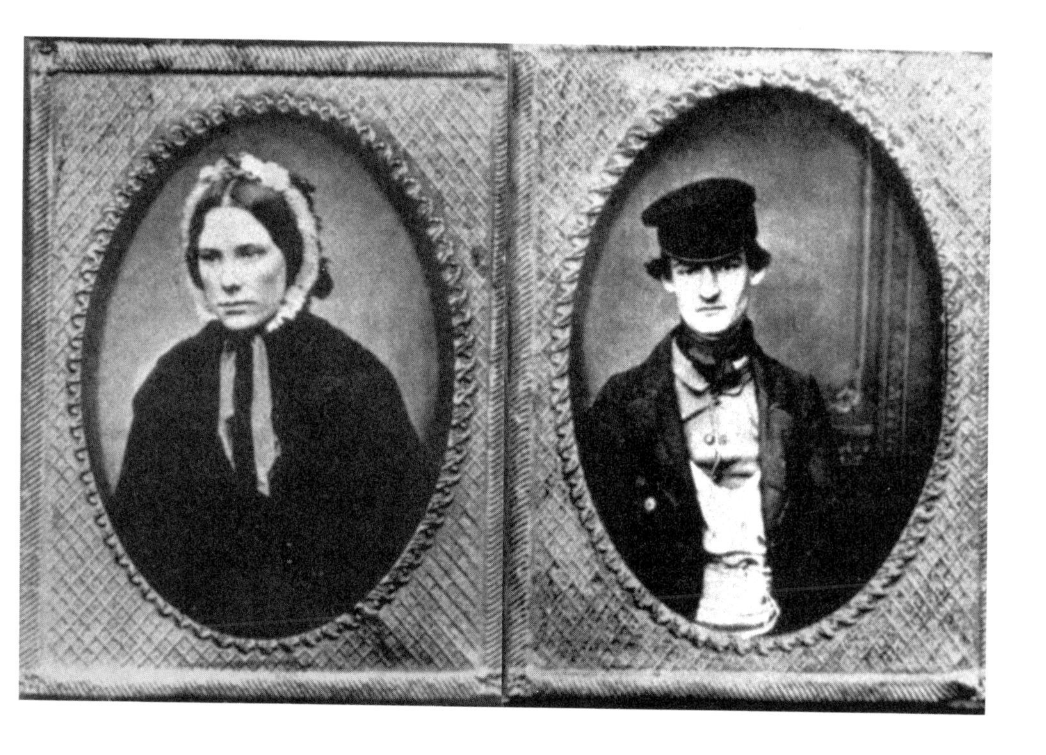

PROSTITUTE AND THIEF

BIRMINGHAM, GREAT BRITAIN, 1848

A prostitute and a thief, photographed for the first time in a seemingly infinite series of prostitutes and thieves captured by the police in Birmingham, Great Britain, in 1848. Daguerre's invention had come out just nine years earlier. It was proof that it was love at first sight for photography and the detention system of the eighteenth century.

These are some of the earliest known police photographs. The police station that originated the idea of eradicating the criminal through photography can be found on Moor Street.

ADALGISA CONTI

AREZZO, ITALY

She was born on May 28, 1887. On November 17, 1913, at age twenty-six, she entered the Arezzo asylum where she would remain for the rest of her life. In 1978, when Adalgisa was ninety-one, she came out of the institution that had contained her entire existence. Her journals, *Manicomio 1914: Gentillissimo Sig. Dottore, questa è la mia vita (Asylum 1914: Dear Doctor, This Is My Life*) were published in 1978 by Mazzotta, edited by Luciano Della Mea. As Italy was preparing the Basaglia reform, the diary, from which we will quote a few passages along with her clinical notes, became a sensation. In the photos on these pages, Adalgisa is pictured at twenty-seven, fifty-one, and in old age.

> Dear Doctor, this is my life. I was born on a mountain called Montalone, my parents took me to St. Leo . . . : when I was a little girl I helped wash the dishes, I went to wash the children's dirty clothes, I watched my siblings, but since I had so little fondness for them, it is quite true that with one younger brother named Aroldo (I think), I covered him with the sheets and blankets with the intention of suffocating him . . .
>
> I grew frail: because I was also wicked from masturbating my girlfriends who lived nearby. I had crusta lactea on the head and the privates, I would have imposed upon a dog, a duck, amusing myself by brooding over them, like a mother hen or a rooster . . .
>
> At age sixteen, in mid-1949, I started flirting with Probo, which, to tell the truth, pleased me, but the first times we spoke I didn't know what to say and if he entered me saying slightly crude things, I became bright red, flustered . . .
>
> For a long eight years I continued this love between peace and discord. After many and many trespasses; most of which were my fault more than ever, because I wasn't made to give in to his desires; material desires, but natural ones.

Anamnestic notes signed illegibly, probably by Viviani:

> She is 26, father a wine drinker, died of poisoning due to pharmacist error, mother alive and sane. She had 17 brothers and sisters, only 7 of whom are still alive: she was the second-born. Of her five brothers and three sisters no one suffers from a nervous disorder.
>
> Her mother had three miscarriages: five died in infancy, but after palsy. At 12 she had a hemorrhage from the mouth that was interpreted as a vicarious menstruation, and considerable enterorrhagia [bleeding within the intestinal tract]. Sensitive, impressionable character: she was the granddaughter of Conti Rosa, institutionalized at Corsi. She began to consort with her husband at 16 and married at 24.
>
> She was always extremely jealous, very affectionate with her husband. She had been affected with anemia since a very young age, her menstruation was irregular and barely noticeable. For about three months she started to complain of pains to the head, she suffered from insomnia, she became melancholic, she expressed ideas of persecution (she did not want to go out, because everyone mocked her, thought badly of her).
>
> She had frequent crying spells. Three days ago, when her husband returned from his evening hunt, she discovered that her mother-in-law had already made plans to bring her to her own house, having shown signs of mental alienation and saying that she had attempted suicide . . .
>
> Taken to his mother's, she stated purposes of wanting to kill herself, being unhappy, no longer being her husband's wife, not being a woman or at least not a well-adjusted woman like the others.
>
> She was made to come into Arezzo:

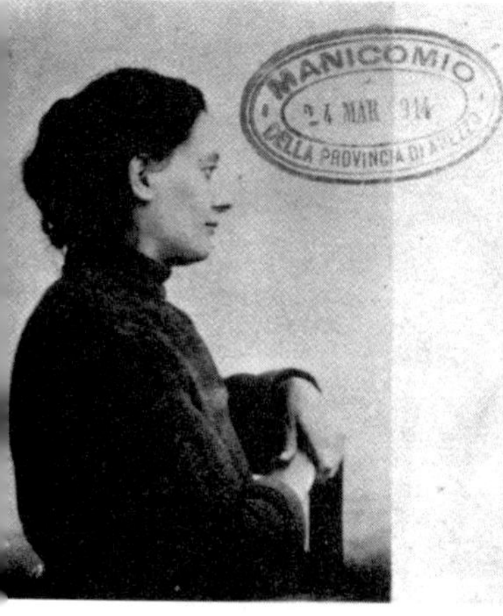

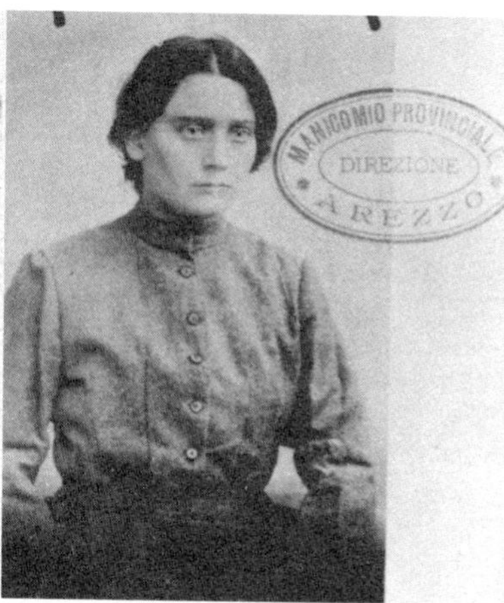

03/24/1914

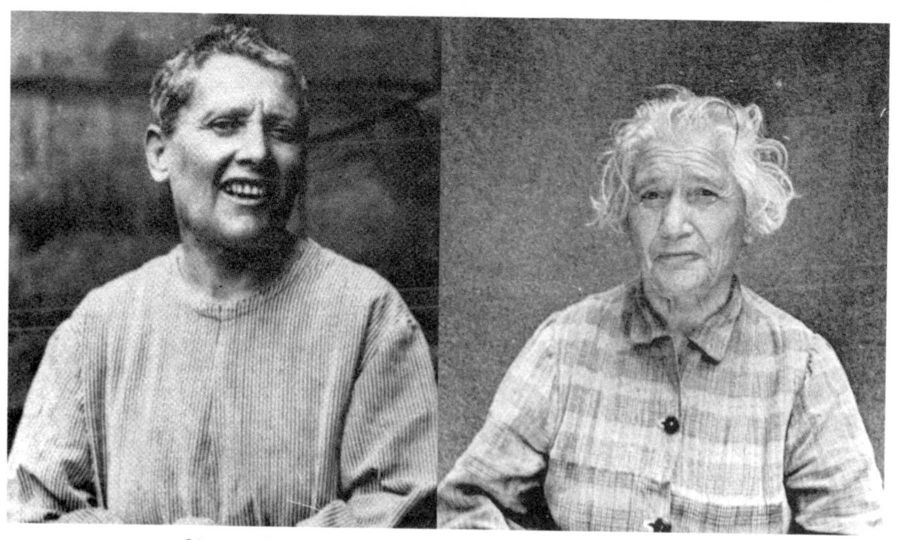

06/03/1938

when I examined her she repeated to me that she was convinced she was not a woman like the others, that she was cursed, that she was condemned to damnation, that she had major sins to atone for, incapable of having children because she never had menses, that she was numb during coitus with her husband, but that she practiced—against religion—masturbatory actions on herself to attain sexual satisfaction . . .

She has not rebelled against the idea of being placed in the care of the Asylum.

On the trip she tried to throw herself under the train; at the hotel to jump out the window.

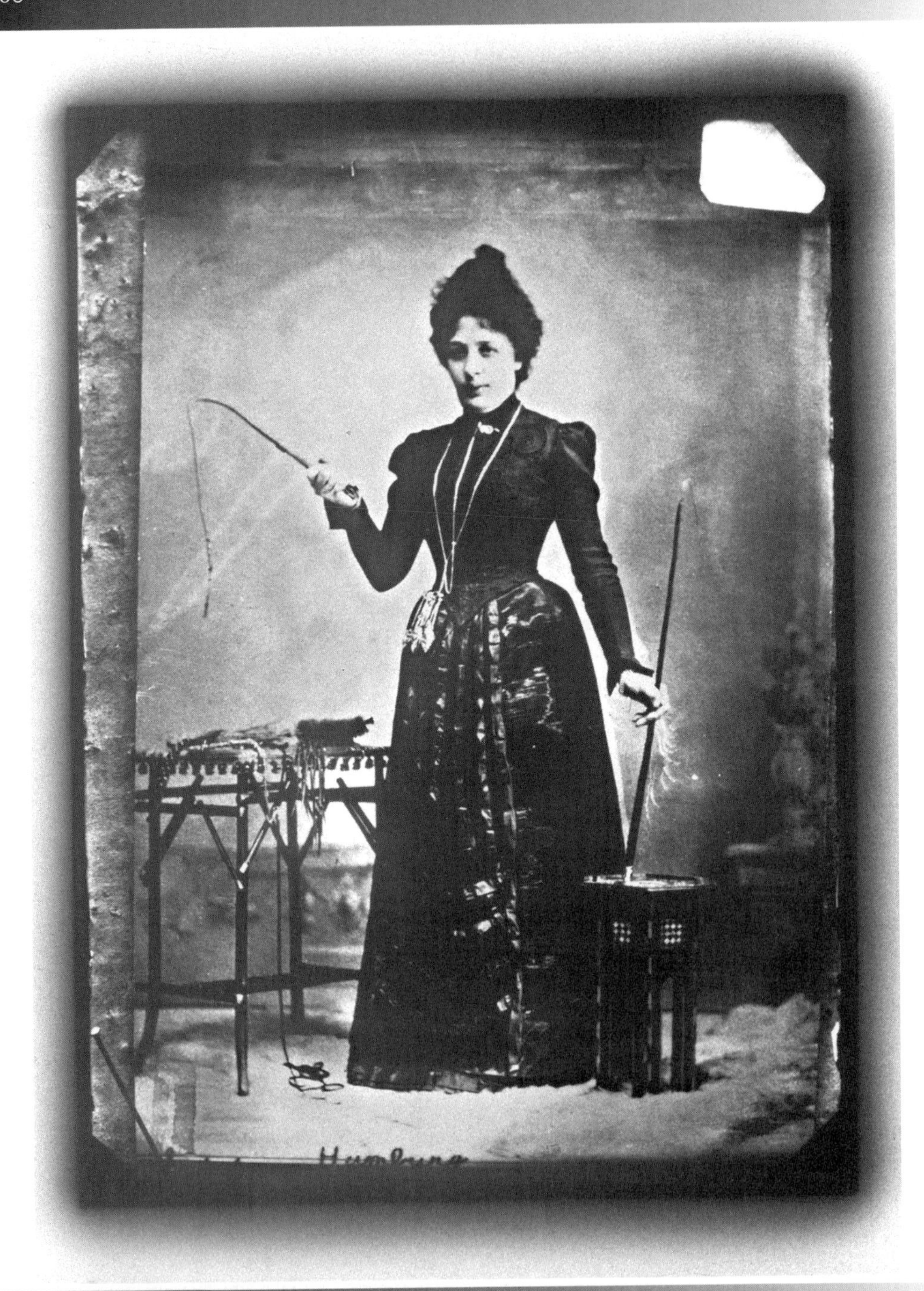

DOMINATRIX

The grand fetishist festival of the twentieth century also passes through, perhaps primarily through, criminal photography. Before fetishism was affirmed and canonized by Bertillon's cult of scientific objectivity, it was common to come across symbolic and aestheticizing embellishments generated by the fervor and imagination of police photographers. The photograph on the left, whose original can be found at the Lombroso Museum, was taken in the early twentieth century. The woman was arrested because she whipped and humiliated her clients for pay. The Hamburg police show her posing with the whip in her hand. On the table, other tools of the sadomasochist trade.

TRANSVESTITE

With the transvestite or hermaphrodite the imagination of the photographer and the criminal archivist is indulged to the point of creating an identification document which, like this one, seems to come from a surrealist dream of Man Ray's.

This story, mentioned in Ando Gilardi's *Wanted!* and reported in the now unavailable *Atlas der gerichtlichen Medizin* by Weimann and Prokop, is beautiful and heartrending. Born as a woman, lived as a man, earned an honest living as a mail carrier. When the man asked for a woman's hand in marriage, the woman underneath was discovered and disrobed.

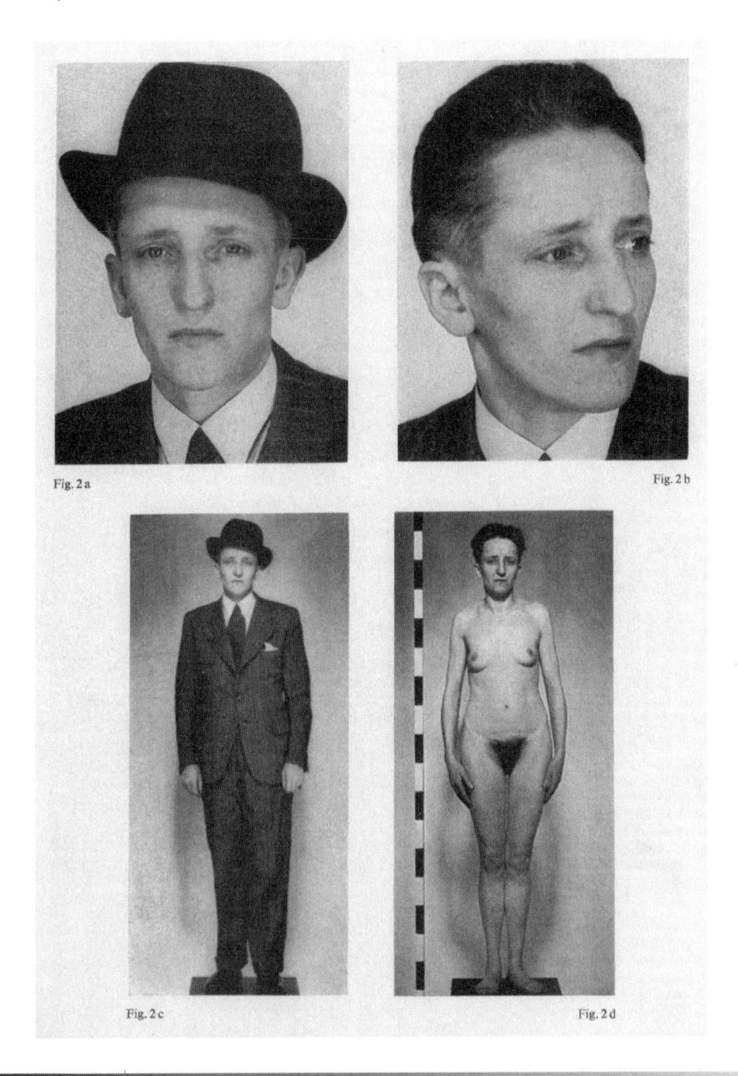

Fig. 2a

Fig. 2b

Fig. 2c

Fig. 2d

TATTOOED MAN

The photograph of this anonymous man with tattooed skin and bandaged face (held at the Rome Criminology Museum) displays tattoos so beautiful and well defined that the photograph is enough to capture them. In similar cases, the classification method is augmented by pieces of paper where the designs etched on the skin of the accused are copied by hand.

With tattoos, especially common in the underworld and the aristocracy, a new type of mug shot was born. This has to do with corresponding "peculiar signs," which, in addition to facilitating future identification, tell the criminal's story to the world. Here is another kind of body language to fixate on and observe. Therefore, the file of a certain Guglielmo Bügler, arrested in Bolzano in 1930 for illegal border crossing, for example, reads: "Left arm decorated with a cross at the center of a heart and beneath the heart the word FAITH . . ."

The tattooed represent the only criminal (and psychiatric) type consistently photographed nude, in full body shots, front and back, or with the forearms turned outward, depending on the location of the designs on the body.

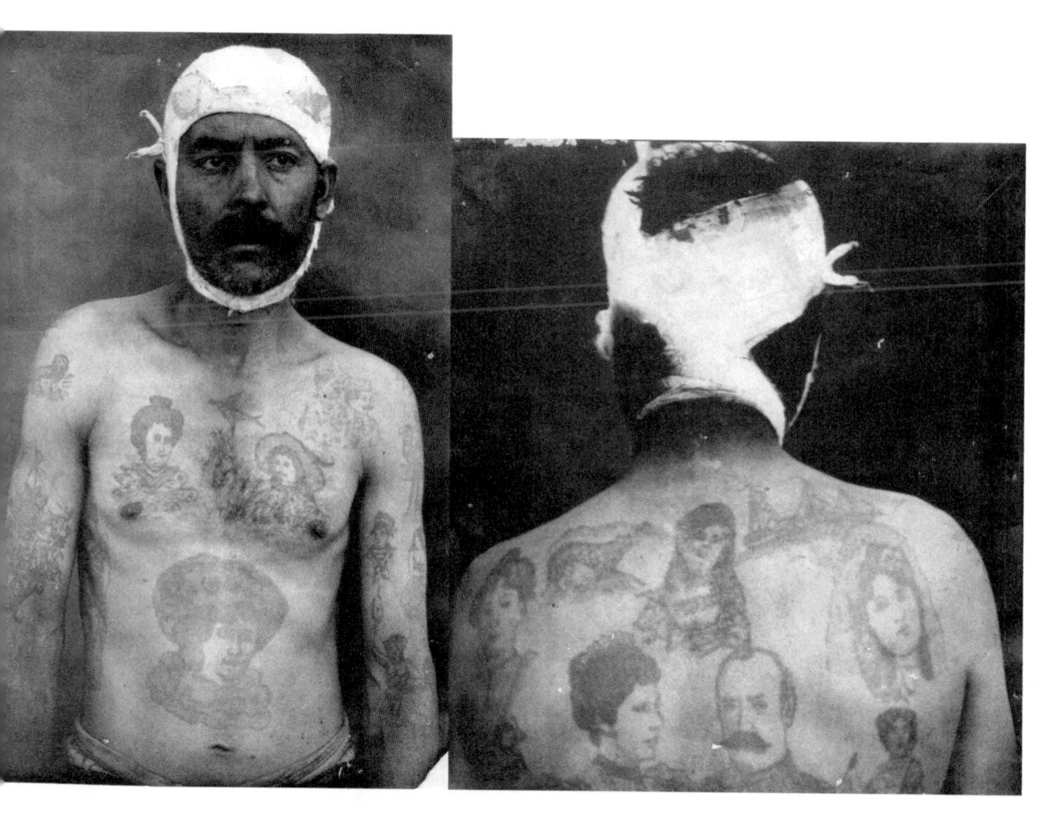

CHILD PROSTITUTES

SHANGHAI, CHINA, EARLY TWENTIETH CENTURY

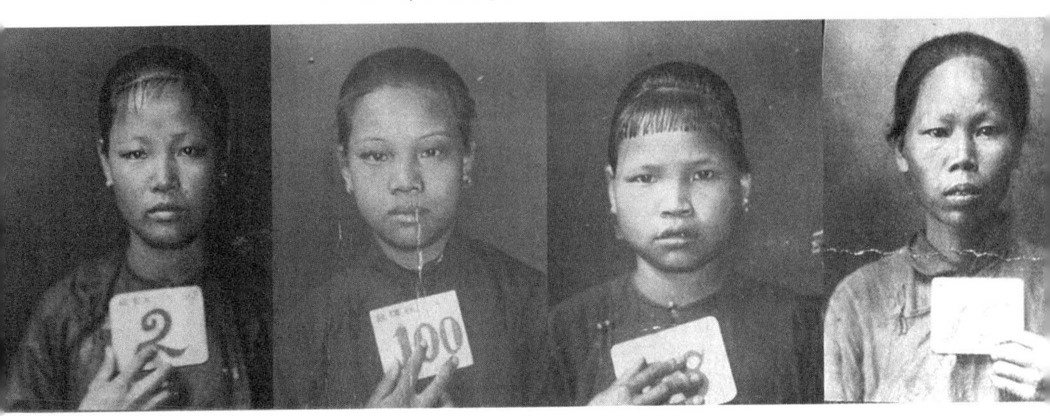

The twentieth century wailed. The world was big. Photography seemed capable of investigating it, capturing it, and making it safe. An Italian diplomat in China thought of an original hobby for himself: photographing and cataloguing, one by one, the child prostitutes (although not just them) of Shanghai. The subject was nothing new; the prostitute, in Birmingham, 1848, had posed for the first daguerreotype mug shot that anyone noticed.

New was the colonial and entomological aspiration that took over our diplomat. The little girls were asked to sit in front of the lens, holding their identification numbers. The only authority the photographer could count on was guaranteed by his Western superiority, by his possession of the means to photograph, and by the money which, in all likelihood, he paid them.

The beauty of these photographs also consists in the exhibition of needs that have occupied criminal photography since its emergence. The shot reveals an act of possession. The compulsion to shoot a series of similar subjects demonstrates an archival impulse and an admiration for the production of series that animates the photographer—a scientific excuse that betrays the voyeuristic desire of he who possesses only with his eyes.

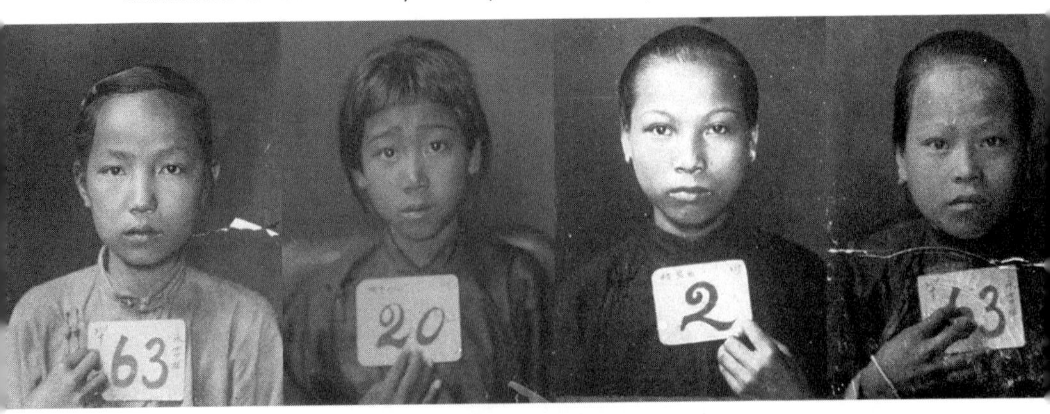

UXORICIDE

"Uxoricide. Chronic alcoholism." This anonymous mug shot, held at the Rome Criminology Museum, provides no other clues. His prison jacket is ironed, neat. Presumably, his hands are in his pockets. This uxoricide wears his uniform as if it were his Sunday best, with his head turned to the right, his gaze distant, his mustache groomed. He seems like a sad yet serene man.

His crime is the same one that devastated the lives of the Italian aristocrat Camillo Casati Stampa and the American athlete O. J. Simpson. What we have here is an age-old crime, made even older by the fact that this uxoricide no longer has a name.

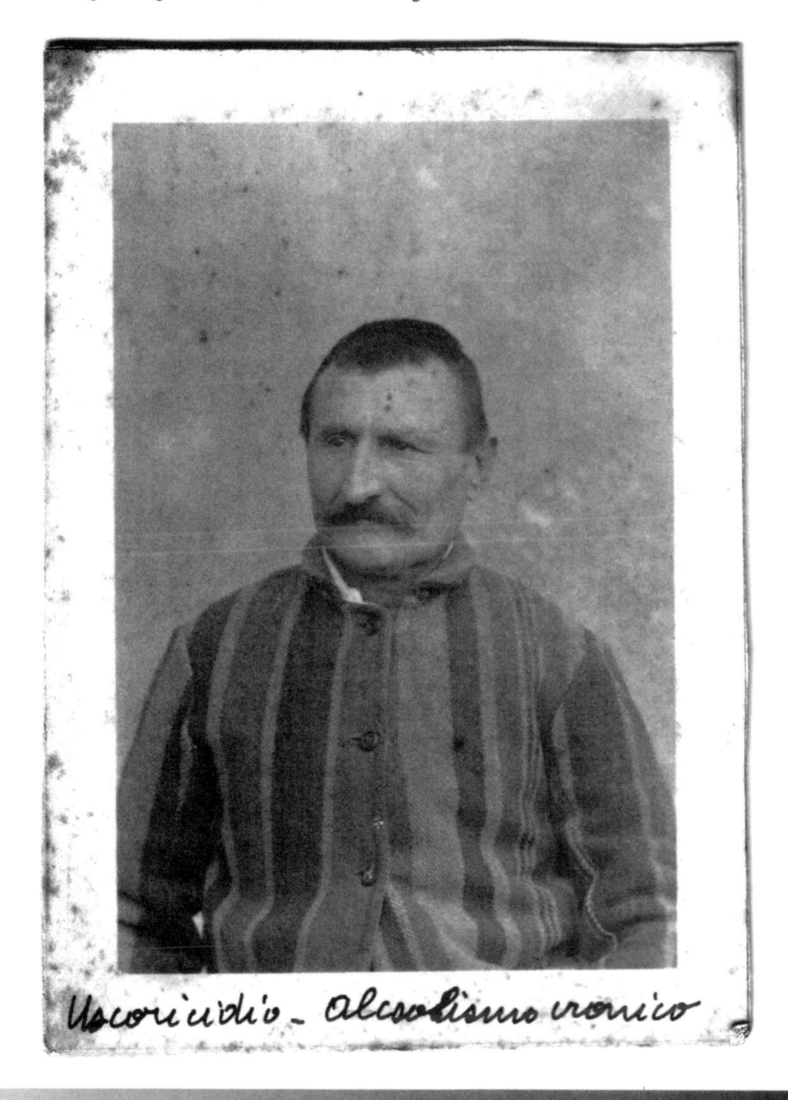

TWO CHILDREN

Two Italian children, twins perhaps, restrained by the adult behind them in a way that allows the picture to be taken. The second half of the nineteenth century was witness to an operation of mass documentation that spread from asylums and prisons to military bases and orphanages. The restraint defeats the purpose. The faces and mouths of the children are unrecognizable because the hands obstruct them. Umberto Ellero, father of police photography in Italy, advised against any coercion that "causes sudden contortions of the physiognomic traits."

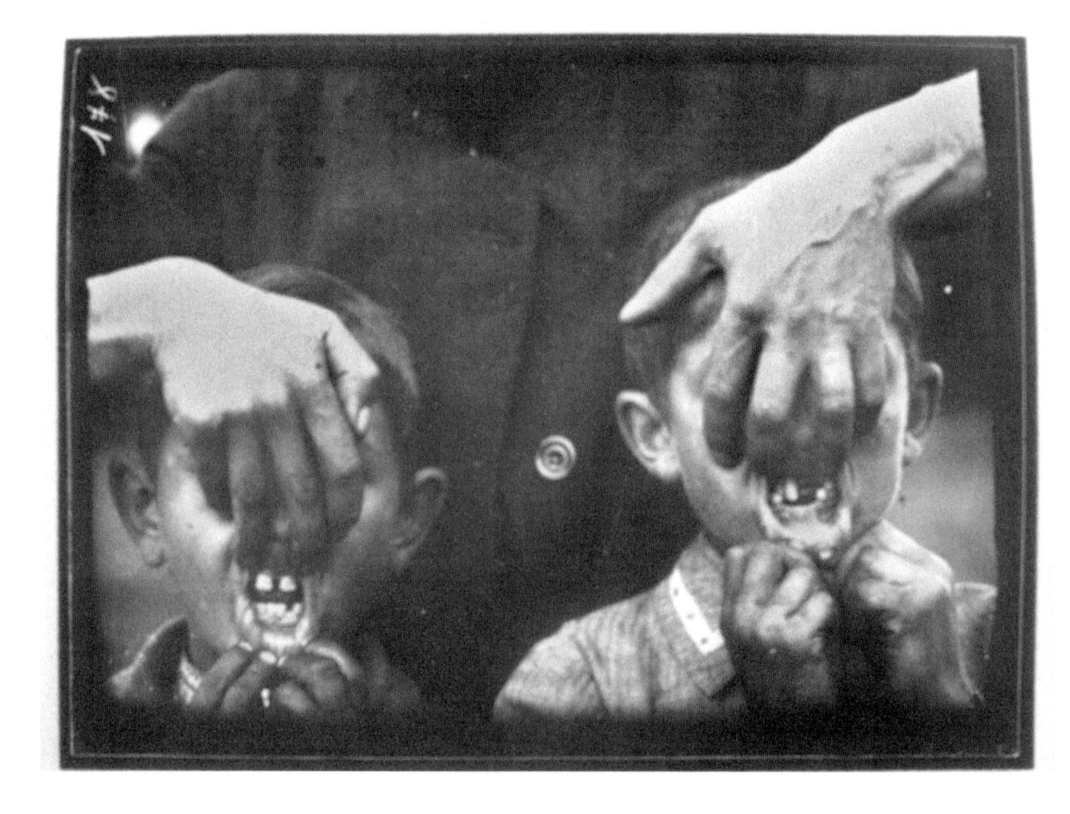

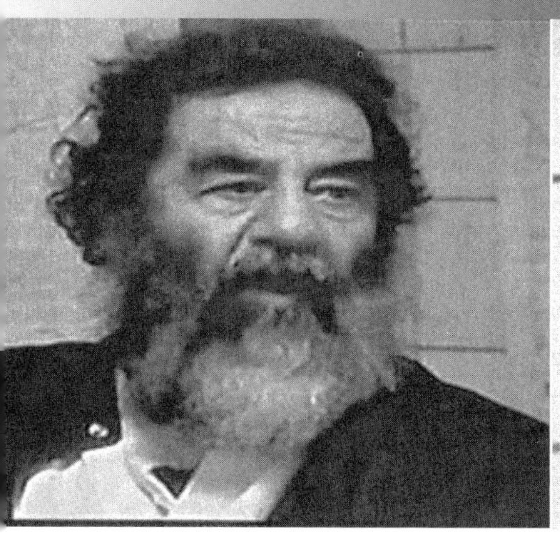

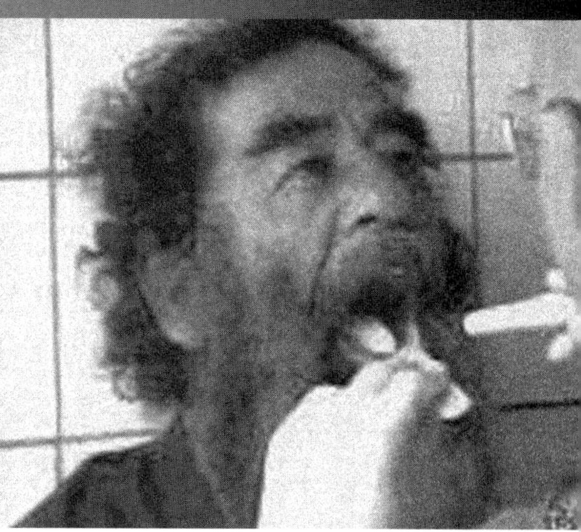

SADDAM HUSSEIN

TIKRIT, IRAQ, 12/13/2003

December 13, 2003, 8:30 p.m. (local time). Look for the devil and you find a bum. Then show him to the world on TV. Saddam Hussein, former Baghdad dictator, was found in a hole in Al-Daur. He was alone. He had a fan, about $750,000 in hundred-dollar bills, two AK-47 submachine guns, and a pistol. To get him, the U.S. deployed 600 men and offered a $25 million reward.

In no modern war have the concept and practice of the mug shot been diffused as widely as in the second gulf war. This change is due to technology, but also to its function: continuously less for prevention and increasingly more for publicity. TV cameras have replaced the photograph.

After the images of the corpses of the dictator's sons, Uday and Qusay, after the exhibition of Saddam, the world witnessed a barrage of footage of kidnapped westerners, tortured Iraqis, and decapitated heads, each time not for reassurance but to display the power of those who made the capture.

The Holy See commented on the footage of the ex-dictator's examination; in Cardinal Renato Martino's words: "What caused me pain was seeing this ruined man, treated like a cow whose teeth are being examined. They could have spared us those pictures."

JOSEPH ESTRADA

MANILA, THE PHILIPPINES, 04/2001

Joseph Marcelo Ejército dreamed of becoming an actor. He left school but in order not to displease his family, he changed his name. For the Filipino public, he was known as Erap (from the reversed spelling of *pare*, Filipino slang for "pal"). His persona was that of the poor, courageous hero who triumphs over evil. His success prompted him to enter politics, becoming the Ronald Reagan of the Pacific Rim

In 1969, at thirty-two, he was elected mayor of San Juan, a municipality in greater Manila. But the new president, Corazón Aquino, removed him in 1986. The following year, he became a senator. In 1998 he was elected thirteenth president of the Philippines.

In October 2000, Luis Singson, governor of Ilocos Sur, claimed he had given the president four billion pesos ($80 million) that were obtained by illegal gambling. Impeachment proceedings began but were stopped on January 16, 2001. Then violence erupted in the streets. Three days later, the army withdrew its support of Estrada, subsequently deposed by the Supreme Court on January 20. The new government, headed by Gloria Arroyo, arrested him for corruption, an offense even punishable by death. In the 2004 elections, Estrada supported Fernando Poe Jr., a former colleague during his stint in acting, but he was defeated by Gloria Arroyo.

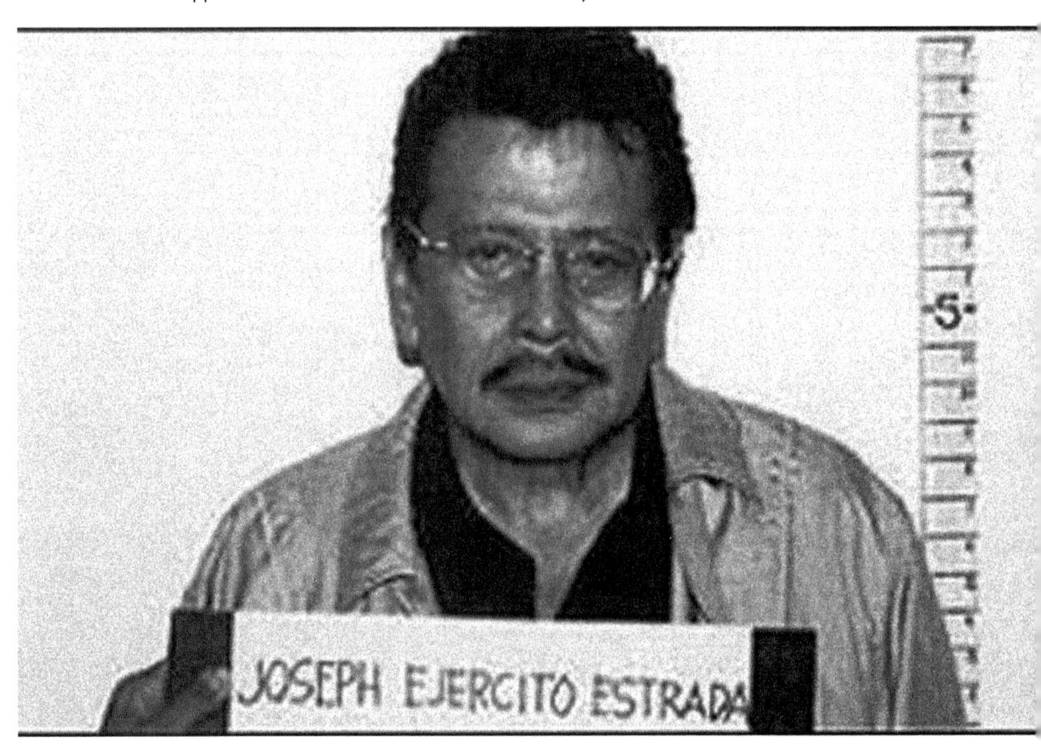

MANUEL NORIEGA

MIAMI, FLORIDA, 01/04/1990

"Pineapple Face" was a good servant. But sometimes even servants get big-headed. Manuel Antonio Noriega, born in Panama City on February 11, 1938, was a general on the CIA's payroll for nearly a decade. Between 1983 and 1989, when he was leader of Panama, he was a U.S. operative in Central America.

He was educated at the Chorrillos in Lima, Peru, and at the School of the Americas in Panama (now in Fort Benning, Georgia). In 1967 he joined the National Guard and participated in the coup on Arnulfo Arias. The new president, Omar Torrijos Herrera, named him head of military intelligence. In this capacity, Noriega organized the repression of peasant guerillas and the disappearances of political opponents.

In 1981 Herrera died in a plane crash. He was succeeded by Rubén Darío Paredes who promoted Noriega to chief of staff. Two years later, he promoted himself to general and took power. Panama, as an ally, became the outpost for U.S. politics in Central America. Thus began the assistance to the Nicaraguan contras and the death squads in El Salvador.

The 1984 presidential elections concluded, thanks to a margin of 1,723 votes real and rigged, with the victory of Nicolas Ardito Barletta, Noriega's puppet president. Panama was always the basin in which Washington dirtied its hands.

The general's romance with the U.S. ended on February 5, 1988, when the DEA accused him of international drug trafficking. On December 15, 1989, Noriega declared a state of war with the U.S. government. Five days later, 27,000 marines invaded Panama.

Operation Just Cause caused, according to U.S. government sources, the deaths of hundreds of Panamanians and twenty-three American soldiers. Other sources calculated 3,000 to 10,000 dead, and another 20,000 homeless.

Noriega took refuge in the nunciature of the Vatican embassy. The American army surrounded the building and for days bombarded it with rock music at full blast, starting with "Welcome to the Jungle" by the Guns N' Roses. The Vatican admonished President George Bush and the music stopped.

Panamanians marched in the streets, and on January 3, 1990, Noriega surrendered. In 1992 a Miami court convicted him to a forty-year prison sentence. In 1999 it went down to thirty years: between parole and good conduct Noriega could get out in 2007. The former dictator—just one of the many heads of state created and deposed by Washington—had himself baptized in prison on October 24, 1992.

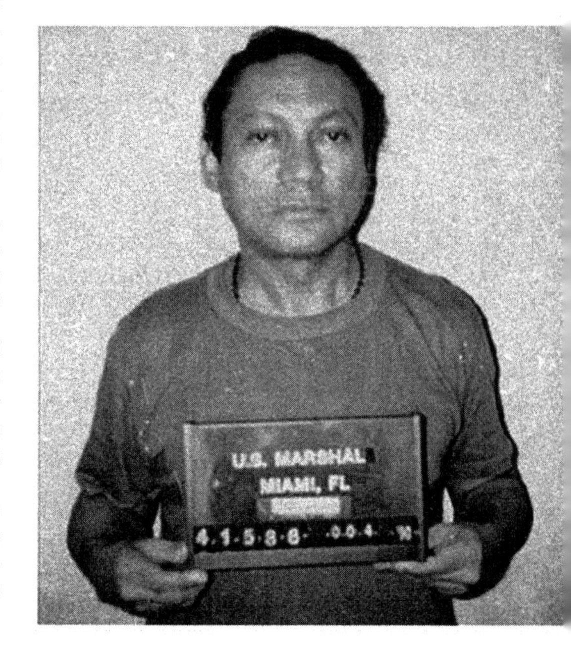

TIMOTHY McVEIGH

OKLAHOMA CITY, OKLAHOMA, 04/19/1995

About three hundred survivors and family members gathered in Oklahoma City to witness the spectacle. On June 11, 2001, at 7:14 a.m., Timothy McVeigh, thirty-three, who served and was decorated in the Gulf War, died by lethal injection in prison in Terre Haute, Indiana. On April 19, 1995, to avenge the Waco massacre, McVeigh blew up the federal building in Oklahoma City, killing 168 people. Many were children who went to daycare there. The testimonies were all the same: before departing, McVeigh lifted his head and searched the onlookers' eyes with his own. He died with his eyes open.

When awaiting the sentence, he gave a few interviews. "I came to terms with my mortality in the Gulf War," he recounted. Then he asked, "What did we do to Afghanistan? Belgrade? What are we doing with the death penalty? It appears they use violence as an option all the time." In prison, he met the Unabomber. "We were much alike in that all we ever wanted or all we wanted out of life was the freedom to live our own lives however we chose to." He also met Ramzi Yousef, orchestrator of the 1993 World Trade Center attack. After McVeigh's execution, Yousef wrote of him, saying: "I have never [known] anyone in my life who had so similar a personality to my own."

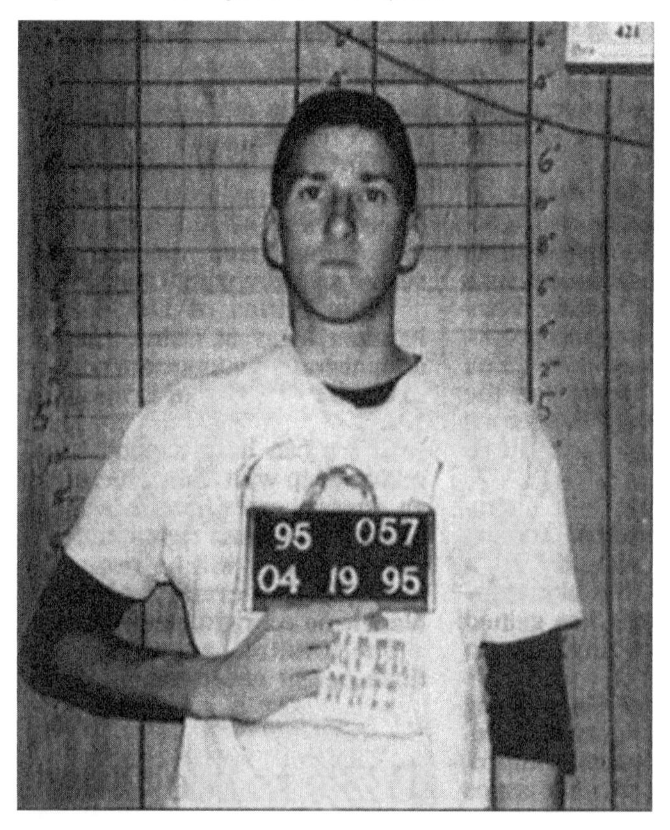

THEODORE KACZYNSKI, THE UNABOMBER

LINCOLN, MONTANA, 04/03/1996

From May 25, 1978, to April 24, 1995, the Unabomber sent mail bombs, injuring twenty-two people and killing only three. It's a miracle that there weren't more. His nickname was coined in 1980 when the FBI connected his first three attacks. Two occurred at Northwestern University in Evanston, Illinois, one on an American Airlines flight, forced to make an emergency landing at Dulles International Airport in Washington, D.C. "Un" stands for University, "A" for Airlines, and of course "bomber."

On September 19, 1995, the *Washington Post* and the *New York Times* published his political manifesto "Industrial Society and Its Future." He was arrested on April 3, 1996. Theodore John Kaczynski, fifty-four, who received a PhD in mathematics in 1967, had been living in a log cabin, without running water or electricity, in the Montana forest. He detested modernity, in the American tradition of Henry David Thoreau. In one of the harsh critiques he wrote while in jail, he said: "I have read Chapters 1, 13, and 14 of *A History of Modern Psychology*." This is amended by a sarcastic footnote: "A pen is a phallic symbol. The flow of ink from the tip of the pen represents ejaculation. My pen ran out of ink at this point because of my unconscious fear of castration."

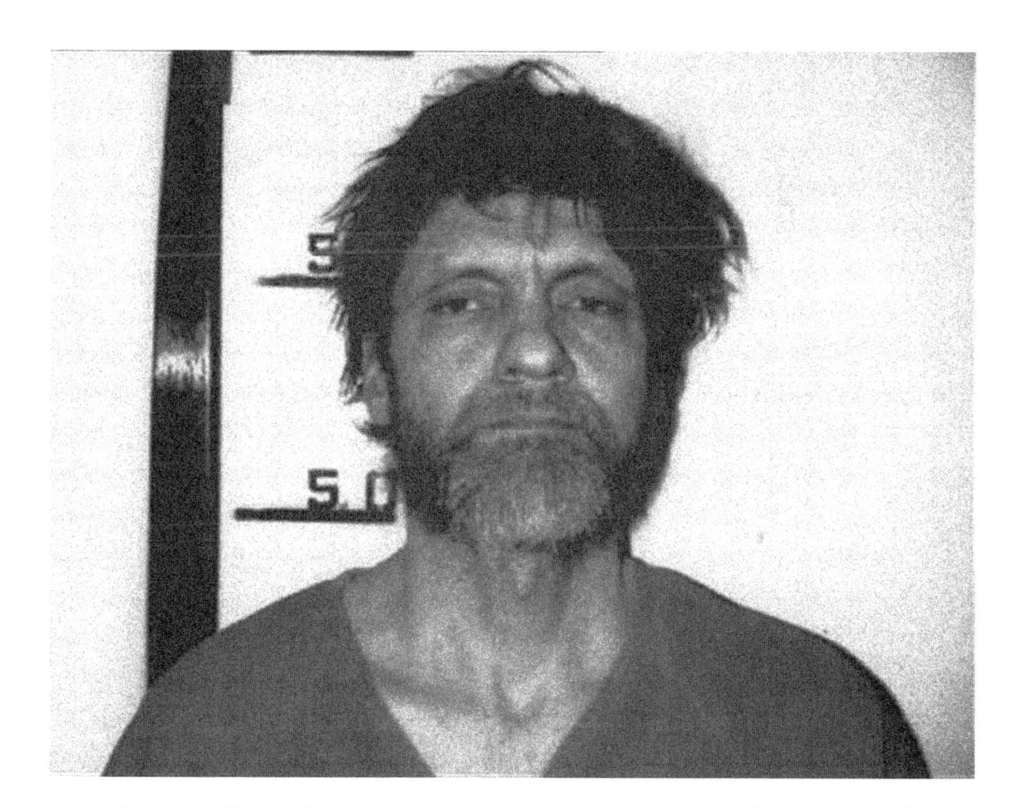

SUSPECTED ISLAMIC TERRORISTS

SINGAPORE, 08/2002

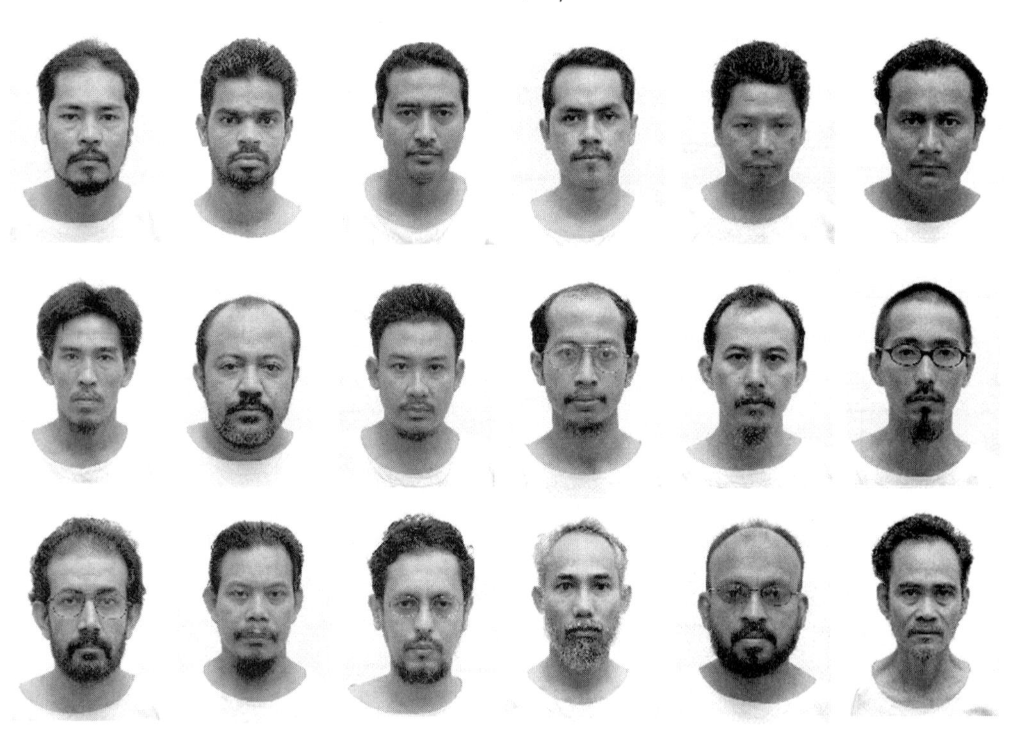

After September 11, all over the world, scores of suspects affiliated with the Al-Qaeda network were arrested and photographed. The small faces you see belong to eighteen of the twenty-one people imprisoned for terrorism in Singapore on August 2002, a year after the American attacks. Reports from Amnesty International on the dangers looming over human rights are increasingly alarming: after the attacks, a greater number of countries have passed laws that allow the almost total annihilation of individual rights for crimes linked to terrorism. In the United States, since 9/11 over a thousand people have been arrested, most of them of Middle Eastern origin. As in Guantánamo Bay, national defense law allows the detention of foreigners for an indeterminate time without specific charges. The European Union plans to pass a collective antiterrorism plan, even if now the definition of the term is so broad that it can be used for many different aims. In many African and Asian countries, the adoption of national defense laws means the suppression of political opponents and Islamic groups.

ZACARIAS MOUSSAOUI

The "twentieth hijacker" of September 11 was the worst student at the Airman Flight School in Norman, Oklahoma. He didn't learn to fly even when he transferred to the Pan Am International Flying Academy in Eagan, Minnesota. After telling him about a fire that broke out on a Saudi passenger plane because a gas stove was on to make tea, the instructor asked him what Ramadan was. Zacarias answered that he didn't know. On August 16, 2001, the French citizen was arrested for violating American immigration laws.

Whether because of his arrest or his boss Mohammed Atta's wariness of his emotional stability, Zacarias Moussaoui didn't take part in the September 11 hijackings. He had, however, traveled to Chechnya, Pakistan, and Afghanistan, where he allegedly spent time in an Al Qaeda training camp. When brought to court in Virginia, he cried out, "I turn to Allah, the almighty, for all the Muslim and all the Mujahedin. I pray to Allah, the masterful, for all my brothers in jail like in Algeria, everywhere in the land of Allah. I pray to Allah for the return of Andalusia, Spain, to the Muslim and the liberation of Ceuta and Medilla." Then he prayed for Islam and "for the destruction of the Jewish people." And he cried out, "So, America, America, I'm ready to fight in your Don King fight."

Four of the six charges against him call for the death penalty.

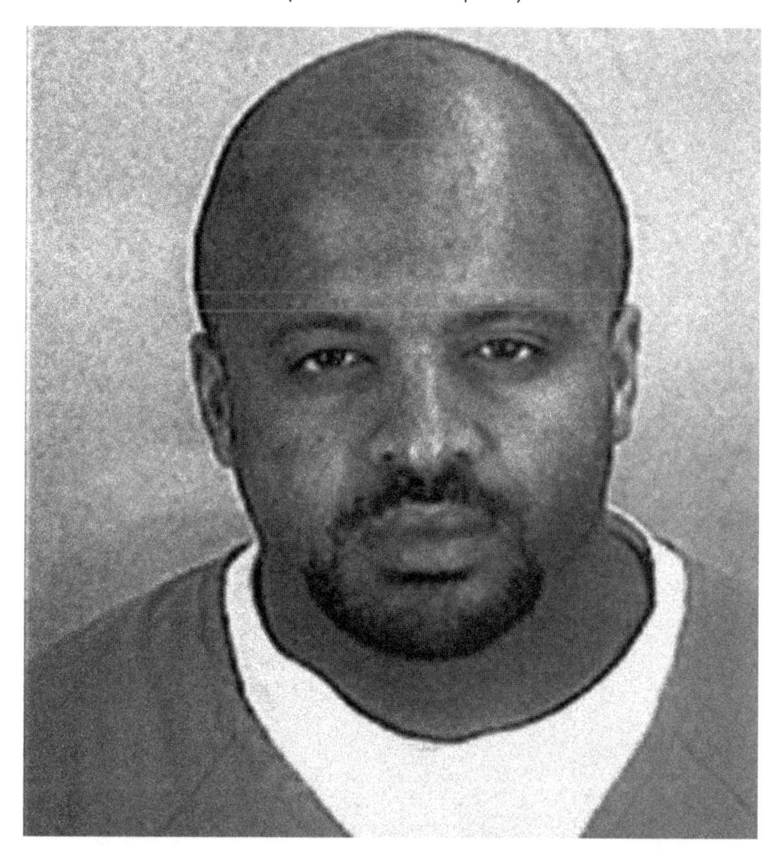

SUSPECTED GUERILLA

RAMADI, IRAQ, 06/21/2003

As in the picture of Martin Luther King Jr., the first in this inventory, the news reporter is outside the frame. A soldier in the American army, first battalion, 124th infantry regiment, photographs a suspected Iraqi guerilla. The image, dated June 21, 2003, was taken in Ramadi, 100 kilometers west of Baghdad, one of the cities in the Sunni Triangle, one of the guerilla bases.

Outside the frame there could also be a TV camera. If so, this single photograph would encompass all the technologies currently used throughout the world, and especially in Iraq, for the task of representing and politicizing the body of the enemy. The digital camera in the soldier's hand, the news photographer's camera, and the television camera. In a sort of dizzying photographic, television, and digital compendium, the nineteenth, twentieth, and twenty-first centuries converge on the suspect, using him and testifying to its own political usefulness.

During the war in Iraq, the mug shot, which for some decades seemed to end its political trajectory, has powerfully returned to center stage. To the center of history. Its function, however, has changed as it has evolved technologically. The illusion of visible control over all potentially dangerous bodies, control exerted for the stability of power, is definitively over, leaving room only for press releases and marketing.

The images of the corpses of Saddam Hussein's sons, just as the images of all the hostages filmed and photographed at the moment of their assassination, the collection of photos of the old regime's most wanted, the footage of the former dictator portrayed like a savage during his physical exam—these images carry the ancient political and military function of a trophy.

They publicly represent the fury and the force of those who hold, in that instant, power over the body of the accused, returning executions to the public square in the age of mechanical reproduction.

Even in its Iraqi manifestation, photography demonstrates the magical belief on which its scientific pretensions are founded. The images of guerillas, dictators, or detainees steal the soul of the condemned. Through the display of weakness, of fear, of the corpse of the victim du jour, the photographer seeks to preserve in the terror of that moment the humanity which he recognizes in himself.

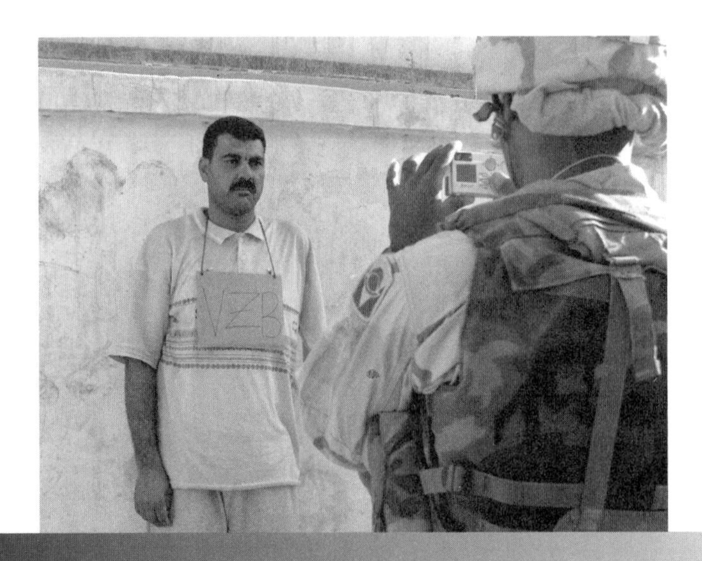

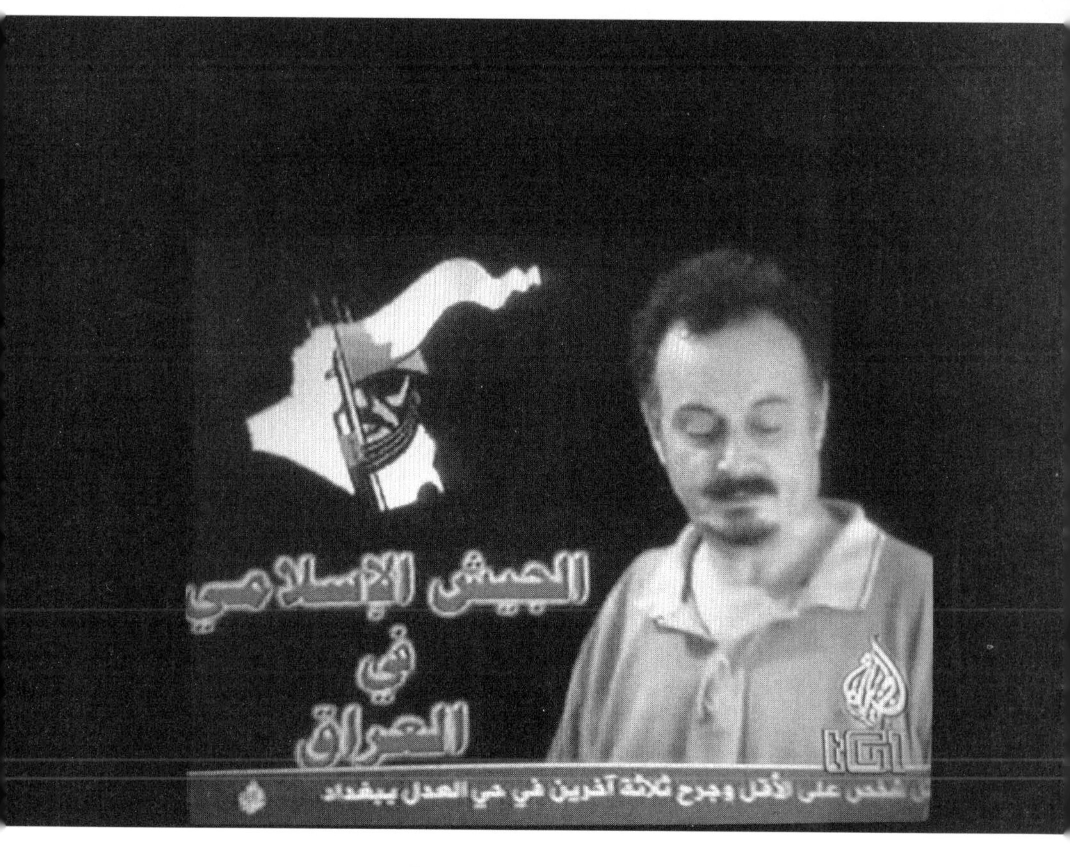

ENZO BALDONI

IRAQ, 08/24/2004

Enzo Baldoni was kidnapped on August 20, 2004, in Iraq, while he was at the head of a convoy of the Italian Red Cross that was bringing humanitarian aid to the holy Shiite city of Najaf.

On August 26, the execution, which occurred in all likelihood about forty-eight hours before, was announced. In a video, aired on August 24 by Qatar-based Al Jazeera TV, he introduced himself: "I am Enzo Baldoni from Italy, I am fifty-six years old, I am a journalist, and I do social work by volunteering with the Red Cross. I came to Iraq to write about the resistance for my new book." We had planned that book together.

FACING THE TWENTIETH CENTURY

The complete inventory of mug shots is infinite. The hundreds of faces in this collection float over a sea of unknown faces. In the 156 years of history from the Birmingham prostitute's gaze (1848, p. 157) to Enzo Baldoni's downcast eyes (August 2004, p. 175), hundreds of thousands of people have interested official history and the institutions that have the task of recording it, but only for the split second of their arrest.

For the most part, these are anonymous existences, but the gallery of famous people who have ended up in prison at least once is just as infinite. During the months when this book was in the works, dozens of worthy candidates were suggested. "Do you have Oscar Wilde?" "Is Adriano Sofri there?" "And the conspirators in the Tokyo subway nerve gas attack?" "Leonarda Cianciulli, the Correggio soap-maker, did you find her?" "And Hitler?" "Pablito Rossi?" "Charlie Parker?" "And Billie Holiday's there, right?"

Some mug shots were discarded during the selection process, others have never been published and will remain forever entombed in police archives. Every absence, however, also serves as a confirmation. We have struck gold. The mug shots of celebrated men, or of people charged with resonant acts, transcend the memory of those who have left the twentieth century behind. Everything that happened from 1848 to today has been part and parcel of judicial photography.

In the parade of faces immortalized by police photographers over the course of the last 150 years, not only the most important historical events or the most heinous crimes march past, but also the subconscious imperatives and secret agendas of the classes who have detained, decided, and sustained the exercise and the stability of power. If at first the faith in photography as an investigatory tool was absolute, not even at its onset was judicial classification of bodies and faces meeting police requirements alone. The need to possess a photograph of the accused always expresses and reveals the need for the symbolic neutralization of evil. In other words, it met the need for magical reassurance. Photographing, classifying, and keeping a picture of the criminal or lunatic represented an act that could reiterate the capture and place it within awareness and eternal possession. The practice of police photography, in short, relieved the taxonomic and taxidermic impulse that lurked in the terrified heart of the nineteenth century.

It was a century that saw the birth of museums for every object in existence, when even the furnishings of bourgeois interiors attempted to express an illusion of containing the vastness of space and the depth of time in the sitting room. As the nation-states pursued their individual colonial vocations, the bourgeois who remained in the homeland arrayed in their most prominent display cases an army of exotic souvenirs and relics torn from the past. An omnivorous need to own and displace suggested strategies of defense and attack to the Europeans, which became so personal and ingrained that they became translated into taste, fashion, styles of furniture and architecture. The aspiration for a sense of safety was undermined, therefore, by the fear that anything could come along one day and suddenly disturb it.

The throng of lunatics, criminals, and poor that, for the first time, tirelessly marched past the windows of the home, demanded a greater theoretical effort, one driven to find an objective method, a technically infallible and "scientific" method to draw the borders between the conformist and the anomalous or the deformed. Only within these borders could the external threat be defined, thereby enabling self-definition. Perhaps it was no accident that Count Charles Tanneguy Duchatel, minister of the French police in 1839, was the one who fought to confer a life annuity to Monsieur Daguerre, who discovered a way to fix photographic images onto plates in 1839. Before the Chamber of Deputies on June 15, 1839, Duchatel made a historic speech: "Esteemed colleagues, we promise to represent the spirit of this assembly, by asking you to acquire, in the name of the State, the property of a discovery as useful as unexpected, and which we consider important to be made available to the public, for the progress of the sciences and the arts."

Parliament approved and Daguerre was able to benefit, until death, from an annual income of six thousand francs, a more than acceptable sum for the State, even if added to the four thousand francs paid to the son of Joseph-Nicephore Niépce, who had developed a similar process some years before.

A sort of marriage of interest was celebrated in those years, based on technology and magic and officiated by the law and police. The newspapers sang photography's praises, this extraordinary invention that seemed capable of arresting a moment forever, freezing it before it could run off and degenerate into crime.

The metropolis, which developed within this context, gave shape to one of man's most ancient dreams. It became more and more like a labyrinth in which, at every corner, evil could lurk and scheme. Therefore, many considered photography the tool able to keep every crevice on earth under control, even the darkest. The great French photographer Eugène Atget almost always captured Paris at dawn, almost always deserted, devoid of the human bustle that made it Paris. For the German literary critic Walter Benjamin, the streets and squares of the "capital of the nineteenth century" in Atget's shots resembled crime scenes.

Thus the new invention represented, even at its first appearance, a powerful and magical alliance of the European police forces working to put a stop to social entropy, impose order on chaos, prevent the dangers looming over the citizens of big cities terrified by the dizzying increase in traffic, by the masses of the dispossessed flocking from the country to the working-class neighborhoods in order to serve the glories of the industrial revolution; frightened, even, by a shocking novelty like the sudden advent of gas lighting at night. If photography was able to immortalize the bourgeois in a portrait that could last forever (as painting did for centuries with the aristocracy), it also held the power to preserve the guilty and their deeds for centuries upon centuries. In 1902, Norwegian painter Edvard Munch bought a Kodak camera and started fooling around with it. He concluded, "The camera cannot compete with a brush and canvas as long as it can't be used in heaven and hell." He hadn't realized that the change was already in progress: God was already dead and the devil had become a bourgeois device.

At first it was like an infatuation. On September 10, 1854, the Losanna *Journal des tribunaux* featured an article called "Noveau moyen d'enquête," which related the capture of a petty sacristy thief identified thanks to his daguerreotype. In 1848, just nine years after Daguerre's discovery, the Moor Street commissariat in Birmingham, England started to file daguerreotypes of thieves and prostitutes. The photographic image gave the enforcers of (disrupted) order the tools to restore, through observation and reason, perfect order.

In the 1880s, small and handy "detective" cameras flooded the market (often the brand used by Sherlock Holmes or Scotland Yard, including the ultracelebrated "photo revolver"), which were invariably advertised with the image of an honest citizen and robbery victim who, by taking the evildoer's picture, enabled his capture. In a few decades, the first theorists of police photography—Alphonse Bertillon in France, Italy's Salvatore Ottolenghi, Umberto Ellero, and, in his own way, Cesare Lombroso—became the priests and custodians of public security.

It was the worst of times; it was the best of times. In this reassuring universe the bourgeois finally felt in "possession"; everything could be displayed in the sitting room to encapsulate the world and amaze relatives or be admired in a museum. Yet, something was still disturbing and refused to be controlled. Something was reluctant to be mummified. This persistent vulnerability was the threat of death, a fear woven into the very fabric of the calming existence that the European bourgeois were constructing for themselves and their children in the second half of the nineteenth century. You expected, Benjamin notes, a murderer's shoes to peek out from behind your old aunt's curtains at any moment. Their attempt was both heroic and desperate: to contain the monstrous in the realm of reason and science. It was clear right away that the effectiveness of this new method left something to be desired. Cases in which the police managed to identify a criminal through a previous mug shot were extremely rare. And even the cases in which a wanted poster effectively led to an individual's capture seemed statistically insignificant. Still, the late-eighteenth-century hopes of eliminating crime through photography, cataloguing, and archiving, and the persistence of evil during an era characterized entirely by progress didn't allow for a change in approach. This didn't diminish the photography craze that had been established during the century's first hopeful decades. Throughout all of Europe, later in America, and then in the whole world, photographing, cataloguing, and archiving the faces of those who, for one reason or another, got themselves arrested still goes on today, as if it were completely natural. In actuality, the encounter between the need for reassurance and faith in science took place on the dance floor of mythology.

To define the conformist, the just, and the honest, one must also define the anomalous, the erroneous, and the criminal. In order for the definition to be infallible and not include the honest man by mistake, it was necessary to construct the myth of scientific objectivity. In the work of obsessive cataloguing and neutralization of the anomalous through the camera, reason found in myth its greatest ally. The old alchemist was reincarnated in the figure of the inventor. As the European bourgeoisie constructed their dominion and the illusion of their own eternity, photography played a role of primary importance right from the start.

The Enlightenment faith in reason turned into fanaticism. Reason became the religion of scientific objectivity. It became positivism. By mathematically defining the law of universal gravity, Isaac Newton reintroduced the concept of action, distant from the alchemists and medieval wizards. With the minor discovery of the pineal gland, French philosopher René Descartes revitalized Aristotle's and St. Thomas's dualism between body and soul. Almost the same thing happened with the invention of photography. The police merits of this revolutionary technological discovery were magnified out of proportion in the attempt to shape a new mythology and to once again affirm society's own faith in the inevitable and the ultimate triumph of good over evil.

The great literature of the time was consequently filled with modern rationalist wizards. The nineteenth century, a century that still had faith in the possible, produced scores of infallible detectives, in the same way that the twentieth, taking refuge in the impossible, would produce superheroes. This is clear in the first chapter of Sir Arthur Conan Doyle's *The Hound of the Baskervilles*, an installment in the Sherlock Holmes saga. Doctor Mortimer introduces himself to Holmes, declaring his admiration for Alphonse Bertillon, the true creator and great cardinal of police photography (pp. 146–147).

The novel, however, in which the police gaze of photography emerges in all its ambiguity is *Bleak House*, one of Charles Dickens's masterpieces. The novel, which marks the appearance of the detective figure in English literature, is filled with photography. An article in London's *The Stereoscope* from March 19, 1853, inspired Dickens. In the text, attributed to William Henry

Wills and Henry Morley, everything is a play on the relationship between the daguerreotypist's studio and the magician's chamber.

The narrator imagines entering a dark, enchanted realm where every word is chosen and measured to express the sense of an unsolvable mystery, based on the apotheosis of a perfect vision. The great immortalizing magician, the photographer, is defined as "the taker of men." In front of their own image, trapped for eternity on plates or paper like an insect in amber, human beings oscillate between the vain desire to remain forever in effigy and the fear of having to give up a part of their soul in exchange.

Again, it is Walter Benjamin who defines this mix of wonder and terror, describing in "Little History of Photography" reactions to Daguerre's first images: "'We didn't trust ourselves at first . . . to look long at the first pictures he developed. We were abashed by the distinctness of these human images, and believed that the little tiny faces in the picture could see *us*.'" The disturbing and miraculous nature of photography seems to consist, then and now, in the capture of the soul through the reproduction of the body. This power encapsulates the attraction and repulsion evoked by the vision of one's own fixed image in the mirror, yet it is altogether free from the fear that the copy, sooner or later, could decide to disobey the original, returning its gaze. Through police photography, in contemplating the photograph of the killer or the lunatic, the bourgeoisie held a mirror up to themselves, fascinated and horrified by the possibility of seeing themselves in the negative.

Being captured by the photographer's eye, however, also meant becoming public, emerging as a face in the tangle of the crowd's bodies and limbs. It meant conquering—even if through evil and criminal deeds—the disgrace of sinking into obscurity. For the poor and the criminal it meant finally being immortalized, obtaining a bit of immortality through their portrait, just like kings, cardinals, and notaries.

In a letter dated October 21, 1859, Jane Welsh Carlyle, wife of English philosopher Thomas Carlyle, expresses this same paternalistic faith in the new tool: "Blessed be the inventor of photography! I set him above even the inventor of chloroform! It has given more positive pleasure to poor suffering humanity than anything that has 'cast up' in my time or is like to—this art by which even the 'poor' can possess themselves of tolerable likenesses of their absent dear ones. And mustn't it be acting favourably on the morality of the country?"

The seeds of the mug shot's future evolution have been planted in the dialectical ambiguity between the manifestation of evil in the effigy of the evildoer and the manifestation of individuality in the resonant, even criminal, act. The photographic exhibition strategically took away the criminal's greatest weapon: secrecy. However, through the exhibition and technical reproduction of his image, the criminal would also attain a public persona and achieve an exemplary significance. In an increasingly factory-like society, he also would become a hero, a myth, an example, a face out of the crowd, a "human being." As Susan Sontag writes in *On Photography*, "To photograph is to confer importance."

Indicative of this point is the case of the bandit Giuseppe Musolino (pp. 60–61): a poor, probably mentally unstable, Calabrian lumberjack, unjustly sentenced to thirty years in prison for a murder he didn't commit, escapes jail and vindicates himself, becoming a popular hero in just a few years. Within a couple of months his mug shots had been turned into postcards. The trend was imported from the United States, where the most famous gangs and bounty hunters, posing in front of their newly dead victims, turned up on widely circulated postcards. The good bourgeois, terrified of evil, death, and insanity had not foreseen that evil, death, and insanity would remain primary sources of attraction, gravitational centers of glamour and seduction even in the emerging mass culture.

The mug shot has always evoked contrary reactions, even from the accused. Mark Chapman (p. 33), in a 1991 interview, eleven years after murdering John Lennon, expresses toward his own mug shot that feeling of nakedness and estrangement that Lombroso attributed to wild places in front of his own photographic portrait: "I remember he told me to remove my sweater. And I was removing it, he just came up and just pulled it off of me, just like, you know, 'Come on!' And . . . and took mug shots of me. One of these mug shots, from what I heard later, had disappeared and turned up in the press. And it was printed in *The New York Post* . . . a very ugly picture. They told me to turn sideways and face forward, and . . . mug shots . . ."

On the other side of the spectrum, there's the actress Juliette Lewis who was photographed in her Los Angeles apartment with her gigantic and prominent—almost a poster or a work of art—mug shot from 1989, when she was arrested for entering a bar when she was only sixteen. The image, recorded and kept by the police, therefore carried out a double function: the first, robbing the soul and face of the evildoer, reducing their entire existence to the execution of a wrong act; the second, conferring their identity, sanctioning the uniqueness of the individual and their act in front of the indistinct masses.

The fascination surrounding evil, especially if validated through legal punishment, is an underestimated element even in the analyses of those who, like the French philosopher Michel Foucault, have occupied themselves with studying the representation of the "deviant" as the primary way to define the "normal." It is almost as if even the most liberal thinkers, in their radical criticism of the bourgeois age, fundamentally remain prisoner to it, implicitly accepting, in the attempt to negate and refute it, the good/bad dichotomy as the single pair of opposites capable of conferring meaning to each other. As he shows that modernity's prison practices were not at all indifferent, but functioned for the class in power, Foucault arrives at a reversal of moral judgment. He places culpability on those who claimed their innocence and considers victims those who were found guilty, again diminishing the myth of the outlaw, the noble savage's latest incarnation. In his conception of society, there is still an irreparable schism between the good and the wicked.

Every strategy of power, even the most refined and efficient, is mythopoeic. All societies symbolically interpret themselves in order to turn themselves into stories, into founding myths of the classes that comprise them. All societies are committed, first and foremost, even before defending and reproducing themselves, to understanding themselves and telling their stories. Crazies, whores, and good-for-nothings were defined, invented, and described as groups (also, but not solely) to define, invent, and describe in a positive manner, the honest citizen inching toward progress. As Robert F. Kennedy said in a 1964 speech, "Every society produces the kind of criminal it needs."

In order for the "total institutions" that were coming into being (asylums, prisons, schools, hospitals) to be based on solid theoretical foundations, it was necessary to define a single ideology that could comprehend, explain, and neutralize, in one fell swoop, each individual outside the established norm, whether a thief, killer, lunatic, or savage. That ideology was the idea of total scientific objectivity.

Jean-Martin Charcot, who began directing the epileptic ward in the Paris asylum La Salpêtrière in 1871, invented the figure of the hysteric (defined by Louis Aragon and André Breton as "the greatest poetic discovery of the late-eighteenth century"), synthesizing in a single symbolic figure the sexual desire for and the repulsion by the female body experienced by the dominant (male) class. During his lessons, the "hysterics" flaunted their submissiveness and their sensuality. There to assist were the students who had rushed from all over Europe to attend the most important neuropathology school in the world. A resource improved upon by Sigmund Freud, Józef Babinski, and Gilles de la Tourette, to name a few. Seven years after the invention of hysteria, Charcot instituted Salpêtrière's photo laboratory.

In the 1890s, Alphonse Bertillon, son of the demographer Adolphe, was nominated head of Criminal Identification Services of the Paris Prefecture and succeeded in making the mug shot the primary tool in the fight against crime. His method, which was based on the statistical premise that two individuals could not have the same appearance and measurements, defined the grammar and the syntax of police photography with the same potency that David Wark Griffith used to define cinema three decades later. During the same period in Italy, Cesare Lombroso, by archiving the photographs and the embalmed remains of thousands of people, tried to trace in a single schema, with his muddled genius, the distinguishing features of the lunatic, the savage, the killer, the thief, and even the genius.

One problem remained: it was necessary to choose the proper framing and the distinguishing body part. But what is a face? When does a face truly express an individual? In a monologue in the film *The Tenant* by Roman Polanski, widower of actress Sharon Tate, who was murdered by Charles Manson (pp. 112–13), the philosophical question is expressed in this way: "At what precise moment does an individual stop being who he thinks he is? You cut off my arm, right? I say 'me and my arm.' You cut off my other arm. I say 'me and my two arms.' Take out my stomach, my kidneys—assuming that were possible—and I say 'me and my intestines.' And now, if you cut off my head, would I say, 'me and my head,' or 'me and my body'? What right has my head to call itself 'me?'"

Whether it has that right or not, the head was endowed with the authority to represent the person. In homage to the pictorial tradition that began during the Renaissance, it is precisely the accused's head, pictured facing forward and in profile (Alphonse Bertillon also used a three-quarter view) that was constituted as the central focus for the photographic and the police gaze. The Renaissance pose, already tested out in renowned paintings, would be abandoned by the bourgeois with the establishment of the mug shot paradigm. The face became, as Ando Gilardi writes in his excellent book *Wanted!*, an "allegory of guilt," a system of signs that could display the irreparability and gravity of the gesture, an encoded text that would reveal, to whomever was able to read it, the mystery of individual evil, which is therefore, in some way, collective.

At this point, another problem arises, no less philosophically dense than the one posed by Roman Polanski. The face is mutable; it has countless expressions. But what is the right expression? What expression must be captured if guilt is to be represented and, at the same time, capture the guilty forever? After testing the defects of coercive methods like straitjackets, handcuffs, straps, and chloroform, Umberto Ellero, founder of the Turin School of Forensic Science and the greatest Italian theorist on police photography, makes some amazing statements. "Given the state of things it is evident that treating the offender with the greatest kindness should be imposed . . . to penetrate the painful situation in which he finds himself . . . A word of encouragement, because even the offender has a heart, matters even more than authoritative methods, of the rules of law, inappropriate threats, etcetera, which by proven fact have resulted in either an increase of acerbity and disquiet and caused sudden contortions of the physiognomic traits." As one can see, the paradigm of the natural borders that of the inexpressible. The act of deconstructing evil starts with the methodical elimination of its expressivity, even before the camera intervenes. This is a grotesque presumption if police photography is thought of as a direct descendant of psychiatric photography, and if one considers the madness of the presumption of studying, cataloguing, and comprehending lunatics by prescinding, to the point of negation, the expressions of their faces. Only if made "natural," only if undressed, can a face speak.

The mania of dressing everything in fabrics, tapestries, and cases that embodied the second half of the 1800s found in the human skin its exact apotheosis yet its only exception. Perhaps this is why, in an essay on German furnishings quoted by Dolf Sternberger in *Panorama of the 19th Century*, the skin is defined as "the most natural clothing." The same paradigm of the natural functions in the identification photo, which was invented in 1854 by André Eugène Disderi as the visual calling card. Even in that case, even in the case of the respectable citizen's identification documents, the ideology of objectivity requires expressivity to be reduced to the minimum, barely revived by the suggestion of a smile.

In short, the human face became the banner of identity for both the guilty and the innocent. It was believed that by divesting the face of its mutable characteristics, it would become a map, it would give shape to a veritable geography of guilt. At that point, it was necessary to proceed to measurements, to the translation of every segment of the face and the body into numbers. Alphonse Bertillon therefore introduced the "portrait parlé," the minute description of the face through five hundred international standard adjectives and twelve necessary measurements that added to the Italian school's version.

Beneath these gestures, then considered eminently scientific and today clearly propitiatory, if not mystical, there were certain impulses at work, which were subsequently much studied, consistent with the era's attitude toward everything in existence. The impulse of the collector who gathers fragments and re-views them with the illusion of making them speak; the absent-minded posture of the flâneur who spends his days observing the crowd in an attempt to confine its vitality within a series of calming tableaux vivants with the illusion that he is outside of it and can enjoy humanity as a spectacle; and finally, the obsessiveness of its most reviled and widespread epigone, the voyeur, who abdicates acting on his own desires to feed off those of others. All these human types act out the same pleasure and the same fear described by the ancient Roman poet Lucretius in *De rerum natura*: to take enjoyment from the spectacle of evil, one must be able to remain on shore watching the sinking ship.

The correct attitude, therefore, is contemplative, as prescribed for looking at a work of art reduced in the museum to one in a series, endless fragments in a succession of the same. The bad and the beautiful become isolated and fragmented in a series of objects that are ultimately desirable because they have been rendered incapable of holding any surprises. In the photographic practices of Bertillon and Lombroso, identity is fractured into an infinite series of segments—of ears, foreheads, mouths, and eyes—now torn from history and from the identity of whomever possessed them.

Seeking to contain every disturbing atom within the confines of a gigantic metonymy, they developed a system in which the detail signifies the whole. The extraordinary flourishing of collecting in those years expressed a simple epistemological theory, in line with the mythology of labor and wealth: the real is known only through possession. To know and to possess, one must shatter the object and observe its parts, hoping that they animate a whole and betting that reality, fragmented thus, can no longer escape control.

This is why police photography, originally structured within the framework of the Renaissance portrait, rapidly changes its construction. The faces alone are no longer enough to define and immobilize the evil. The wicked body must explode within the molecules that constitute it. In a fetishist fervor, the body of the anomalous is fractured. As the pre-Socratic philosopher Empedocles writes: "Many heads sprung up without necks and arms wandered bare and bereft of shoulders. Eyes strayed up and down in want of foreheads." In a certain sense, the technology and the knowledge of the late eighteenth century achieved this vision.

I have discussed early police photography from its beginnings because only by starting from its original or deepest motivations is it possible to understand some of the transformations that occurred in the following century. To be perceived as controllable, the universe becomes petrified and the contemporary becomes archaeology. This celebration of the secularized relic is repeated, time after time, in the twentieth century, going from its foundations to the modern cult of the brand name. It is an era that, like ours, clings to everything new and that doesn't understand that the very nature of the "new" consists in, as French poet and philosopher Paul Valéry recalls, its intrinsic mortality.

It is not by chance that the first attempt at worldwide documentation took place in 1914, with the approaching carnage of World War I. To identify corpses more quickly, an edict from the Italian government required all soldiers to pose for photos before leaving for the warfront. These portraits, tens of thousands of them, were still constructed according to the aesthetic ideal of the bourgeois photograph sittings from the end of the 1800s: Doric plaster columns springing up impossibly next to fake Persian rugs, exotic *trompe l'œil* at the bottom, pressed uniforms, cigarettes between their fingers, waxed moustaches. Yet, death was still the hidden impetus.

At the same time, mass use of the identification document as an image of a moment that can shed light on an entire existence, continues today on gravestones in cemeteries throughout the world. The late nineteenth century, and much of the twentieth, have been obsessively intent on finding a magical device that could fix the essence of a moment eternally. Photography, in its endurance and its instantaneity, has been the primary instrument of this obsession with preservation.

Over the course of the twentieth century, the need to extract something from nothing emerged thanks to the technology omnipresent at any potentially memorable event. To be remembered, to have really happened, rites of passage—weddings, first communions, and graduations—must take place in front of a lens. With the spread of technology such as videophones and web cams, the ritual of the pose is substituted by the ritual of the capture. Evidence of really "having been there," now consists of the act of taking the photo, rather than having it taken. Today, proof of "being there" is in the act of using photography or video (even during a trip or the birth of one's own child) to halt the unarrestable flow of reality.

Space and time, not only criminals or lunatics, must be neutralized and archived photographically. "To photograph is to appropriate the thing photographed," writes Susan Sontag, adding, "As photographs give people an imaginary possession of a past that is unreal, they also help people to take possession of space in which they are insecure." The unfolding of the identifying function, instead of separating the normal from the monstrous, ends up absorbing the one into the other. Sontag, again, writes: "The freakish is no longer a private zone, difficult to access. People who are bizarre, in sexual disgrace, emotionally vacant are seen daily on the newsstands, on TV, in the subways. Hobbesian man roams the streets, quite visible, with glitter in his hair." Photographs "trade simultaneously on the prestige of art and the magic of the real."

If in the 1800s there was a large-scale attempt to reduce the universe, including the social one, to a system of comprehensible, transmittable signs, in the 1900s the inherited signifying universe is emptied little by little of every cognitive ambition; the fragments no longer refer to anything. The sole fact of being possessed and available is enough to give the illusion of extensive and constant control, which no power believes it can exert anymore. The exponential increase in the signifiers necessarily leads to the futility of the signifier itself.

If interpretation is also impossible, the availability of images is enough to calm. German philosopher Arthur Schopenhauer notes in *Parerga and Paralipomena*: "That the outer man is a picture of the inner, and the face an expression and revelation of the whole character, is a presumption likely enough in itself, and therefore a safe one to go by; evidenced as it is by the fact that people are always anxious to see anyone who has made himself famous by good or evil . . . Photography, on that very account of such high value, affords the most complete satisfaction of our curiosity."

Over the course of the nineteenth century, the camera and the printing press, meanwhile, became less and less expensive and more and more widespread. Thanks to the advent of cinema, publishing, and the news media, the photographic image is found everywhere. Technical reproducibility "confers importance" to the photographed. In the thirties, in the United States, Henry R. Luce created *Life* (and later, *Time*), the glossy magazine, as Gilardi writes, whose "incredible fortune was based largely on agreed journalistic appropriation of police photography."

The world is narrated and sold as the grand photographic spectacle of its tragedies, its deaths, and its arrests, like history gathered by a panoramic lens. The "rogue's galleries" that started in America were photo exhibits of criminals displayed to the public for general curiosity, but also to enable their capture. In just a few years, the photos were so numerous as to render that purpose vain. Nevertheless, in any given political system on the planet, millions of human beings continued to be documented.

Documentation continued at Auschwitz and in all the extermination camps (pp. 140–41) where, consistent with the Nazi dream of applying industry even to death, an extremely sophisticated photographic device was at work, which moved the inmate in front of the lens rather than requiring the kapo photographer to expend the effort of moving. The Nazis understood better than anyone else the political nature of the photographic image and its power over the body of the photographed. They also understood that a prisoner's photograph empowered its owner and that the spell was broken and the significance altered if the picture was returned. For this reason, as their defeat approached, they destroyed millions of identification shots.

Documentation continued in Stalin's Gulags (pp. 51–53), of the millions of inmates forced to contribute slave labor in order to build communism, the classless society that would one day, paradoxically, culminate in liberation from labor. These identification photographs, therefore, appeared grainy, similar to company badges made by a business that was still primarily agricultural.

Documentation continued in the United States, of millions of people, no matter how venial the crime of which they had been convicted. Everyone falls into the net of American mug shots: future Microsoft magnates, relatives of presidents, singers and actors, managers and killers. In a country where twelve million people are arrested every year, with a prison population that wavers around 2 million annually (the currently accepted number of people that the Soviet Gulags held at their peak of development in 1950 is 2.8 million), where the penitentiary industry, financed by the state coffers, has created a satellite industry that has made the California union of prison guards the most important in the country, the mug shot truly comes to be a photograph of the entire society.

In no place does the mug shot make history and become a story like in the United States. Rendered almost unusable for police purposes (given their unusual diffusion), today's American "rogue's galleries" reveal how much the social function of police photography has changed over the course of the twentieth century. It has distanced itself more and more from its preventative aim and is now limited to the capture and display in effigy of the accused. In the gallery of photographic portraits taken by the American police one can, therefore, follow how people's poses in front of the lens and their perspectives on the photographic portrait have changed in the last 150 years.

The increasing availability of technology has extended the ritual of viewing life's moments through a lens, even the moments of death or of arrest. Slowly, the habit of posing for the photographer has taken over, even if the photographer is a prison guard. Little by little, the expression of the guilty has changed as well. As early as the 1930s the mug shot became a rite of passage. This is clear when looking at the photos of golden-age American gangsters (pp. 70–76). In one shot, Al Capone smiles impudently. In another he is positioned in such a way that the frame cuts him off. Lucky Luciano exhibits a gaze of defiance. Meyer Lansky poses with the professionalism of a banker being photographed for a company badge. Bugsy Siegel has an air of annoyance. The mug shot has become an opportunity to carve out one's identity before the public eye, rather than allowing it to be taken away by whomever holds official power.

This isn't an attitude limited to those who have developed, through their chosen career, a certain proclivity for prisons and police stations. It explodes with the affirmation of popular culture in the second half of the twentieth century, when the hero is no longer defined by conforming to the ideals of bourgeois tactfulness, but rather by breaking away from them. Steve McQueen raises his hand in a peace sign (p. 20). Jane Fonda holds up a fist (p. 17). Michael Jackson's expression resembles a Peter Pan mask (p. 89). Frank Sinatra poses like a model (p. 94). Elvis Presley, who in real life sided with the authorities so that they wouldn't make him pay for his excesses, asked for a souvenir mug shot when he visited the White House in 1970 (p. 93).

The sanction of guilt has become, in short, exhibition of the self. Police photography has changed its function: if in the late-nineteenth century it could determine the exclusion of the accused from civil assembly, in the second half of the subsequent century it was absorbed, as an extreme case, into the general tendency to establish the extraordinary merely on the basis of visibility.

One witnessed, therefore, an inversion of tendency. If since the eighteenth century, by gaining power, the hegemonic bourgeoisie felt a need to hide themselves, in the late twentieth century, those who have power of any kind must return to displaying the signs of their dominance. The first part of this analysis, synthesized so briefly as to become imperfect, is derived from the French philosopher Michel Foucault. In *Power/Knowledge* and later in *Discipline and Punish*, Foucault historically, philosophically, and architecturally structures the idea of a central, pervasive, and omniscient gaze on the subject; this is a gaze already formulated in literature by George Orwell in *1984* with Big Brother. The magnificence of a sovereign leader empowered by divine right was replaced by the gray clothing and drab appearance of a mid-ranking state official. Public displays of torture, which showed the people the divine sovereign's power over the body of the condemned, were replaced by total institutions, increasingly anonymous and invisible. Foucault, however, chooses as the founding paradigm of modernity the Panopticon, an architectural model designed at the end of the eighteenth century by English utilitarian Jeremy Bentham, which was composed of a central tower inhabited by guards and an all-glass exterior, where prisoners exist under the guards' constant gaze. The agenda of the Panopticon is manifested, for Foucault, not only in the hundreds of prisons, schools, and hospitals constructed according to Bentham's blueprint, but also through a "microphysics of power," indicated by minute regulations, records, documents, and identification photos.

In leafing through the mug shots in this book, registering the progressive transformation in the gaze of the accused—progressively less estranged, less guilty, more sure of themselves—the suspicion arises that Foucault's grand analysis has only taken account of part of the process, stopping at the threshold of the establishment of popular culture. Here is a society that enables the visibility of each of its members, a society of mass-produced exhibitionism, a drive founded on the need to exert control by imprisoning everything and everyone within a single glance.

If Charles Dickens and Arthur Conan Doyle helped to construct in literature the myth of the political alliance between forensic science and photographic objectivity, the literature of the twentieth century questions this faith right away. For Raymond Chandler, a writer who has built at least one novel on the collision between the photographic image and investigation, the world is forever changed. Chandler's is a world in which good and evil, conformity and anomaly no longer exist, a world in which everyone is guilty and no one can ever be definitively identified or fully believed. Chandler's pessimism isn't enough, however, to explain the reversal of the mug shot's function. His still seems an affirmation of disillusionment, of a betrayed hope, which falls back onto the very ideology from which it distances itself. It represents a critique, a refutation of the previous world, yet does not reach a description of a different world.

However, history always retraces its steps. Today the Sun King wears sequins and wants to be on prime time. The attempt to impose order and stability on the masses is a failed attempt. Not even the greatest critics of modernity (and we should also add Carl Schmitt to the list, one of the extremely rare cases of an intelligent Nazi) managed to understand that in the second half of the twentieth century the primary source of power went back to being extensively visible and no longer omnisciently invisible.

Attaining visibility is today a mass aspiration. Descarte's great bourgeois motto ("Bene vixit qui bene latuit," "He who lives well hides himself well") seems less appealing with every passing day. A vulgar exhibitionism has replaced the discreet fetishism of the nineteenth century. The central power, though there has never truly been one, no longer has to remain invisible because everybody believes they're being watched. The people rush, out of their own free will, to be observed. It has literally gone from the Orwellian Big Brother to the television show *Big Brother*.

Photography and documentation continue, incarceration at gulag proportions continues, but the mug shot's function is no longer the same. American prison culture increasingly resembles a branch of the economy and continuously less a preventative strategy taken to establish law and order. The modern concept of privacy (another concept that began with the bourgeoisie and was probably destined to fade along with it) represents, in this case, only an attempt to regulate a change that seems unstoppable. Andy Warhol, the artist who perhaps best foresaw and embodied the mythology with which the twentieth century is saturated, made the frequently quoted statement: "In the future, everyone will be famous for fifteen minutes." The myriad of objects—celebrities, athletes, soup cans—that Andy Warhol transformed into pop icons, naturally includes mug shots.

In 1964 Warhol salvaged the pictures for his piece *Thirteen Most Wanted Men* (p. 64) from the refuse of the twentieth century—America's most sought-after criminals from the annual FBI list—and used them to decorate the exterior wall of the pavilion at the New York World's Fair. They were almost all Italian and for this reason it was feared they would offend the governor's Italian constituents, but the giant posters of those thirteen accused, up for almost a month, finally started to watch the passersby, instead of being watched by them.

This fifteen minutes of fame coincides with the time it takes to pose for a police photographer. But set on paper or film, or published electronically, they contain within themselves the power to last forever. It is in this juxtaposition, in a single representation of the fleeting and the eternal, that technical reproducibility pushes the gaze toward the primal fear of death and the desire for immortality. This need is embodied today in the aspiration to fame as the great enterprise, as a significant moment capable of giving sense to everything.

Those who attain visibility are, today, "bigger." It becomes desirable in itself. Visibility, like money in Karl Marx's *Economic and Philosophic Manuscripts,* is the "great subverter," the wizard capable of making the fat thin, the old young, the bald bushy. This transformation is also narrated, perhaps especially so, in the history of mug shots, from the scores of adoring admirers that unfailingly gather around the murderer of the hour, around "bel René" Vallanzasca (p. 62) in Italy to those in the United States around serial killer Richard Ramirez (p. 118).

Perhaps there is a development implicit in the mug shot's very function, as demonstrated by the fervor with which the disorderly precursor to pop art that was Cesare Lombroso approaches the genius and the lunatic, the thief and the regicide. The dance between genius and lack of self-control stimulates European romanticism but blossoms completely, becoming trade and trademark, only in the subsequent century: in music, yet also in art, likewise in film and architecture. This is why the images in this collection still have a seductive effect.

The conquest of visibility is, in short, the existential, aspirational, almost artisanal form of the advertisement. As German philosopher Jürgen Habermas asserts in *The Structural Transformation of the Public Sphere,* advertising represents the sign of the decline of the public dimension upon which the bourgeoisie built its best and most civilized conquests, but it also represents the only public dimension still possible. Whoever wants to recount something today must do so on the stage of this simplified public dimension.

The essence of the advertisement is to draw the gaze onto the self, eliminating the other from the field of vision. In other words, the advertisement polarizes. It communicates the self at the expense of the other. It's not just about Pepsi vs. Coke or Nike vs. Adidas, it's about a new means of doing politics. It is no accident that advertising has adopted a vocabulary of war, filled with targets, blitzes, and campaigns. Yet again, it is the history of police photography that has led the way.

If one wished to indicate the last act of the eighteenth-century mug shot's function, as well as the first signs of its metamorphosis, it would require going back to the late seventies, to the kidnappings of Aldo Moro, president of the Italian political party, the Christian Democrats, by the Red Brigades, and Hanns-Martin Schleyer, president of two German industrial associations, by the Red Army Fraction. The two men, kidnapped and later "brought to justice," were photographed by the "tribunal of the people" in an exact replica of the gesture used by the "bourgeois tribunals" to catalogue lunatics, anarchists, and criminals. In Italy and Germany, the "vanguards of the proletariat" found no better approach than to replicate the very detention strategies they opposed.

After Moro, after Schleyer (and after Roberto Peci, the informer Patrizio Peci's brother, who was filmed, murdered, and photographed with a Polaroid by the Red Brigades in 1981), nothing else happened for the next twenty years. Parading through the newspapers and the internet are the classic mug shots of ordinary serial killers, pedophile singers, violent actors, athletes, con artists, the intoxicated relatives of American presidents. It will be important to watch the second Iraq war because the historical motivations and ambiguities previously described synthesize, if not a new grammar, then at least a new function of police photography. It is as if the continuation of a thread that existed at its beginnings, with the postcards of dead brigands and bandits, has again gained the upper hand.

During the Iraq War an orgy of mug shot–like images have come onto the scene, mostly video, but also digital photographs of corpses (of kidnapped Westerners and the deposed dictator's children), which in the renewal of the older function of judicial photography as proof of capture, express an altogether new polarization. A polarization, essentially, of publicity.

The digital self-portraits taken by American soldiers while they tortured prisoners at Abu Ghraib, the image of the bloody dictator turned bum (p. 167) examined "like a cow" with his mouth agape, the horrendous visual ritual of the video transmitted by Al Jazeera, the dance macabre of the endless throat-slashing, implorations, and proclamations no longer have only the function of communicating to one's own that a battle has been won, but also and above all that of throwing in other people's faces that they have been crushed and humiliated in the battle.

The observers and informers, the guards and the thieves have been replaced by the primitive division between victims and executioners. Publicity does not take into account the desires of those who have bought you or can choose you. The recipients of the message are only the friends and the enemies, those who, essentially, have already chosen sides. From one place to another, the identification image, now digital or often video, is no longer an expression of a social detention strategy, but has transformed into an opportunity to garner publicity, newsreels about its own power and military might.

For the torturers at Abu Ghraib and the kidnappers standing before their victims, the image functions as proof and advertisement of having been there, of being strong. It attests that they were present in that moment and that they held power because they detained human beings: that they existed only insofar as they detained. The mug shot has shifted from the face of the accused to that of the accuser, often hooded like the executioner of Berlin (p. 126).

Before the chain of gazes flaunted like trophies to the television audiences of both factions—the perpetrator of genocide, his sadistic sons, the tortured Iraqi, the English engineer, the decapitated young American, Nepalese immigrants with slashed throats, the Italian journalist—it can truly be affirmed, again according to Benjamin, that "the gaze is what remains of a man."

Milan, November 2004

BIBLIOGRAPHY

BOOKS

AAVV. Gulag. *Il sistema dei lager in URSS*. A cura di Marcello Flores e Francesca Gori. Milan: Edizioni Gabriele Mazzotta, 1999.

AAVV. *Memoria dei campi. Fotografie dei campi di concentramento e di sterminio nazisti (1933–1999)*. A cura di Clément Chéroux. Rome: Contrasto, 2001.

AAVV. *Nascita della fotgrafia psichiatrica*, a cura di Franco Cagnetta, con la collaborazione di Jacqueline Sonolet, Venice: Marsilio editore, 1981 (I ed.).

AAVV. Nella rete del regime. *Gli antifacisti del parmense nelle carte di polizia (1922–1943)*. A cura di Massimo Giuffredi. Rome: Carocci, 2004.

Benjamin, Walter. *Angelus Novus*. Turin: Einaudi, 1962.

———. "Little History of Photography." In *Walter Benjamin: Selected Writings, Volume 2, 1927–1934*. Edited by Michael W. Jennings. Boston: Belknap Press, 1999.

———. *Parigi capitale del XIX secolo*. Turin: Einaudi, 1986.

———. "The Work of Art in the Age of Mechanical Reproduction." In *Illuminations*. Edited by Hannah Arendt. Translated by Harry Zohn. New York: Schocken Books, 1969.

Bertillon, Alphonse. *La photographie judiciaire avec un appendice sur la clas sification et l'identification antropométrique*. Parigi: Gauthier-Villars, 1980.

Bettin, Gianfranco. *L'erede*. Milan: Feltrinelli, 1992.

Chandler, Raymond. *The Big Sleep*. New York: Vintage, 1988.

Chomsky, Noam, and Edward S. Hermann, *La fabbrica del consenso*. Milan: Marco Tropea, 1998.

Colombo, Giorgio. *La scienza infelice. Il museo di antropologia criminale di Cesare Lombroso*. Turin: Bollati Boringhieri, 1975.

Conti, Adalgisa. *Manicomio 1914. Gentilissimo Sig. Dottore questa è la mia vita*. Milan: Edizioni Gabriele Mazzotta, 1978.

Diario. *La medlio gioventù*. Accadde in Italia 1965–1975. 2004.

Dickens, Charles. *Bleak House*. New York: Penguin Classics, 2003.

Doyle, Arthur Conan. *The Hound of the Baskervilles*. New York: Penguin Classics, 2001.

Echols, Alice. *Scars of Sweet Paradise: The Life and Times of Janis Joplin*. New York: Metropolitan/Owl Book, 2000.

Ellero, Umberto. *La fotografia nelle funzionidi polizia e processuali*. Milan: Società editrice libraria, 1908.
Empedocle. *I presocratici*. Bari: Laterza, 1990.
L'Europeo. N. 4, July 2003.
Fasanotti, Pier Mario, and Valeria Gandus. *Bang Bang*. Milan: Marco Tropea, 2004.
Foucault, Michel. *Microfisica del potere*. Turin: Einaudi, 1977.
———. *Discipline and Punish: The Birth of the Prison*. New York: Vintage, 1995.
———. *Storia della follia nell'età classica*. Turin: Einaudi, 1976.
Freund, Gisèle. *Photography and Society*. Boston: David R. Godine, 1979.
Gates, Kelly. "The Past Perfect Promise of Facial Recognition Technology." Champaign: ACDIS, University of Illinois, 2004.
Gilardi, Ando. *Wanted!* Milan: Bruno Mondadori, 2003.
Gilman, Sander L. *Disease and Representation: Images of Illness from Madness to Aids*. Ithaca: Cornell University Press, 1988.
Ginzburg, Carlo. *Miti, emblemi, spie*. Turin: Einaudi, 1986.
Gramsci, Antonio. *L'albero del riccio*. Rome: Editori Riuniti, 1989.
Habermas, Jürgen. *Storia e critica dell'opinione pubblica*. Bari: Laterza, 1994.
Hoess, Rudolf. *Commandant of Auschwitz: the autobiography of Rudolf Hoess*. Translated by Constantine FitzGibbon. Introduction by Primo Levi, translated by Joachim Neugroschel. London: Phoenix Press, 2000.
Kracauer, Sigfried. *La massa come ornamento*. Naples: Prismi editrice politecnica, 1982.
Korber, Dorothy. "Language Gap Key Element in Soltys Case." *Sacramento Bee*, September 10, 2001.
Lombroso, Cesare. *Delitto, genio, follia. Scritti scelti*. Turin: Bollati Boringhieri, 1995.
Marx, Karl. *Economic and Philosophic Manuscripts of 1844*. Moscow: Progress Publishers, 1967.
Melograni, Pietro. "1914. La festa delle armi." *Il Sole 24 ore*, July 25, 2004.
Murray, Charles Shaar. *Crosstown Traffic: Jimi Hendrix and the Post-War Rock'n'roll Revolution*. New York : St. Martin's Press, 1989.
Orwell, George. *1984*. New York: Plume, 2003.
Palazzolo, Salvo and Ernesto Oliva. *L'altra mafia*. Catanzaro: Rubbettino, 2001.
Pavese, Cesare. *Disaffections: Complete Poems, 1930–1950*. Translated by Geoffrey Brock. Port Townsend: Copper Canyon Press, 2002.
Poe, Edgar Allen. "The Murders in the Rue Morgue." In *Complete Stories and Poems of Edgar Allen Poe*. New York: Double Day, 1984.
——. "The Man of the Crowd."
Posner, Gerald. *Killing the Dream: James Earl Ray and the Assassination of Martin Luther King, Jr.* New York: Random House, 1998.
Proll, Astrid. Baader Meinhof, *Pictures on the run 67–77*. Zurich: s/l, Scalo, 1998.
Ragon, Michele. *La memoria dei vinti*. Milan: N.E.I., 1998.
Ross, John. *Murdered by Capitalism: A Memoir of 150 Years of Life and Death on the American Left*. New York: Nation Books, 2004.
Schopenhauer, Arthur. *Parerga and Paralipomena: Short Philosophical Essays*. Translated by E. F. J. Payne. New York: Oxford University Press, 2000.

Sciascia, Leonardo. *The Moro Affair and the Mystery of Majorana*. Translated by Sacha Rabinovitch. New York: Carcanet, 1987.
Semper, Gottfried. *Der Stil in den technischen und tektonischen Künsten oder praktische Ästetik*. Monoco: Bruckmann, 1878.
"Sketches of Gangland Figures Named by Valachi in Senate Testimony." *New York Times*, September 28 1963, 6.
Sontag, Susan. *On Photography*. New York: Anchor Books, 1990.
La Stampa. *Prima pagina* 1867–1981, 1981.
Sternberger, Dolf. *Panorama del XIX secolo*. Bologna: Il Mulino, 1985.
Streissguth, Michael. *Johnny Cash at Folsom Prison. The Making of a Masterpiece*. Cambridge: Da Capo Press, 2004.
Tagg, John. *The Burden of Representation*. London: Macmillan, 1987.
Thomas, Bernard. *La banda Bonnot*. Milan: Squilibri edizioni, 1978.
Thomas, Ronald S. *Detective Fiction and the Rise of Forensic Science*. Cambridge: Cambridge University Press, 2000.
Veblen, Thorstein. *La teoria delle classi agiate*. Milan: Rizzoli, 1981.
Violi, Alessandra. *Le cicatrici del testo: l'immaginario anatomico nelle rappresentazionii della modernità*. Bergamo: Edizioni Sestante, 1998.
"Walk to Death Calmly." *New York Times*, August 23, 1927,1–2.
"Wealthy Farmer, 3 of Family Slain." *New York Times*, November 16, 1959, 39.
X, Malcolm. *The Autobiography of Malcolm X*. New York: Ballantine Books, 1987.

WEB SITES

http://sunsite.berkeley.edu/Goldman
www.absolutecelebrities.com
www.answers.com
www.bbc.co.uk
www.berlingeschichte.de
www.cbsnews.com
www.cnn.com
www.crimelibrary.com
www.diario.it
www.fbi.gov
www.gobelle.com
www.google.com
www.guardian.co.uk
www.imdb.com
www.law.seattleu.edu
www.law.umkc.edu
www.mugshot.com
www.nba.com
www.news.bbc.co.uk
www.pbs.org
www.pertini.it
www.rotten.com
www.time.com
www.usdoj.gov/foia
www.thesmokinggun.com
www.washingtontimes.com
www.womenshistory.about.com

CREDITS

AP Images
Willie Earle
Martin Luther King

Associazione Nazionale
Sandro Pertini

Bettmann/CORBIS
Berkeley Students
Chu Chin Kuay
Angela Davis
Duquesne Case
Albert H. Fish
Carlo Gambino
Helen Gillis
Arthur Hosein
Nazamodeen Hosein
Malcolm X
Vincenzo Perugia
Charles Ponzi
Richard Ramirez
Red Brigades
Georg-Hans Reinhardt
Sirhan Sirhan

Reuters/CORBIS
Chu Chin Kuay
Nikolaj Soltys
Suspected Islamic terrorists
Suspected Guerilla

Hulton-Deutsch Collection/CORBIS
Renato Vallanzasca

*Don Cravens/TimeLife Pictures/*Getty Images
Martin Luther King Jr.
Laura Ronchi

Farabola
Vito Genovese

Fotogramma
Mara Cagol
Camillo Casati Stampa

Fototeca storica Gilardi
Bradel
Child Prostitutes
Giacchino Di Pasquale
Dominatrix
Prostitute
Thief
Transvestite
Two Children

Museo crimiologico di Roma
Luigi Brancaleone
Teresa Crupi
Fragments
Marcello Micheluzzi
Parricide
Tattooed Man
Uxoricide

Museo di antropologia criminale "C. Lombroso" dell'Università degli Studi di Torino
- Katharina Milek
- P.G.

Raccolta stampe Bertarelli
- Giuseppe Musolino

State Museum of Auschwitz-Birkenau
- Maks Königsberg
- Rozalia Kowakczyk
- Noachim Leiman
- Émile-André Poupleau
- Russian Prisoner
- Maria Smilek

Ullstein Bild
- Rudolf Hoess
- Erich Honecker
- Guxtav Völpel

ABOUT THE AUTHOR AND TRANSLATOR

GIACOMO PAPI is the author of several previous books, including *Era una notte buia e tempestosa* (*It was a dark and stormy night*), an anthology of the best opening lines in world literature, with a preface by Umberto Eco; and *Papá*, a best-selling humorous guide for expectant fathers. Since 2000 he has worked as a journalist for *Diario*, an Italian weekly newsmagazine. Together with Massimo Coppola, he runs ISBN Edizioni, an imprint of the Italian book publisher il Saggiatore.

JAMIE RICHARDS holds an MFA in Literary Translation from the University of Iowa and is currently pursuing a doctorate in Comparative Literature at the University of Oregon. Her translation of a short story by Laura Pariani was published in *Words Without Borders*, and selections from her translation of Giancarlo Pastore's *Meduse*, for which she received an ALTA fellowship in 2004, have appeared in *Two Lines*, *Absinthe*, and *eXchanges*, an online magazine that she formerly co-edited.